THE WORLD
OF THE WITCHES

Julio Caro Baroja was a Spanish Basque anthropologist and historian who was best known for his ethnographic studies of Basque and Spanish traditional cultures and folklore. He was a nephew of the well-known novelist Pio Baroja, was a member of the Spanish Academy of History, and is well-known as the author of the classic ethnography of the Basques whose activities in witchcraft inspired the present work. Dr Baroja died in 1995.

Also by Julio Caro Baroja

The Basques
Los Pueblos de España
Los Vascos
Las Brujas y su Mundo
Los Judios en la España Moderna y Contemporánea
Vidas Mágicas e Inquisición
Los Baroja
Las Formas Complejas de la Vida Religiosa

THE WORLD
OF THE WITCHES

Julio Caro Baroja

Translated from the Spanish by Nigel Glendinning

PHOENIX
PRESS

5 UPPER SAINT MARTIN'S LANE
LONDON
WC2H 9EA

A PHOENIX PRESS PAPERBACK

First published in Great Britain
by Weidenfeld & Nicolson in 1964
This paperback edition published in 2001
by Phoenix Press,
a division of The Orion Publishing Group Ltd,
Orion House, 5 Upper St Martin's Lane,
London WC2H 9EA

A CIP catalogue record for this book is available
from the British Library.

Printed and bound in Italy by
Grafica Veneta S.p.A.

ISBN 1 84212 242 8

CONTENTS

INTRODUCTION

PART I

THE CLASSICAL BACKGROUND

v

PART II

THE RISE OF WITCHCRAFT

PART III

THE CRISIS OF WITCHCRAFT IN THE BASQUE COUNTRY

PART IV

THE DECLINE OF WITCHCRAFT

ILLUSTRATIONS

BC 400 Cabeiric cup with a scene representing Circe offering a potion to Ulysses (Reproduced by kind permission of the Ashmolean Museum)

Witches' banquet

Witch riding to a Sabbath on a monster

Baptism by the Devil at the Sabbath

Homage being paid to the Devil

Devils, witches and sorcerers dancing

Witch producing a storm

Sorcerers changed into animals cast their spells

Jan Ziarnko's plate for De Lancre's Tableau de l'inconstance (Reproduced by kind permission of the Bodleian Library)

Engraving by Jacques Callot of The temptation of St Antony (Reproduced by kind permission of the Bodleian Library)

Illustration of a sorceress casting spells by Jan van de Velde (Reproduced by kind permission of the Bodleian Library)

Print of a witchcraft scene by David Teniers the younger (Reproduced by kind permission of the Bodleian Library)

Plate illustrating the Sabbath from Laurent Bordelon's L'histoire des imaginations extravagantes de Monsieur Oufle *(Reproduced by kind permission of the Bodleian Library)*

Goya's Capricho 60—*Practice*

Capricho 67—*Wait until they've anointed you*

Capricho 12—*Hunting for teeth*

Capricho 68—*Attractive teacher*

Early nineteenth century woodcut of witches (Reproduced by kind permission of the Bodleian Library)

PROLOGUE

This book is, in one sense, the fruit of childhood thoughts and recollections. Had I not spent the formative years of my life in the Basque Provinces I might never have written it. In those days, many people in that part of Europe still believed in magic and witchcraft. Holiday-makers in the great modern seaside resorts like Biarritz, St Jean de Luz or San Sebastián might find this hard to accept. But the families who lived an isolated existence in the valleys and mountains just inland from the coast had no contact with modern ways of life. They were cut off and protected from the world outside by their strange language, and so they still clung to the same conception of the world as their forefathers, a view of life rooted in antiquity, full of mystery and poetry and even, at times, humour. Witchcraft and magic were still very much realities for them.

Before I was twenty I spoke with elderly people born between 1850 and 1860 living not more than a mile from my home, who were convinced that there were men and women who could change themselves into animals, fly, and do other things which, for want of a better name, we generally call witchcraft. What is more, I was living in the part of Spain where many of the witches and sorcerers of the sixteenth and seventeenth centuries had been born. They were supposed to have held their meetings and covens in Zugarramurdi, and were condemned and some put to death for it at Logroño in 1610. Not far away, in the Labourd region of France, the extraordinary events described by the brutal witch-hunter Pierre de Lancre had taken place at much the same period. For de Lancre, the legal proceedings he instigated were not enough, and he published records of his experiences which can still surprise and shock the reader even today.

The part of the world I come from, in fact, has a not unimportant place in the history of European witchcraft. But my early surroundings were not the only things which stimulated my interest in the subject. There were numerous books on witchcraft in Europe in general and in the Basque countries in particular, in the library of my uncle, the novelist Pío Baroja. Those of Pierre de Lancre were among them. And I could read them when I spent my summer holidays at his house, called 'Itzea', in Vera de Bidasoa.

Between 1931 and 1934, although I was still in my teens, I already reckoned to be something of a specialist on witchcraft. As is the way of specialists (and young people too), I did not wholly understand all I read and made notes about. But I continued my researches until the Civil War in 1936 and finally my university career and other activities compelled me to put them on one side. And although I have worked from time to time on witchcraft in the Basque country and in Spain, I have been reluctant to return to the wider field of research I had covered earlier, and to the rather incoherent notes I had made and locked away in an old cupboard.

It was a visit to London a few years ago, when I bought and read several recent books on witchcraft, which made me turn to the subject with renewed interest. Subsequently, at the request of a friend and colleague, I tried to make some use of the material I had collected many years previously, bringing my earlier theories into line with my present views on the subject.

The process has not been an entirely pleasant one. It meant going over again a great many old projects which had never come to anything, fruitless investigations, and difficulties which I had not been able to overcome. But if everybody has a destiny, books have theirs too. I have said enough about my personal reasons for being interested in witchcraft and can go on to explain briefly the standpoint I have adopted in writing the present book.

The title of the book—*The World of the Witches*—gives some indication of my initial intention, which was to examine a specific group of people in relation to the world around them. The witches' world, like that of any other social group, changes considerably from one generation to the next. And witches are thought to exist in a variety of historical circumstances, in countries with different cultural backgrounds and changing patterns of society. It might be thought that the witch ought to change with her environment. But, in fact, witches tend to be much the same whenever and wherever they happen to be. By studying the changing circumstances in which they live and move we come to realise how radically the concept of reality itself—all that man believes to be real and to exist—varies in the minds of men in different societies and at different periods. So that ultimately this book, written by someone whose chief interest lies in the the study of social history and anthropology, comes to touch on a subject which has been discussed by many historians of philosophy and science, but which deserves further study in the view of the present writer: the nature of reality itself.

The fact is that the nature of witches and the acts they are believed to carry out cannot be determined without taking into account the concept of reality of the times and circles in which they move. And this is very difficult to determine. For modern man, with his scientific education, words like reality and realism have a significance which several hundred years of investigation and thought have given them. How is he to appreciate the notion of reality which existed and exists in the minds of people untouched by scientific thought?

This is the essential problem for those who investigate witches and witchcraft. What is the nature of reality in a world where there are witches? Above all, what do those who believe themselves to be the victims of witchcraft believe to be real? Much more is known about sorcery and witchcraft from the point of view of those who believe in witches than from the witches themselves. And we have to analyse the mentalities of such people: the mentalities of whole communities gripped by a specific fear, not simply individuals convinced of their own unnatural powers.

My investigations will cover two main fields: the societies of classical antiquity and those of the modern era. My approach will be primarily historical. But I have made some use of material drawn from the works of modern anthropologists, and have discussed present-day people and communities in the final chapters. This means that the book is relativistic, and not everybody will approve. But I think that there is no lack of justification for my position, since the rigid approaches of scholars in the past have led to an oversimplification of the whole question of witchcraft.

In many books of the nineteenth and twentieth centuries, European witchcraft was studied purely and simply in relation to Christianity. There is something to be said for this approach. But it should be noted that there is no one consistent Christian view of witchcraft and sorcery, and that the views of outstanding Christians at different periods have varied very considerably. Many measures taken in the name of religion and supposed to be authoritative prove to be *ad hoc* and circumstantial. Catholics of the late Middle Ages were at odds with those of the early Medieval period on certain questions relating to magic; just as, subsequently, there were differences of opinion among Protestants.

The philosophical and legal interpretation of the facts of witchcraft worked out by other writers is equally tendentious. It neglects the theological ideas involved and attaches, in my view, too little importance to the historical circumstances of the communities which believe in the power of witchcraft: who are often the victims of war, pestilence or other disasters. Such matters influence the beliefs of an individual, as do also the structural characteristics of societies in which magic is practised. These need to be carefully examined so that the psychological effect of the social environment can be adequately taken into account.

Too little attention has, I think, been paid to the historical background of witchcraft. At the end of the nineteenth century, it was all too easy to criticise the inquisitors, judges and other persons in authority for the way in which they had dealt with witches. But the rationalistic and somewhat anticlerical scholars who were so ready to condemn them might have looked more carefully at the nature of the people they were judging and the communities in which they lived. The inquisitors were certainly unsympathetic characters, but no worse than other persons who have to make legal decisions in cases where there is an element of doubt. Had scholars examined their situation more rigorously, they would have found, if not a full justification for their actions—and no historian is required to justify extreme prejudice—at least an explanation for them; much as modern anthropologists studying similar cases (the Trobriand Islanders, for example, brilliantly investigated by Malinowski, or the Azande of Africa analysed by Evans Pritchard) have found that the activities of sorcerers, witches and enchanters are so bound up with the actions of the other members of their society that neither can escape the demands of the social order—which is as much or more an order of social action as of religious or intellectual ideas.

For witches, sorceresses or enchanters to exist in a society, in fact, it must possess certain structural characteristics. And throughout the present study of witchcraft problems of social structure will repeatedly occur, as will also problems of 'change' and 'conflict' (two clichés of modern anthropology). I shall also consider aspects of human existence which require psychological rather than historical explanations, as will be seen in my first chapter.

JULIO CARO BAROJA

INTRODUCTION

CHAPTER 1

A PRIMARY CONCEPTION OF THE NATURE OF THE WORLD AND OF EXISTENCE

Sky, sun, moon and earth – The moon and its sphere of influence – Magical thought; the conception of man and the world

Sky, Sun, Moon and Earth

In the following pages I want to try to give some idea of the historical background of magic and witchcraft, and the nature of certain facts connected with them. Although the present book is not, of course, the only work on the subject to appear in recent years, I believe that it is still possible to throw some new light on the vast complex of facts which tend to be put under the general heading of witchcraft or magic in encyclopaedias and books on the history of religion, anthropology, sociology and so on.

I think it is first necessary to analyse, however briefly, certain basic aspects of the mentality of those who have believed in magic or practised the magic arts, frequently separated though they are from one another by time and space, and differences of social environment. No historian or anthropologist today would maintain that people as far apart in as many different ways as, for example, a medieval peasant in South Germany and an inhabitant of classical Greece—both of whom believed in magic—could conceivably have the same mental make-up. However, it is possible for historical and anthropological investigations to show that the beliefs and, above all, the actions of very different people have something in common, just as Greek, German and many other

European languages have Indo-european in common, according to the philologists. The only advantage we have over the philologists in our attempt to find some common basis for so elusive a thing as the psyche of Europeans of different countries and periods, is our belief that certain rudimentary experiences can account for similarities: experiences which are much the same in everyday life today as they were in the past.

To find out what these rudimentary experiences and feelings are, we must try to imagine ourselves in an environment that is not merely primitive but primeval—elemental—looking at things around us for the first time. Our environment will clearly be a rural one, and the most basic things in it will be blue sky, sun and moon, day and night, and the earth herself. What impression will such things make on us? What impressions have they made on people in the past? What are the associations they normally have for people, and what desires, experiences, emotions and religious beliefs have usually been linked with them?

Creeds and systems of religious belief vary in different communities and at different periods, so we can hardly rely on them for such information. The findings of philologists interested in European languages, on the other hand, of students of folklore and the history of religion, and latterly of psychologists also, can help us to identify the fundamental associations which natural phenomena have.

Even in a scientific age such as ours, a clear blue sky, a starlit night and storm clouds massing on the horizon, have power to move us. And everyone is affected in some way by these things however specialised or elementary their education is. But for primitive man the elements were far more powerful. He was emotionally involved with them, and in recognition of their closeness to him he addressed them as equals, not as mere objects: as 'thou', not 'he, she, or it'.[1] He addressed them as he would God, in the second person singular, with some familiarity. And only one or two poets are on those sort of terms with nature nowadays.

For primitive man, however, the attributes of the elements were more than just poetic. To the early Indo-european the sky was a superior force which ordered existence: a supreme father. When he was angry he looked stormy and sent out flashes of lightning, preceded by menacing claps of thunder.[2] The Romans and the Germanic peoples looked upon the sky in much the same way. Jupiter and Thor are merely different ways of expressing the same basic belief. And we can see their parallel nature in the world today, where the English *Thursday* (or Thor's day) and the German *Donnerstag* (Thunderday), are the equivalents of the Spanish *jueves* and French *jeudi* which both mean the *day of Jupiter* (from the Latin 'dies jovis').

As for the sun, it was held by these same ancient European peoples to be a deity of the first importance, although it had more varied attributes than the God of the Sky.[3] Most frequently the sun was associated in rituals with the idea of strength, beauty and vigour: life itself, in fact. The summer and winter solstices consequently became periods of tremendous significance. The latter was considered to be the birthday of many of the gods, including the sun itself, and the former marked the moment of the apogee—their triumph—a propitious time for celebrating all manner of protective rites.[4] Shakespeare's *A Midsummer Night's Dream* reflects some of the traditional magic associations of the summer solstice. And in Europe today, country people still perpetuate the rites with bonfires and flowers and by bathing in streams on St John's day.

But just as the blue sky, sun and day traditionally have certain sensual, emotional or religious values, so also do the moon and the night, which form, as it were, the other half of a system of opposing forces. The sun is male and the source of life. The moon on the other hand, almost invariably thought of as female, presides over the night and protects the dead. Not only are the ideas of 'moon' and 'month' connected in English and several other languages (not only those of Indo-european root), but often the word for death is related to them as well. The moon is a measure, above all, regulating human actions not motivating them; her light is a cold light, indirect, reflected, dead.

It is during the day that the life of man advances. During the night, life is considered to be in a state of suspended animation, a necessary lull during the hours of the dominion of death. Evil comes to be associated with death and night (for reasons which I believe to be instinctive) and so does everything that is contrary to the normal course of life. Night is something to be feared, and this impression of fearful mystery is felt even by those who have no form of religious belief at all.[5]

It was at night, men believed—as they still believe—that the

5

ghosts of the dead appeared and walked abroad. It was then that
the spirits which normally lived in another element, the earth,
emerged from their caves and hollows. The earth is the mother of
things, just as the firmament is the father. The sun and moon in
their daily cycle rise and go down by turns, taking over from one
another.[6] But the earth herself is associated with a belief in beings
who live beneath her, in regions that we may call 'infernal'
without necessarily meaning to be pejorative.[7]

What we have briefly discussed here is the bedrock on which
are constructed not one but several complete religious systems;
the basis of the various elements common to all religions; the
heart of a body of mythical beliefs, of a logical and ethical order,
and the centre of a system of love and hate in social life! What
might be called the Mythos, Logos, Ethos and Eros of things.
Let us, therefore, make a few observations of a historical nature
about the various religious systems and the societies which evolved
them.

The Moon and its Sphere of Influence

In the early years of this century several writers held the view that
moon myths were all-important and fundamental for the understanding of mythology in general. Scholars like Ehrenreich,
Siecke and Winckler agreed about this, in spite of the fact that
they started out from totally different positions. Others, however,
favoured the sun myths, and there were those who supported
theories which one might call 'meteorological'. All these views
have long since been considered extravagant.[8]

Almost equally dated are the views of certain German and
Austrian ethnographers, who formed a group that was famous
in its day. They thought that there were various 'cultural cycles'
which centred round cults of the gods of the sky, sun and moon
respectively. Each cult was held to have characteristics similar
to those to which we have already referred. But the truth of the
matter is that the existence of cycles is by no means proven in
the religious field any more than in the social or economic fields.
It is certainly unlikely, in any case, that they are as rigidly independent of one another as the authors of the theory maintained.[9]

But even though such theories are now largely discredited there
is no lack of evidence to support the existence of a connexion of

some sort between certain female functions and certain conceptions and beliefs. Even the so-called 'functionalists', who are most opposed to these 'cyclic' theories if I am not mistaken, have reason for pause here. For this connexion is based not on facts which can be studied under the heading of 'culture', but on real functions, physical rather than social.

The close relationship which exists in many communities between the moon, the lunar month, the idea of the month itself, and the menstrual cycle of the woman, must have decisively influenced the view that the moon as a divinity and the woman as a human being are closely linked. This basic relationship may well have led on to more complex ones, in less obvious, subconscious ways which involve sexuality. But this has not been the subject of my research.

It can be assumed fairly concretely that throughout what archaeologists call the European Neolithic period, communities existed here and there in which the woman cultivated the land, and consequently matrilineal systems came into being. In them the woman also served as a priestess, and the community worshipped 'Mother Goddesses' of a cthonic or moonlike nature. There is archaeological data which leads to this conclusion; and material about peoples who were considered archaic or primitive by the Greek geographers and historians, also supports it.[10] Strabo, for instance, in certain passages of his *Geography*, describes the way of life of the Cantabrian peoples in the northern part of the Iberian peninsula. He tells us that their communities were organised on matrilineal lines, and that the woman had considerable power and economic importance as she was the cultivator and property-owner. The Cantabrians were also clearly moon-worshippers.[11]

Bachofen, in a book that is packed with classical erudition, romanticism and extraordinary insight, used nearly all these texts to emphasise the connexions we have already mentioned and to construct his own theory of matriarchies or primitive maternal law. It was also Bachofen who first drew attention to the startling links between women and the moon.[12] Inevitably, since his time, our knowledge of the so-called matrilineal societies has considerably increased.

No one has demonstrated better than Malinowski the role of myths in daily life, nor attached more importance than he (perhaps excessive importance?) to the utilitarian significance of myth, quite contrary to the view held by the naturalist, symbolist and poetic schools of mythology, and contrary, too, to the theory of myth as history.[13] Although I believe that students of the religions and myths of ancient Europe can learn a great deal both from his criticism and from his own theories, I also believe that they will come to realise that the myth in his view is much more than the mere traditional, poetic or symbolic explanation of natural phenomena. Rather is it the expression of an order which embraces nature itself; an order which is ultimately evolved by man according to his own criteria and conventions.

Magical Thought; the Conception of Man and the World

The religions of the most enlightened communities, as of the least, conform in some way or other to the primitive world order we have outlined. Thus when the Catholic child learns his prayers and recites the Lord's Prayer or the Creed, he automatically arranges the cosmos with God the Father in heaven, and with hell in the depths of the earth along with the kingdom of evil. And the child may add to these basic ideas others which, although they are not included in any dogma, possess a life-force which is stronger than chance or circumstance, or historical and epistemological considerations.

This primitive conception of things can be represented diagrammatically in two complementary systems. (Fig. 1)

In the first system, we have the heavens on the one hand as a masculine element, symbolising paternity, a superior authority; and, on the other, the earth, the symbol of motherhood and fecundity. In the second, sun and day are associated with Life, Strength and Good; and the moon and night with Death and Evil. The moon is a feminine element like the earth, but without the latter's fecundity.

Thus the development of man and his world depends on a series of elemental facts, systematically linked together, and involving all created beings, including those in communities that are far from primitive. These facts comprise two systems which include both physical and moral phenomena. And in reality it seems impossible to find real barriers between these two types of phenomenon. This elemental world is representational—an expression of will, as Schopenhauer wanted it to be. Only by processes of the intellect can distinctions be drawn between the 'natural' and the 'moral'. In fact the intellectuals of today manage, with an almost Alexandrian virtuosity, (similar as they are in many respects to the thinkers of the Hellenistic world) to make endless distinctions; they speak of culture, society, history, and so on, as if they were entirely independent concepts, in opposition, what is more, to the concept of nature. These intellectuals carve up religious experience in a wholly arbitrary fashion.

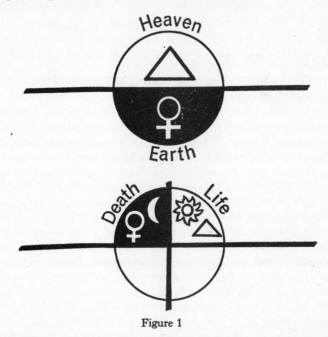

Figure 1

But to return to our systematised world, broken down into large categories in the simple way we have described. These spatial and temporal patterns of the cosmos and the world condition the nature of magic acts of particular individuals and particular communities, more especially those that can be put under the general heading of *sorcery* and *witchcraft*. Every myth, whether it relates to heaven or earth, has some sort of moral or even utilitarian value in the life of the community; the community must necessarily,

9

therefore, have some significance in relation to magical activities. Let us clarify this idea by going further into the question of magic in general.

At the beginning of this century, many of the investigations being carried out into magic in antiquity were affected by the view that magic was an isolated fact. In the early 1900s sweeping anthropological definitions were the fashion, and many were invented then or widely used, such as animism, preanimism, totemism and so on, despite numerous debates about their exactitude.

Nowadays, these definitions are thought to have a much more limited value; it is felt that they only bring out one aspect of what is in reality a complex of ideas more easily described than defined. It is clear that the anthropologists who were responsible for the 'theories and definitions of magic' evolved at that period had to work rather hard to keep their observations within the bounds of the definitions and classifications they favoured.

Some of the most famous of these theoreticians (in agreement with Hegel) believed that magic in itself reflects a more primitive and ancient concept of things than religion. And because of the ease with which evolutionary hypotheses were given universal validity in those days, the facts which emerged from vast research projects (taking in all kinds of different countries and periods) were always arranged in such a way that those which seemed to be related to magic were put earlier in time than those connected with religion. When magical and religious practices were found together (as they quite frequently were) it was readily assumed that the former corresponded to a separate and earlier phase of evolution than the latter. Inevitably Frazer, who was responsible for working out the best known general theory of the period based on a broad survey of sympathetic magic with its two branches ('homeopathic' and 'contagious' magic), had to write a chapter on the relations between magic and religion. But he went no further than explaining them as the results of a 'mixture of magic and religion' which occurred at later periods: a 'fusion' or 'amalgam' of pre-existing processes.[14]

The fact is that when he proceeded as he did—in all good faith and with the best of objective intentions—he was methodologically at fault, and broke up the unity of a series of separate systems in order to make them fit into a hypothetical time pattern or correspond to completely rationalistic combinations.

In any case, it was already difficult at that time for the less doctrinaire-minded to separate what was magical from what was religious in systems like those of the Egyptians, Chaldeans and other ancient peoples. And what was finally deduced from Frazer's vast fund of information and from other similar sources was the fact that not only were religious rituals linked with considerable frequency to magical practices, but also that each group of religious beliefs had its own special magic. It is reasonable, therefore, to suppose that public acts of magic, carried out for the benefit of society (rain-making magic, or magic to improve harvests, etc.), correspond to particular myths which have their Ethos and Eros within a religious system, just as black magic fits into another kind of system.

In the world of classical antiquity there was a striking succession (which Frazer himself described) of rain-making priests, of priest-kings, and of kings who were incarnations of the gods (even of Jupiter himself); they all had important ritual duties to perform, although they might themselves be the object of mysterious rites. All this makes us realise that very special types of magic must have evolved in the *highest* spheres of Greek and Roman society in relation to the *celestial* and *solar* divinities: a system of magic which was frequently hereditary, which justified the existence of royal and priestly families and which served to solve public problems. This form of magic was the product of social pressures.

We cannot hope to give an adequate idea of all this here. Our aim is less ambitious. We are going to put forward certain concrete facts to show how, in this same world of classical times, the ideas of moon, night and death are very closely linked, and how with them one finds also certain feminine factors. Ultimately, these ideas are connected with acts of Black Magic in which a certain type of woman was believed to take a specific part.

In the society of antiquity, as in other societies which are observable today, magic was not really an isolated system to which one could have recourse as one does to a specific science. In each case magic is man's answer to a particular situation. We may be able to diagnose with greater accuracy than the ancients when something involving a concept of magic occurs. In the case of female witchcraft our eyes can see still more clearly, and we do not need to have recourse to abstract ideas.

11

Our examinations of witchcraft in the Graeco-Roman world will also serve as a basis for a broader historical investigation of the phenomenon in later periods, following the same pattern. Furthermore, witchcraft itself presents us with a problem to which we have already referred in the prologue to this book; one that has broad implications for philosophy as well as for religion. Since the myth content of witchcraft is so varied, the logic of the acts performed in connexion with it so extraordinary, and the moral intentions underlying it no less equivocal, witchcraft has seemed almost incomprehensible to many of those who have been concerned with the nature of human thought at different periods. It has consequently given rise to numerous conjectures, polemics and arguments.

Thus, for example, we may note that Plotinus (whose point of view could hardly be said to have much in common with that of a scholar with rationalist leanings, like Frazer, in the early years of the present century) could already hold the view that magical acts could be explained by the sympathy or harmony which exists between like things, and the antipathy which exists between those which are unlike. Consequently, Plotinus believed that certain forces could interact without human intervention, although he added that the magician is able to establish contacts as he wants them, as a result of his special knowledge.

The same philosopher—something of a thaumaturge—also held that the magician could only attack the irrational part of an individual. Consequently the wise man, whose reason was paramount, was unsusceptible to the effects of magic.[15]

Is there, perhaps, in reality some sympathy, some affinity, something in common between moon, night and woman which explains the system that we are about to describe? If there is, who brings out this sympathy or affinity? Is it the woman herself when she performs acts of witchcraft, or is it the people who watch her at her work, who seek her aid, or who persecute her when they find her at her witchery? Personally I believe that in this, as in other matters, *public opinion* is more worth while taking into account than the witch's own views of herself. For our purpose, what a person is said to do carries more significance than what that person actually does.

And here I must once more insist that the frontiers between physical reality and the world of the imagination and myths have not always been so clear cut as some people seem to believe today. Between what physically exists and what man imagines, or has in the past imagined to exist, there lies a region in which the evidently real and the imaginary seem to overlap. As a result, people—not to mention other kinds of animal life—could be thought to have certain characteristics of an unnatural kind. Sorceresses and witches have existed in this region of *experience*; and they have played the most extraordinary parts in a world in which animals, planets and stars, light and darkness, were all felt to be close to man and to be capable of human passions. However arbitrary such a view of life may appear, and however hard our task, it is clear that certain distinctions and qualifications have to be made between one kind of consciousness and another, if the personality of the witch is to be understood.

So far we have been examining only the central figure or figures in our discussion of magic: the magicians and sorcerers and witches. But it is impossible to form any clear idea of magic, sorcery and witchcraft, without considering the people among whom they work, or more accurately, the people among whom they are believed to work: those members of a society or community who benefit from or suffer as a result of their acts of witchcraft or sorcery.

The role of society in witchcraft can be called a passive one. But it plays an extremely important part in the problems we are about to study. In the last instance, the reality of acts of magic is a consequence of the belief that an illness, a storm or some other misfortune or setback on the one hand, or a success on the other, are directly attributable to some other person or persons, with malevolent or benevolent designs.

The effects on a society of consistently believing itself the object or victim of magical acts are incalculable. The whole system of religious and legal sanctions in that community will need to be adjusted to what may be called a magical sense of life.

But witchcraft varies from one period to the next in its social significance. At one stage it is treated as an accepted practice and at another as the activity of a dissident and feared minority; sometimes it is seen as a means of satisfying envious designs, at others as an indulgence in sexual abandon; now it is an individual performance and now a collective cult; the cult of a false Deity or a real Devil; a reality or a delusion.

13

In this book one of our main objects will be to describe how, as a result of appalling and tragic experiences, European societies finally came to eradicate this magical sense of life altogether, deleting the so-called crimes of magic, witchcraft and sorcery from their legal systems and codes at the same time. Even those who look upon our subject as utterly unimportant and even absurd have to admit that it has ramifications of some consequence.

PART ONE

THE CLASSICAL BACKGROUND

CHAPTER 2

THE NATURE OF THE WITCH IN GRAECO-ROMAN TIMES

Theories about magic – Magic and religion in the classical world – Maleficent magic – Amatory magic – Mercenary magic – Metamorphosis – Conclusions

Theories about Magic

Several theories have been put forward to explain the phenomenon of witchcraft. According to one it had historical origins in the cult of Diana, and witchcraft as found in Europe at the time of the major persecutions was merely a development of this cult. Others have linked witchcraft with the Devil of Christian theology, and yet others have held that it was the product of specific social conditions which obtained in the Middle Ages. The subject has also been connected with magic, and studied in the light of the various general theories about magic evolved by anthropologists in the latter half of the nineteenth and early years of the twentieth century.

Anthropological investigation and research has made great strides since then and not all the theories of that period can be accepted without reserve today. Yet all of them contain elements of truth. Generally speaking, however, they tended to over-simplify, and witchcraft is more complex than they would have us believe. The problem is to find some new thesis which will satisfactorily take into account the views that still hold water.

It seems to me that the best way to approach the subject is to take a specific social context about which we have adequate historical information, and investigate the relationship in it between night, the moon and nocturnal spirits, and the belief that certain women have the power to perform certain acts connected with them. We must also try to ascertain the real nature of the acts she was believed to perform.

Magic and Religion in the Classical World

Let us start by studying the situation as it was in classical times.[1] According to the leading authorities on magic in Greece and Rome, processes believed to be specifically magical are known to have been employed in both these societies to produce rain, prevent hail-storms, drive away clouds, calm the winds, make animals and plants prosper, increase wealth and fortune, cure sickness and so on. But magic was also used in Greece and Rome for more obviously perverted reasons: in country areas, for instance, it might be used to ruin an enemy's crops or make his cattle sicken; in the city, it was used to strike down an enemy when he was on the point of making a speech or taking an important part in some public celebration; or it was used to prevent a rival from winning a race or some other event in the public games. Death was quite frequently considered to be the result of witchery, and such beliefs were not confined to any one sector of society.[2] What we might call erotic magic is a whole world in itself.[3]

It is important to realise that any description or analysis of Graeco-Roman magic which fails to take into account the intention, whether good or bad, underlying specific acts, or the social stratum in which they take place, is bound to be invalid. Acts may be produced by similar processes, and yet be essentially and radically different in their ends.

Thus the practice of magic for beneficent purposes was considered legal and even necessary in Greece and Rome. It was commonly practised by a great variety of people; the priests of specific deities on the one hand, and professional people, such as doctors, on the other.[4] The state itself supported those whose business it was to augur the future or make prognostications for special occasions, and those who, in the public interest, discovered by divination what had happened or what was about to happen. A variety of techniques was used for this purpose, and these have been studied in detail in books on the religion and cults of the

18

Greeks and Romans. It is not, therefore, necessary to go over the same ground here.[5]

Even the austerest Roman authors included magic formulae for obtaining useful and beneficial results in their work. Treatises on agriculture and medicine and the offices used by priests for certain cults and rites, contain collections of spells and obscure writings probably of an invocational nature.[6]

Occasionally it is possible to detect a kind of scepticism even there. For the same technical treatises warn farmers and country-folk not to believe foreign diviners and sorcerers[7] nor women referred to as *sagae*.[8]

What of the magic and spells which were intended to cause harm? These were always held to be illegal. From the earliest times and even when there was some doubt about the spells' effectiveness, it was considered a serious criminal offence to make them. Plato made a distinction between those with a professional knowledge of maleficent practices and mere amateurs. Doctors were included among the professionals, but, speaking as a states-man rather than as a religious individual, Plato thought that pro-fessionals who tried to do evil should be condemned to death. Amateurs, on the other hand, ought to be let off more lightly.[9]

But that is not all. Although almost anyone might use spells in moments of violent stress, it was generally felt that they were more usually used by a particular type of person and in very specific circumstances. And Plato attacked those who believed they could summon up the dead and even bend the gods to do their will by spells as well as by prayers.[10] It is possible that the passage which contains this particular attack is a specific reference to followers of the Orphic cult. But it should be remembered that there were a number of divinities in the ancient world known to be propitious to evil actions, however odd this may seem to us today, brought up as we are, whether believers or agnostics, in an era of Christianity.

In the Christian religion, God is the very image of Good, and the Devil of Evil. But the gods of the pagans—and some pagans were shocked by this—were subject to the same forces of evil and passions as men; even to the same fleeting and capricious desires. Maleficent magic has to be seen in relation to this kind of god. And this is not easy. The simplest thing to do is to examine the concrete forms which magic took, and see whether they were the

19

result of belief in the power of spells and invocations, or belief in the power of supplications. But the whole relationship between magic and religion in antiquity appears complex, even if we follow the views put forward by classical authors themselves.

Take Lucan for example. He was a man who liked mystery and was keen on posing questions it was difficult to answer. In the course of discussing the objects, which were capable of *forcing the gods to do something* ('vim factura deis'),[11] owned by a sorcerer called Erichtho, and after enumerating the more extraordinary unnatural acts which it was possible to perform with the aid of Black Magic, Lucan asked himself how it was possible to force the gods in this way. Did the gods like obeying the spells of the sorcerer, he wondered? And did the power of these spells lie in some unknown form of piety, or were they the result of some mysterious ability to threaten?[12]

These are some of the fundamental problems of magic common to many different peoples. Lucan has expressed them very clearly. But he has not solved them. He merely presents us with three hypotheses which the student of magic and religion must constantly bear in mind.

When the magician invokes, curses or threatens the gods, he assumes that they have certain weaknesses he can exploit. This is either because the gods are capricious, or because the magician knows their secrets, which are witheld from other mortals, sometimes because of their shameful nature. Or there may be other explanations still stranger than these, such as, for instance, the existence of some strange *kinship* between the magician and the gods, or a certain affinity and sympathy with them, such as those to which Plotinus refers.

In order to understand the mentality of the magician it must first be realised that the gods of the Greeks and Romans were held to be largely subject to the same physical and spiritual laws as men. The ideas of good and evil were related to physical feelings and experiences even in the case of the gods. In other words, nature and morality, divinity and humanity could not be put in the same watertight compartments as they are today, in the philosophical and religious systems of a world ruled by science and largely secular in character.

What then was the nature of the Greek and, more particularly, the Roman gods?

In Greek and Roman times, according to Otto, the spirit-world was thought to be so all-embracing that the most insignificant human actions were held to be the expression of something divine, while the celestial and terrestrial bodies were gods in themselves. Nature could not possibly, therefore, be thought of as a separate entity with an independent system of laws. And with such a view of nature as this, there could be no absolute frontier between magic and religion. Minds which believed in the existence of so many gods, and which were dominated by a magical conception of things, could hardly be expected to distinguish radically between nature and religion.

The view that magic in general (and the magic of antiquity in particular) is only marginally connected, if at all, with religion —susceptible, therefore, of being studied independently—is quite invalid. The truth of the matter is that the two are much more closely interrelated than is generally thought to be the case; their two fields of influence overlap. But it is possible to agree that, in general, magic is connected with man's *desire* and *will*, and religion with feelings of *respect, gratefulness* and *submission*.

However, the issue is not as simple as this. Whichever of the two dominates a situation there is always a third force which comes between the individual, who wants something in the course of everyday life—whether good or bad, and motivated by either love or hate—and the object of his desire. This third factor sometimes involves a magician or sorcerer and sometimes a priest. The former make conjurations, the latter normally prays or makes a sacrifice. There are occasions, however, when the priest will resort to magical practices like conjurations, and the magician will use prayers and sacrifices. But it is at least clear that in neither case is the approach in any sense 'naturalistic,' involving a concept of nature like our own. This is not to say that the societies of classical times did not believe in natural events. But the only ones they believed in were those everyday-life occurrences devoid of all religious significance or magical purpose. A religious or a magical element at once transformed the events in question, making them mysterious, secret, awe-inspiring. In fact, Otto was right, I believe, when he suggested that magic was an aspect of what he called 'numinosity'.[13] He was also right in thinking that natural things—from the point of view that concerns us at present—were quite simply whatever was not 'numinous'.[14]

21

The simplest pattern of action involving an individual who desires something, the object of his desire, and an intermediary, can be expressed in the way shown in diagram 2. A second case could be expressed as in diagram 3 and a third might be represented by diagram 4.

With only a slight modification of the pattern we could obtain a fourth possibility. Diagram 5.

It would also be possible to combine a spell with a prayer, or for the one to take place after the other. But in any case it is plainly impossible in the present instance to make a rigid distinction between what is religious and what is magical, given the lack of rigidity of human thoughts and emotions. Nor is it possible, for the same reason, to fix a chronological order and say that one

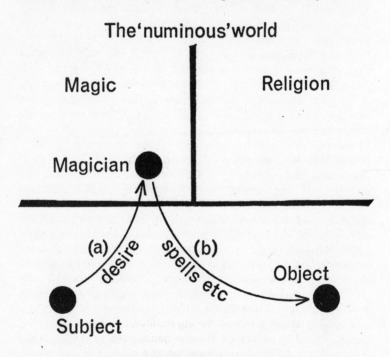

The 'numinous' world

Magic

Religion

Magician

(a) desire   (b) spells etc

Object

Subject

The natural world

Figure 2

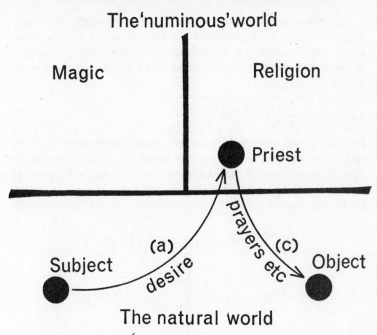

Figure 3

process (the magical one, for example) takes place *before* or *after* the other (the religious one in this case).

Nor can we say that religion is exclusively concerned with good, and magic with evil or what is morally indifferent (neither good nor evil). The civil authorities in classical times sometimes thought that the cults and rites which were practised at the period were a threat to social order,[15] yet it is equally true that Christianity has sometimes led to error and sacrilege. Magic and religion cannot, I repeat, be separated as simply as people used to think.

The only real distinction that can be made is between White and Black Magic. These terms, which have become part of every-day usage, reflect an intuitive appreciation of the dual role of magic: useful to society on the one hand, done in the open and in the broad daylight; anti-social on the other, evil and secret, done under the cover of night. Each of these roles would produce a totally different pattern of relationships between the individual, the object desired, and the intermediary.

We must now discuss the second of the two magics. For Black Magic is much more relevant for our purpose than White—even in the way in which it is connected with religion and mythology. We shall refer to this kind of magic as witchcraft for the sake of clarity.

Maleficent Magic

Evil has its own proper setting—the night. And gods who are propitious. It also has its own qualified ministers. For evil is ultimately achieved by combining a series of techniques which have been passed down from one generation to the next. It would be out of place to mention here all the Greek and Roman texts

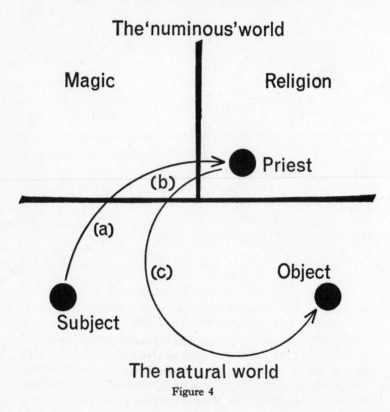

Figure 4

24

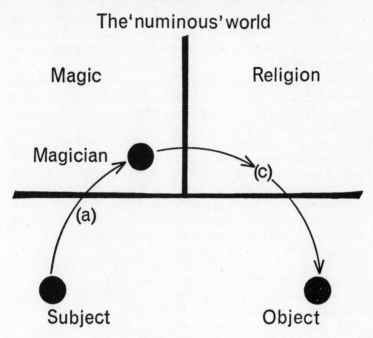

The 'numinous' world

Magic

Religion

Magician

(c)

(a)

Subject

Object

The natural world

Figure 5

which prove that the night was looked upon as the proper time for committing evil deeds, because of its silence and the atmosphere of secrecy that surrounds it. However, some of the more important and significant passages are perhaps worth quoting.[16]

It is certainly a commonplace in classical poets for witches to appear at the most obviously secret hours. As Ovid has it:

> *Nox, ait, arcanis fidissima, quaeque diurnis*
> *aurea cum Luna succeditis ignibus, astra*[17]

In these well-known lines the Latin poet is in fact describing Medea, one of the greatest witches of classical mythology, when she is on the point of committing a particularly evil action.

Horace's witch, Canidia, invoking the powers of night, is also well worth quoting for the realistic qualities of the passage:

'Night and Diana, ye faithful witnesses of all my enterprises, who command silence when we are celebrating our most secret mysteries, come to my assistance, and turn all your power and wrath against my enemies'.[18]

Here we find two of the deities who preside over magical acts mentioned in the same text. But the qualities of night are always less clearly defined than those of the moon. The moon, perhaps because it changes shape, changes its name. In Horace it is Diana: since, whatever the origin of this Roman goddess, she was held to be the equivalent of the Greek Artemis. In Theocritus, we find a similar invocation addressed to Selene.[19] But there is another name which is also associated with the moon: that of Hecate, a goddess with more than one side to her nature. She was primarily looked upon as queen of the spirits of the dead, and was believed to be present both when the spirit entered the human body and when it left it; that is, at birth and at death. She lived in tombs, although she could also sit by the hearth, perhaps because that was at one time the place for family burials. And she also appeared at cross-roads on clear nights with a following of spirits and dogs who set up terrifying howls.[20]

At these cross-roads offerings were placed each month to propitiate the goddess. These consisted of the remains of purifying sacrifices. Initially Caria (in Asia Minor) seems to have been the centre of the Hecate-cult, but it also existed in Thessaly. This is particularly interesting because Thessaly was always well known for its witches. Hecate is, in fact, a deity around whom secret cults and ideas of terror could easily develop.[21] Her help was sought in cases of madness, since madness was believed to be caused by the souls of the departed.[22]

A whole group of ideas that might be termed 'cthonic' evolved around the deities Selene, Hecate and Diana. And even today the power of the moon in relation to the mind continues to find expression in such common terms as 'lunatic,' referring to someone who is thought to be under the influence of the moon, and 'moon-struck' etc. But there is more to it than that.

In my view it is clear that a particular sexual significance was attached to these deities. They are either virgin goddesses or goddesses of erotic mysteries; not mother goddesses, for whom love meant principally fertility.

Now let us turn to their ministers. The existence of two

sorceresses, the celebrated sisters Medea and Circe, who are even believed to be *daughters* of Hecate, traditionally dates back to heroic times.[23] Circe symbolises seduction and is the archetype of the woman who by being 'enchanting' or 'bewitching' as well as by her skill, makes all men bow to her will. (It is interesting to notice the sexual significance which we attach to these words, regardless of their original magical connotations.)[24]

Circe turns Ulysses' companions into pigs, but they still retain as animals the mental faculties they had as human beings—νοῦς.[25] In Homeric times, then, people believed the reverse of what St Augustine was to believe. For the latter, metamorphosis was the direct result of a mental derangement induced by the Devil, but with no physical reality. Circe ends up by falling in love with Ulysses, who turned out to be her equal in diplomacy.

Medea is perhaps less complex: she is the archetype of the tragic female and has been immortalised as such in drama. 'You have knowledge and wisdom'—she says to herself in the soliloquy in which she declares her intention of avenging herself on her unfaithful husband. 'Besides,' she adds, 'nature has made us women absolutely incapable of doing good and particularly skilful in doing evil.'[26] In the same soliloquy she admits her reverence for Hecate above all other gods and speaks of her as her helper.[27] In this short text, in fact, we have a woman, albeit a particular type of women with a violently sensual and frustrated nature, who is bent on doing evil, in possession of recondite knowledge, τέχνη, and a vassal or dependent of a feminine goddess associated with terror and the night. This is the basis of a system: the 'logos' of maleficent magic or witchcraft. But Medea, like Circe, is the protagonist of events which took place in legendary times. So let us turn to texts which refer to a less obscure period.

Other texts speak of the τέχνη or *scientia* of the more ordinary witches. Even Horace, in *Epode* 17, when writing a satire on a witch he frequently attacked elsewhere, begins by speaking of the science itself. After mentioning its patrons, Proserpina and Diana, he refers to the books of incantations, *libros carminum*, and to the chief instrument used in making spells of all sorts, the *turbo* or ρόμβος (which had only to be rotated in the reverse direction to undo what had already been done). He goes on to list the various arts that are the witch's pride, such as the ability to call down the moon from the sky with her chanting, to make waxen figures move, to invoke the spirits of the dead, to make love philtres[28]—all the skills, in fact, mentioned time and again by earlier and subsequent writers.

The magic arts are passed down from one generation to the next: a point which need not be laboured in view of what anthropologists have already said on the subject. As Malinowski wrote in a well-known essay: 'Magic never originated, it was never made or invented.'[29] The use of mythological allusions and invocations to certain deities can, perhaps, be explained if magical formulae are passed down from ages in which man was closer to the gods. The fact that the most ancient and archetypal witches of classical times, as has already been pointed out, date from a period when heroes and demigods (the sons and kinsmen of the gods themselves) walked the earth, tends to bear this out. This transmission of knowledge about witchcraft would also explain why certain parts of the ancient world enjoyed a particular reputation for magic—maleficent magic. The Greeks believed, as we have already said, that Thessaly had a particularly high population of witches. At a later date Apuleius speaks of the power that these witches had over the forces of nature.[30]

Witches would change themselves into dogs, birds or flies,[31] the better to carry out their deeds; they would shrink their bodies to enter houses,[32] and use the entrails of the dead to make their spells.[33] These spells would frequently be used to attract men or women to whom they had taken a liking,[34] and they generally avenged themselves savagely on any who resisted their attentions,[35] although at times they were satisfied with turning them into frogs, beavers or lambs for long or short periods of time,[36] and with urinating on the faces of any terrified individuals who happened to see them carrying out their evil deeds.[37]

This quintessence of witchcraft could equally well be applied to many other parts of the world. In Italy, the Sabines and the Marsians were reckoned to have the highest proportion of witches among them. But the spells of the Marsians at one time seemed unsophisticated to experts.[38]

Let us now turn our attention to the deeds which Apuleius attributed to the witches of Thessaly, and compare them with those found in other places. First of all, the magical rite itself; the substances used and their preparation are all important. Some serve to simulate the object desired, others are used because of their contact with the object, to produce sympathetic magic; yet others have only some intrinsic virtue which, in appearance at least, seems to have no possible connexion of cause or effect, contact or similarity, with the object. Poets, even in the most premote times (such as Laevius for instance), liked to list these strange substances:[39] φάρμακον, ἀγώγιμος, ριλίρον, *poculum*, are some of the names used to describe their, concoctions.

But there is another point of technique which is more significant than this. The magician, and to a still greater extent the sorcerer or the witch, are impelled by their emotions and desires to work themselves into their part, rather like actors on the stage, except that theirs is a deeper involvement. Dramatisation is essential. Even more so if we accept Malinowski's thesis that magic is an answer to the sense of despair which men and women feel in a world which is beyond their control.[40]

Malinowski has been criticised for his utilitarianism in defending this point of view, and for basing his general theories on a limited field of observation.[41] However, this criticism loses its force when it is a non-utilitarian magic that is under review, one that has no positive or public purpose: a witchcraft that is merely intended to satisfy the violent passions of individuals, always the same in men and women regardless of time and place.

A woman in love casting a spell to attract a lover who spurns her, is as good an example as any of the effects of despair and impotence on a person dominated by an ardent but unrequited sensual passion. But let us look at some concrete instances. Here, for example, is a story told by Theocritus in one of his most beautiful poems:[42] Simeta lives the life of a normal girl until she falls in love with Delphis (who is a classic example of the good-looking young man who lets women love him). She gives in to him only to be deserted subsequently, and in her state of passionate despair decides to regain her lost love by means of magic. Aided by a slave, she plays her part dramatically and does nothing to conceal her passions and desires. First, she calls on the most propitious gods to help her to win back the beautiful Delphis. These are Selene and Hecate. And to do the will of these gods there is a mysterious bird called Jynx, who is referred to rhythmically in the conjuration, where he is begged and commanded in the following terms: 'Jynx, bring this man to my house . . .'

The command is repeated as often as ten times.[43] Simeta,

29

while she speaks makes motions with the *rhombus* or 'bull-roarer ', and throws flour and salt on the special fire, on which a branch of laurel is also burning and a figure of wax is melting; for Delphis will have to be consumed with love as the laurel is consumed with fire, he will melt away like the wax and will circle Simeta's house like the *rhombus* circling in the air.[44] This is imitative (sympathetic) magic, certainly, but it has been preceded by an invocation and by a kind of formal confession of Simeta's desires. To whom does she make this confession? Naturally to the divine Selene: to the moon. In the second part of the poem, when Simeta relates how she fell in love and how her fortunes changed subsequently, she also chants several times the line: 'August Selene, consider my love and the object of my affection',[45] as if its repetition were a vital part of the ritual.

The line is repeated twelve times, and at the end there is a short, final prayer to the moon and the stars and to the night herself.[46]

Much more horrifying than Simeta's invocation is the one which occurs in a work called *Philosophumena*. It is addressed to Hecate and reads as follows when translated: 'Come infernal, terrestrial, and celestial Bombo, goddess of the cross-roads, guiding light, queen of the night, enemy of the sun, and friend and companion of the darkness; you who rejoice to hear the barking of dogs and to see blood flow; you who wander among the tombs in the hours of darkness, thirsty for blood, and the terror of mortal men; Gorgo, Mormo, moon of a thousand forms, look favourably on my sacrifice.'[47] The invocation always conforms to certain poetic forms, with special rhythms and even onomatopoeia. This is an essential part of the logos of magic.

Incantations are, in fact, to a large extent 'carmina', songs; similar to poetry. And the line of poetry, like an incantation, has a specific power or force for the poet.[48] The magical value of the line may be enhanced when its meaning is not absolutely clear. The dramatic manner of its recitation, its rhythmic quality and hermetic significance, all contribute to its emotive force. Some modern poets have come very close to the sorcerers of classical antiquity in their views of poetry.[49]

But apart from the 'mythos' and 'logos' of magic and sorcery, there is still the 'ethos' and 'eros' to be considered. We have already suggested that it is the negative ethos of witchcraft which makes it sensibly different from other magical and religious forms of expression. In most instances it runs counter to the interests of society as a whole. And when love is involved, it is violent and uncontrolled. Love, for the witch, is a consuming passion, never love for one's neighbour. When she works for someone else, it is for some perverted purpose or for financial gain.

Amatory Magic

Personalities need to be particularly strong in a world swayed by desire and ruled by violent passions. And sorcerers and witches have, as a rule, nearly always been strong characters, from the time of Simon Magus down to the eighteenth century, when the magician, Count Cagliostro, had the French court at his feet. Witches of antiquity were equally forceful characters, with overdeveloped personalities. Their talents and learning may not have been very highly developed, but one side of their character certainly was: their bad character, one might say.

Perhaps the most hair-raising description of such a personality dating from classical times is given by Lucan when he relates how Sextus Pompeius, while in Thessaly, came to consult Erichtho. We have already referred to a part of this poem.[50] Sextus Pompeius, in despair, no longer seeks to employ the more or less orthodox methods for telling the future used in pagan times, but has recourse to the 'savage practice of sorcerers' (*saevorum arcana magorum*):[51] the emphatic form of the phrase is obvious.

But Erichtho had raised these criminal rites to a degree of perversity not previously known. Not satisfied with the usual rites performed by the witches of Thessaly—such as calling down the moon from the sky[52]—she made use of the dead. She is, in fact, a much magnified image of the typical witch who appears in stories, mutilating corpses horribly in order to acquire the materials for her spells. The poet voluntarily allows himself to be carried along on the flow of horrors—a trait which some might think to be typically Spanish—describing in perverse detail the foul acts of Erichtho.[53]

Lucan also believed in the existence of gods who preside over magical acts.[54] And which of these could be more propitious to black magic than the moon? Erichtho even gives momentary life to a corpse by blowing a 'lunar virus' into it.[55] After inserting the virus and making the most revolting concoction, and after chanting the menacing invocation to the spirits, the shade of the corpse appears.[56] But it is frightened to rejoin its body, so what will happen? The sorceress breaks into long and threatening imprecations against the gods in order to complete the spell, treating them as if she were in a position to harm them. The pagan gods, as we have already said, have their weaknesses, and are so human, in fact, that they can feel shame. So the witch uses her skill and knowledge to force them to act in the way she wants, by referring to their failings if necessary.

Apart from using her skill, the witch may also put herself into a strong position *vis-à-vis* the gods by pacts: secret pacts, as Lucan himself believed. These enabled her to approach the gods on a different footing from the customary deferential one. Or she might have some inherited kinship, affinity or sympathy with the gods which gave her power over them.

Each person in the drama has his proper setting, each act is duly narrated. Homer puts Circe in a mysterious and remote geographical situation; Euripides makes Medea the avenger of a past offence. Lucan places Erichtho in the grim setting of civil wars. But the ordinary witches of classical times are most skilfully portrayed by non-epic poets; poets who delight in observing human passions, or satirists who take an ironic view of the effects of passions in the world around them. There are, in fact, more references to amatory magic (and those who cultivated it) in certain classical poets than in any other class of writers. Theocritus among the Greeks, Horace and Ovid among the Romans were great authorities on the subject. Later on, novelists and satirical prose-writers like Petronius, Lucian and Apuleius (each with their own individual viewpoint) were attracted by the witches and the acts they claimed to perform. Let us see what such writers as these, more realistic in their outlook than the epic poets, have to say about the motives of witches.

The world of Black Magic—and this is a point which cannot be too much stressed—is the world of desire. The great witch figures of Greek tragedy appear to be dominated by violent passions. Medea, inflamed with her blind love for Jason, betrays her own people; later her love turns to hatred when she realises that Jason loves another woman,[57] and the revenge she takes is terrible.

Other women, deceived or abandoned in their love seek rather to regain their lovers. Theocritus's Simeta is one of these, and her careful preparations to attract Delphis have already been described.[58] But sometimes instead of the attractive figure of a girl in love we find a mature woman motivated by erotic desires sharpened by advancing age: the critical period sexually for both men and women. The best known picture of a witch with long years of erotic experience behind her is to be found in Horace.

The Fifth Epode describes how a child who has been carried off from his home by Canidia the witch, begs her and her companions to do him no harm. Later, when he realises that they will have no pity on him, he lays curses on them. Canidia has, in fact, met together with other witches—Sagana, Veia and Folia of Ariminum—with the intention of employing magic to regain at all costs the love of Varus or Varo, her former lover. The first spell is brewed from maleficent substances such as a wild fig which has been growing on a tomb, funereal cypress, toad's blood, the bones and feathers of a screech-owl (*striga*), herbs from Iolchos and Hiberia (particularly poisonous countries) and bones snatched from the mouth of a hungry bitch.[59] Later, there will be a chance to use the liver and marrow of the unfortunate child for a strong love potion (*poculum amoris*), if other spells prove ineffective.[60]

To commence, the witch invokes the propitious spirits—the moon and Diana as we have already said—and after a short time she is able to see what is happening elsewhere. The lover is on the move; but he is off to see a woman who has used subtler magical methods than hers so far.[61] The child has therefore to be killed, and the child's curse follows. In it there are two enigmatic lines which seem to imply that the witches will be overwhelmed with remorse[62] and will be pursued by crowds through the streets in their old age, and stoned.[63] Early commentaries on Horace suggest that Canidia was really a Neopolitan perfume-seller called Gratidia.[64] Horace evidently had several accounts to settle with her since he brings her into his work on more than one occasion. Once in another of the *Epodes*; and again in the Satires,[65] where she appears with Sagana, who has also been mentioned before, hunting for corpses. Witches who went about Esquilinus by night were, like Pamphilia in Apuleius's *Golden Ass*: '*maga primi nominis et omnis carminis sepulchralis magistra*'.[66] But for every case—like that of Apuleius himself—in which a man is accused

33

of winning a woman's love thanks to his own knowledge of magic, there are many others of a different kind.[67]

Mercenary Magic

Persons of both sexes who love or physically desire someone else but are unable, like Simeta or Canidia, to make magic themselves, have recourse to a third party—the classical or professional witch who earns a living by her arts. In her activities as a go-between the witch may indeed use magic, but she does not entirely discard more conventional methods of seduction. Ovid has described a witch like this in a poem remarkable for its profound psychological insight.

Before going on to discuss this work, it should be remembered that, even amongst primitive peoples, natural methods of achieving ends were not entirely disregarded in favour of magic. If a straightforward study of human desires and passions suggested that other methods might be effective a sorcerer would use them.[68] According to an old Spanish proverb one should 'call on God for help and strike with one's mace at the same time'. And this would not be a bad summary of the magician's point of view, with minor modifications. But let us look at Ovid's witch.

Dipsas, as she is called, is a drunken and spiteful old lady. Her name itself suggests her qualities, since *dipsa* means thirst in Greek[69] and *dipsada* refers to a certain type of viper in Latin. She was known to work magic and was skilled in the art of conjuring spirits; her knowledge of the properties of herbs, and magical substances in general, was extensive. It was said that she took the form of a bird and flew about by night; and the poet adds that she had two pupils in one of her eyes and practised necromancy, summoning up the spirits of her ancestors.

Dipsas's achievements, however, did not stop there. She lived in a city society where women did not think morality very important, so she could be a useful go-between. Her smooth tongue and attractive propositions helped her, and she would try to procure any woman who fell into her clutches for financial advantage.[70]

Dipsas is by no means unique in the poetry and novels of classical times. Petronius's Proselenos, an older woman than Dipsas, is one of her kind, and she is connected with the moon, as her name suggests.[71]

Lucian refers to a similar type of person when he makes the Athenian lady Mellita ask Bacchis if she knows of any old woman who could bend others to her will. There were supposed to be many of them in Thessaly according to Mellita, and she wanted one of them to win back Charinus's love for her.[72] Tibullus, too, had earlier made use of the skill and cunning of a woman who claimed that she could help him to have an affair with Delia without her husband finding out.[73]

In addition to her skill in the magic arts, and her activities as a go-between, the witch acquired a rich store of experience. And this in turn enabled her to make poisons and perfumes—whose manufacture was often the work of a single person as late as the Renaissance, and even later, to some extent. In this respect, the witch is almost a forerunner of modern chemists and scientists, although she was hardly disinterested or objective in her approach. But at least there was no lack of herbs and 'simples' in her laboratory, and, indeed, by using particular herbs she may well have induced her own dream-states and those of her victims.[74] Certainly, as we shall see later on, specific information about the properties of plants was handed down by witches, at least, until mediaeval times.

When they wanted to change themselves into animals—above all into birds—the witches of classical antiquity which Lucian and Apuleius describe, would undress completely, put two grains of incense into a burning lamp, and remaining erect, mutter a few words over it. Then they would open a small chest or box holding various phials, and, choosing one which contained an oily liquid, rub the contents all over their bodies from the tips of their toes upwards. Wings and beaks would then sprout instantly, and uttering harsh cries they would float out of the window.[75]

Scholars have wondered whether this oily liquid or ointment could have had some special effect on the person using it. Could it for instance, have produced a dream-state in which the individual imagined he or she was taking part in witches' covens and 'sabbaths'? Writers at the time of the Renaissance, as we shall see, spoke of ointments which could dull the senses. The special use of such ointments must have been handed down from earlier times and this would imply that one generation of witches did indeed pass on its knowledge of herbal properties to the next. But it is always possible that the ointments had 'numinous' or spiritual properties.

35

Every spell has an antidote or can be rendered useless by one more powerful. A skilful rival was able to beat Horace's Canidia at her own game.[76] And a spell to awaken sexual desire could always be countered by one inducing frigidity or impotence.[77] Sometimes the witch or sorcerer made use of genuine scientific knowledge, at others pseudo-scientific information was employed and substances were held to have properties which, in reality, they do not have.

In order to make a man impotent both spells and poisonous substances might be used. Ovid in one of his poems describes a case of temporary impotence very similar to one which occurs in the *Satyricon*,[78] and suggests that the state could have been induced by a poison from Thessaly, a 'carmen', a herb, or even by someone holding aloft an image inscribed in red wax with the name of the victim.[79]

It is conceivable that this exceptional knowledge of herbs has a historical explanation, and was the result of the time spent by women collecting wild plants to eke out the food produced by the community, while the men hunted or robbed what they could. They would have learnt to recognise harmful as well as useful plants. Certainly there is often more logic in the witches' world than one might think.

Metamorphosis

It is more difficult to find acceptable historical hypotheses for the persistent belief that witches can change themselves or others into animals, in order to go on nocturnal expeditions, or wreak vengeance.

These two reasons for metamorphosis are important because they are the origin of two stock characters in literature and folklore: one is the *striga*, the other *Lucius* the ass or ass-man. When someone makes a speciality of one particular metamorphosis, such as the wolf-man (*Licanthropos*[80]—*loupgarou* in France, *lovisome* in Portugal) or the classical witch of antiquity who turns herself into a nocturnal bird, there arises a popular belief in dual natures, with some doubt as to which is the basic one. Some hold that the *striga* is primarily a nocturnal bird, others that she is really human.

Ovid has given a good description of the *strigae*, who under cover of night fed on babies, and uttered harsh cries as they flew about. He put forward three theories as to their origin:

1 They were born like it (*sive igitur nascuntur*).
2 They were enchanted (*seu carmine fiunt*).
3 They were old hags whose shape had been changed by spells (*Naenique in volucres Marsa figurat anus*).[81]

Petronius, on the other hand, puts into the mouth of a low-class character a classic incident in which the *strigae*, after beating up a strong man, substitute a straw doll for the body of a young child. The narrator ends up somewhat sententiously by saying that there are certain very wise women who are able, under cover of darkness, to overthrow the natural order of things: '*Rogo vos, oportet credatis, sunt mulieres plussciae, sunt Nocturnae, et quod sursum est, deorsum faciunt.*'[82] It is clear that in this case, the wise women of the night are specifically the *strigae*. Many views expressed in classical times are equally ambiguous. This is not to say, however, that such ideas are necessarily the product of a pre-logical mentality. For it is precisely in spiritual matters (those which are numinous) that facts which cannot be fitted into the so-called logical 'law of identity' chiefly occur.

The relative frequency with which this happens is of small consequence. But it was those who were prepared to believe in the existence of a pre-logical mentality (one which preceded logic in time, they would have us believe) who invented this law of identity. In fact, the ideas of 'simple identity' and 'complex identity' relate to quite different systems of thought, which can, however, be reconciled in the minds of people in the present as well as in the past. Just as the law of identity $(A = A)$ is valid for the common or 'natural' world, so the law of complex identity $(A = B)$ holds good for the spiritual or 'numinous' world:

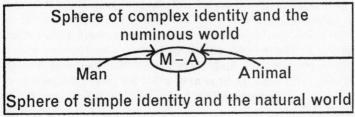

Figure 6

The struggle between the two systems continued until much more recently than is generally believed, not only among the uneducated majority but equally among the intelligentsia, because the naturalistic conception of the world has become increasingly influential with the course of time.

The *striga* of poets and novelists is quite clearly a product of the system which involves a complex reality. And there is evidence of belief in the power of witches' spells even in inscriptions on tombs, such as the one which refers to the boy Jucundus and reads, '*Eripuit me saga crudelis. . . . Vos vestros natos concustodite parentes.*'[83]

Probably the death of the child in question was due to the Evil Eye (*fascinum*, βασκανία). This was commonly attributed to witches at the time, and amulets were worn for protection against it in the First Century BC not unlike those which are still used today.[84] But more must be said later about cases where such beliefs have persisted.

Sometimes the terror that the witch could cause—and which Horace and Lucan exploited—gets mingled in some strange way with very different feelings, apparently diametrically opposed to terror: laughter and mockery. Petronius achieves an extraordinarily realistic effect in the passages already quoted, by making two of the guests at Trimalchio's feast tell terrifying stories about witches and lycanthropes, much to the horror of the lower-class people present. In another passage Petronius makes the old witch Oenothea speak lines of grandiloquent poetry when she is drunk: 'Everything you can see in the whole world obeys me . . .' she says. 'The land dries up, the plants wither and die, the seas are stilled and the wild beasts are pacified . . . The very moon comes down to earth.' It is for all the world as if the squalid old lady were Medea or one of the wise women described by the epic poets.[85] In both these cases the satirical intention of Petronius is obvious and serves to show that already in classical times there were intellectuals who were prepared to mock the world in which elemental desires held sway. Even a writer like Apuleius, who is known to have been religious and who admitted he believed in magic, was not above including comic touches in the middle of relatively serious passages in the many episodes relating to witches.[86]

I suspect that even in societies far more primitive than those of

classical antiquity there existed sceptical people, men with out-
looks similar to those of Petronius and the libertines of the Renaissance and subsequent periods, men who realised just how much
sham and frustrated desire underlies magic. But the majority of
people pander with what they wish to happen. Erotic appetites, ill
will, fear, all passions and vices, pave the way for magical processes, worked through a divine power which is not always so
awe-inspiring or maleficent.

Gods of a specialised kind within the Roman religion were
favourable to, and patrons of, particular categories of spells. Ovid,
in a not unironic passage from the *Fasti*, describes an old woman
sitting in the middle of a group of girls. She is making a sacrifice
to Tacita, nymph or goddess of silence, but cannot stop talking.
With three fingers she places three grains of incense on the ground
at a spot where a mouse had made a hole. Then she joins three
magic threads to her bull-roarer and turns over seven black
beans in her mouth. Finally, she dries the head of a salt fish
(*maenae*) over the fire, stopping its mouth with another fish before
putting it into a tin frying-pan. Afterwards she pours a little
wine on it, and drinks to her own health and to that of her
companions (mostly to her own) with what is left: 'Lo!' she
concludes, 'we have tied up the tongues that speak evil, we have
sewn up the mouths of those that hate us.' And she goes off, a
little drunk perhaps.[87] Imitative and homeopathic magic one may
say. Certainly, but also a religious ceremony with a moderately
respectable minister.

Conclusion

In conclusion, there is documentary evidence of the existence over a
period of *centuries* of the belief that certain women (not necessarily
always old ones) could change themselves and others at will into
animals in classical times; that they could fly through the air
by night and enter the most secret and hidden places by leaving
their body behind; that they could make spells and potions to
further their own love affairs or to inspire hatred for others;
that they could bring about storms, illness both in men and
animals, and strike fear into their enemies or play terrifying
jokes on them. To carry out their evil designs these women met
together after dark. The moon, night, Hecate and Diana were the

deities who presided over them, helping them to make philtres and potions. They called on these goddesses for aid in their poetic conjurations, or threatened and constrained them in their spells when they wanted to achieve particularly difficult results.

Apart from these powers, the women who were believed to attend such meetings were supposed to be experts in the manufacture of poisons and also in cosmetic arts; sometimes they were used as go-betweens in love affairs.

In fact, a whole series of nouns can be found in the classical Greek and Latin languages which refer to the various acts, operations and materials carried out and used by the witches. And these constitute a nucleus which has its place both in the history of witchcraft and in the history of humanism. Indeed, we can put forward the theory that when Fernando de Rojas, during the Renaissance, described in his *Celestina* the kind of woman we have been discussing and what has come to be called her 'laboratory', he could do so without being thought a pedant, in spite of the fact that he based himself on Horace, Ovid and other classical writers. His literary sources provided him with material about witchcraft that was still valid in his own time, as it had been in that of the Romans.

Another important point is the condemnation of magic for evil purposes which we find in pagan laws. This was formally laid down from the very earliest Roman times,[88] and continued to be the case at the period when the Roman authorities had still not accepted Christianity officially. Tacitus has painted a brilliant picture of the terror felt in Rome when the spells which were believed to have caused Germanicus's illness (some of them described as *devotiones*) were discovered.[89]

Ammianus Marcellinus has also referred to prosecutions for crimes of magic in the reigns of Constantius,[90] Valens and Valentinian I.[91] His writings and others on the same subject were later the basis for some of Gibbons's most eloquent pages—pages which reflect only too clearly the disbelief in magic common in Gibbons's time.[92] But when we come to these obscure figures of the Roman Empire's declining years we are already in a new world, with a new view of the beliefs we have been discussing.

CHAPTER 3

CHRISTIANITY, PAGANISM AND WITCHCRAFT

Christian and pagan views of early magic — Legal and theological doctrine — Witchcraft during the decline of the Roman Empire — Witchcraft amongst the German and Slavonic peoples — The nature of civil and religious laws

Christian and Pagan Views of Early Magic

Inevitably, with the triumph of Christianity in Europe, there was a fresh evaluation of earlier creeds. Finding it necessary to condemn paganism, the spiritual leaders of the Christian faith treated their predecessors' beliefs in much the same way as pagans had treated Christianity in earlier days; they mis-represented them slightly to make them appear more obviously evil.

In the past, the pagans had claimed that Christians worshipped an ass's head, that they killed children, and committed other atrocities at their gatherings.[1] The Christian could criticise the pagans with more justification, pointing out the stupidity and irrationality of some of their myths and rites, whose obscenity and crudeness had, in fact, already been condemned by the moral philosophers of classical antiquity. Men like Arnobius and Lactantius made good use of the writings of sophists such as Lucian, although the latter had had quite different ends in view.[2]

Thus, with scant regard for nice distinctions, the gods of antiquity were equated with devils; or, after the inevitable process of simplification had taken place, with the Devil himself. The elements of piety, morality and decorum in the private and public worship of the Greeks and Romans were forgotten. And only recently (now that total disbelief has become the greatest enemy of the Church) have some churchmen come to recognise openly the piety of antiquity, of paganism in fact, which is apparent in many of the writings of classical authors. 'Who would lose by a Christian world except pimps and procuresses and all who make profit from vice? Paid assassins, poisoners, magicians, soothsayers, fortune-tellers (*arioli*), and astrologers (*mathematici*).' Such was the view of Tertullian as expressed in his famous Apology[3] long before the triumph of Christianity. He never suggested, however, that the religion of his choice would also seek to stamp out all others, equating all pagans and gentiles with those whose arts and activities were criminal even by the standards of pagan morality.

The conflict is over now, and we can see it objectively. It is difficult to imagine how it felt at the time for those involved. The historical evidence seems overwhelming. But it is possible that the radical distinction which we make between Christianity and Paganism prevents us from seeing clearly the deeper spiritual values of the latter. The triumph of Socratic philosophy had long before confused people's views of earlier systems in precisely this way and even today, in spite of several attempts to do justice to the Pre-Socratics, they are less appreciated than they ought to be.

In the first battles between pagan emperors and those with Christian sympathies the important question was which faith proved the more effective in supporting military action. And when Constantine's efforts were rewarded with victory, he simply thought that he ought to give God his due, since He was partially, at least, responsible for it. For his successors this was not enough: gradually they proscribed paganism altogether. And they also proscribed beliefs and practices which the pagans themselves had considered criminal offences, and had made punishable by law.

Law acquired a religious character which it had probably not had in the period immediately preceding the Christian era. And in the place of the law which applied to the Greek *polis* or Roman city—a law which was essentially empirical and pragmatic—there arose the law for believers as opposed to non-believers. The concept of public morality, the morality of the *polis*, was replaced by the concept of morality within a religious community. The change is considerable from any point of view, although it must be acknowledged that once the change-over had

42

taken place, legal and theological doctrines still developed independently up to a certain point.

Legal and Theological Doctrine

There were several laws forbidding the practice of most kinds of magic in the Christian legal system under the Roman Empire, just as there were others condemning what were already called idolatrous forms of worship. Some of these laws were, if anything, more severe (though less specific) than those of other periods. The *Interpretatio* of Law 3 title 16 in Book IX of the Theodosian Code for example reads:

> '*Malefici vel incantatores vel inmissores tempestatum vel iis qui per invocationem daemonum mentes hominum turbant, omni poenarum genere puniantur.*'[4]

Amongst other laws in the same code, dating from different years of the fourth century, there is one which makes it a capital offence to honour or to invoke devils.[5] The laws of Book IX, title 18, in Justinian's Code,[6] and other ancient legal codes, adopt much the same position.

What was the point of view of the chief authorities of the time, the Church Fathers? Well-known passages in their writings on the subject show that belief in witchcraft was widespread.[7] The magic arts were much the same as they had been in earlier periods —astrology, divination, spells and enchantments, so-called mathematics, necromancy, the manufacture of philtres and phylacteries, belief in the power of sorcery, etc. But where the activities of witches (as described by Apuleius and others) are concerned, there was an attempt to interpret them from a theological point of view as phenomena not wholly *real*. Such an attempt—a memorable one on many counts—was made by St Augustine himself, speaking in the light of his own direct experience: 'When we were in Italy,' he wrote in a well-known passage of his *De civitate Dei*, 'we heard of certain women, innkeepers by trade, who were so learned in the Black Arts that by giving cheese to travellers of their choice they could change them into beasts of burden.'[8] Evidently stories like those told by Lucan and Apuleius (to whom St Augustine subsequently referred) were considered plausible in the fourth and fifth centuries. However, St Augustine, in the comments which follow the story, showed that he was doubtful about the *physical* possibility of these changes taking place. He believed that the Devil had induced a special dream-state in those who believed themselves transformed. While in this trance, the person involved believed that certain things were really happening to him. Although, in fact, they were not, they *might* have been. St Augustine illustrated this belief in the power of the spell involving cheese, which we have already mentioned, by citing a case which had been told him by a certain Prestantius.

The latter related how his father, after eating the enchanted cheese at home, had fallen into a deep sleep from which it was impossible to rouse him. Finally he woke up after several days and explained what had happened to him in the meantime: he had been changed into a horse and had been carrying provisions for the troops in Rhetia. Subsequently it was possible to establish that supplies had been taken up to the army in the way which he described. . . . Clearly this is very different from the case of Apuleius. For St Augustine, although he believed that witches (*veneficae*) were able to make people fall ill or restore them to health, did not believe that metamorphoses could really take place. Nor did he believe that it was possible to make spells to summon up the souls of the departed and carry out the various things it was supposed to be possible to do with them.[9] Leaving these last points on one side, it is important to remember that the *trance* theory of metamorphosis proved the most acceptable one to the authorities of the Western Church during the whole of the early Middle Ages. The theory also had its defenders in later periods as an alternative to the view officially held, which acknowledged both the reality of metamorphosis itself and the reality of other occurrences like the night-flights and cavalcades of witches, of which more will be said later. The Church Fathers in the early days of Christianity fought pagan views of reality as well as other pagan attitudes. But the Church in later periods felt itself under no such obligation, and readily accepted what many pagans had earlier believed.

Witchcraft during the Decline of the Roman Empire

If the effectiveness of the Black Arts could not be entirely denied (particularly since the Bible considered their powers genuine) it was possible in certain instances to limit the scope of the Devil's power. But what had been common enough before the advent of Christianity was thought to be less likely afterwards. Furthermore, the physical effects, formerly believed to have been caused by the Devil, could now be attributed to his spiritual rather than physical dominion. One need hardly add that St Augustine and the other Church Fathers who had views on magic, were living in a period of both individual and collective insecurity, when absolute credulity could easily flourish. And there are a large number of specific cases which provide evidence of belief in Black Magic during this period. But if we restrict our inquiry to the magical powers of women, it is perhaps worth while quoting, as an example, the account given by the historian Zosimus of the way in which Flavius Stilicho's wife made use of a witch to prevent the Emperor Honorius from consummating his marriage with one of her daughters.[10] After the fall of the Roman Empire, the power of the *strix, stria, striga* or *masca* (as the witch was variously called in low Latin) lived on for centuries in the minds of the people.[11] The acts they were believed to be capable of doing were always much the same, if not identical. Such is the force of stereotyped patterns that centuries after Lucian and Apuleius, and centuries after St Augustine and the unfortunate Emperor Honorius, as late, in fact, as the ninth century, there could still be a great argument between Pope Leo IX and Peter Damian about the case of a young man who was supposed to have been changed into an ass by some women. An English author gave the following version of the story at a much later period. One night a young minstrel asked for lodging in the house of two old witches, who lived on the outskirts of Rome. While the unfortunate young man was asleep they changed him into an ass and, since he retained his faculties in spite of the transformation, made a lot of money by exhibiting him in public and making him do tricks. Finally they sold him for a considerable sum to a rich man who was fascinated by his tricks. The witches advised the new master not to let the ass bathe in water. The young man lived for a long time in his 'translated' state until one day, when the master had relaxed his vigilance, he went to a pond, dived into it and recovered his original shape and form. The minstrel told his story openly and the Pope, after Damian had convinced him that such things were possible, sentenced the witches.[12]

If witches were particularly prevalent in parts of the old western Empire, their effect on the lives of numerous people in the eastern, Byzantine Empire, was hardly less remarkable. One of the more aggressive Fathers of the Greek Church constantly preached against superstition in general. But in some of his sermons he attacked women, who used magic, with particular vigour.[13] 'You are not satisfied with spells and sorcery,' St John Chrysostom said to the people of Antioch on one occasion. 'In addition you invite drunken and palsied old women into your homes to work spells.'[14]

Nor did the preacher's attacks stop short at the higher levels of society. His position *vis-à-vis* the excesses of the Empress Eudoxia is well known.[15] And if the practice of Black Magic was rife in the latter's court, there was as much of it, if not more, in the courts of other Empresses subsequently. Procopius tells us that Antonina, Belisarius's wife, 'made use of philtres which her family alone knew how to make,' (φαρμακεῦσι τε πατρᾶις πολλά ωμιληκυιώ) as if her family consisted of a dynasty of witches.[16] And once she had attracted Belisarius and married him, she used magic for other ends.[17] According to Procopius, Theodora had help from the Devil in connexion with magic.[18] And men as well as women were accused of similar activities.[19] Some centuries later, another Byzantine historian, Nicetas Acominatus Choniates, refers to the spells which Euphrosyne, wife of the Emperor Alexius III, used to learn the future. Amongst other things these spells involved whipping a statue of Hercules (a valuable work by Lysimachus), and mutilating a Calidonian hog by breaking its muzzle.[20]

Other courts were perhaps quite as cruel and even less refined, and witnessed many equally sinister scenes—the court of the Frankish kings, for example. The Germanic peoples above all were liable to be influenced by magic during the slow process of their Christianisation. Some authors think a kind of cultural index can be worked out on the basis of belief in magic. The more a people or society accepts the objective reality of magical acts, the more backward it is.[21] According to them, any attempt to consider the most common magical acts unreal, as St Augustine did for example, may be taken as a positive sign of progressiveness. Let us turn, then, to the so-called barbarians.

Witchcraft amongst the German and Slavonic peoples

The type of witch known in classical antiquity is not very different from the one with which we are familiar today. She continued to exist in Europe a long time after the fall of the Roman Empire and even down to our own times. The same, as we shall see, is true of the witch amongst European peoples who were not part of the classical world.

In the first place, let us consider those peoples of Germanic origin whose magical interests and activities are well documented. If we accept the evidence about them, it would appear that, among the Germanic tribes too, each individual social class had its own particular brand of magic; even the gods used magic in certain circumstances. The practice of magic in these tribes also corresponded to their logical and social order (the 'logos' and the 'ethos'), however surprising this may seem. This is also true, of course, of other communities which have recently been studied in detail; maleficent magic flourishes during certain states of tension.

In the highest levels of Germanic society the kings practised magic publicly, and their success was more or less generally admitted.

Among the Swedes, Erick 'of the windy hat' had remarkable powers as king and magician.[22] In other cases, the trials and misfortunes of the community were attributed to the fact that the reigning monarch lacked the necessary magical power to deal with the adverse circumstances. But coming down in the social scale we also discover that in ancient Scandinavia every magical activity was thought to be the property of a particular family. Thus, 'all' the sooth-sayers, 'all' the witches and 'all' the magicians could be traced back to three specific forebears, just as the giants could.[23]

The division of human activities according to families presupposes the handing down of knowledge from the period of myths. Witchcraft or maleficent magic has its own special terminology, and is completely defined by the word *seid*.[24]

There are passages in Icelandic Sagas in which whole families are accredited with the power of witchcraft: father, mother and children.[25] However, as in the classical world, women, or particular types of women, were belived to have more special powers.

The passage in Tacitus's *Germania* which relates how the men of that country believed women to be sacred and always attached great importance to their opinions, warnings and advice,[26] has been the object of numerous conflicting interpretations—like other parts of that work.

But if the cases of Velleda[27] or Ganna,[28] both heroines of German history, can be adduced in support of this view, there is also good reason to believe that fear as well as respect and veneration was sometimes felt for women; fear of the spells of which they were held to be capable.

Both early Germanic literature and historical works, written in Latin about the Germanic peoples at a later date, make frequent references to the ambivalent position of women in that society.

There are, for example, numerous passages in the *Edda* which allude to the skill of women in magic and the dangers run by those who allow themselves to be dominated by women.

'Flee from the dangers of sleeping in the arms of a witch; let her not hold you close to her. She will make you disregard the assemblies of the people and the words of the prince; you will refuse to eat and shun the company of other men, and you will feel sad when you go to your bed': such were the supernatural warnings given to Lodfafner.[29] These and other passages seem to support the case for the existence of a 'Circean complex' which has completely controlled men's actions at various periods.

The picture of the *old witch* is also extremely common in the *Edda*. Such a one, for example, was Angerbode, mother of the wolves who will ultimately eat the sun and the moon:

> 'East of Midgard, in the iron forest,
> Sat the old witch.
> She fed the fearful race
> of Fenrer . . .'[30]

At the same time, witchcraft, or magic for evil ends, is the constant subject of criticism as one of the most anti-social activities possible.

But it must be emphasised that in the pagan German world the gods were not only aiders and abetters of witchcraft but sorcerers themselves. Loke or Loki, the evil one, was able to say to Odin, the Father of the gods: 'They say you have practised magic in Samsoe, that you have made spells like any *Vala*: you have wandered through the country disguised as a witch. What, I say, could

48

be viler in a man than this.'[31] The same Loki could shout at Freya: 'Be silent! You are a poisoner and you work magic. Thanks to your spells the powers that were propitious to your brother have turned against him.'[32]

There can be no doubt, therefore, that magic has its place in the life of gods as well as men. The question that Lucan asked himself about the gods on Olympus might well have been put by a German about those in Valhalla. A *vis magica* exists which fascinates or coerces 'them' just as it controls the strong and the meek in the world.

Several legends which have survived in more modern versions than those which have so far been quoted, prove that the Germanic peoples were dominated by fear of witches in their everyday life.

They frequently attributed the misfortunes of their kings to witches. One of the best known of these legends is the one about the death of the Danish king Frotho III. The usual source for this tale in books on magic is the German historian, A. Krantz.

The king, who is said to have lived at the same time as Christ, seems to have used magic in much the same way as other more or less legendary figures. He had a witch at his court who was famed for her magic. Her son had great faith in her powers and plotted with her on one occasion to rob the king's treasury, since the king was advanced in years. When they had carried out the robbery, they went to an isolated house they owned far from the court. The king, following the hints of a number of people, connected their flight with the robbery and decided to go in person to look for them. When the witch saw him coming she used her magical powers to change her son into a bull who went out to meet him. The king sat down to look at the animal. But the witch gave him little time for contemplation. The bull charged him violently and killed him.[33]

This is roughly the story as Krantz has it, although it should be borne in mind that there are other slightly different versions.[34] For present purposes, however, this will serve. The important thing in this instance is the general outline of the legend. It is also worth while pointing out that the person chiefly responsible for popularising the story believed that old witches were perfectly capable of achieving the same or even more astonishing results in his own times (i.e. in the fifteenth and sixteenth centuries).[35]

The Germanic world was dominated by belief in witchcraft

from its northern extremities to the shores of the Mediterranean where the Visigoths, and Lombards lived; from the steppes of eastern Europe to the Atlantic islands. Even at the height of their power, men lived in constant fear of witches.

This fear and hatred led the Germans to accuse their enemies of practising witchcraft or of being descended from evil witches. An example of this is the traditional story about the origin of the Huns. This was first written down by a historian of the Goths called Jornandes, or Jordanes, in the sixth century, and it was later reproduced and modified by many other historians. According to the legend, King Filimer, after conducting a survey into the customs of his people at a very early period, discovered that a number of sorceresses lived among them. These he banished to the remote and deserted regions of Scythia so that they should have no ill-effect on others. However, as a result of the contact between these women and certain foul spirits who wandered about the same deserts, the Huns were born.[36] Those were the sorceresses called *alrunae* or *haliurunnae* which also appear in other texts. To call someone a 'son of a witch' is a very ancient insult.

It is an equally hallowed custom to attribute black powers to one's nearest communal enemy. So far as the specific case of the Huns is concerned, it is highly probable that witchcraft was common among them (just as it later was among the Magyars and Hungarians). But their bad reputation may have been partly due to the intense fear they inspired in others; in other words, it may have been due to the feeling of comparative impotence that others felt in their presence.

More or less mythical stories about the power of specific witches are also to be found in the old Slav chronicles.

There is, for instance, a legendary episode in the earliest history of Bohemia which is worth recording. A certain chief named Krok died at the end of the seventh century, in 690, and left three daughters. The first, Kazi or Brelum, had a considerable knowledge of medicinal plants which she put to practical use. The second, called Tecka or Tekta, was a sooth-sayer and diviner; whenever there was a robbery in the country she revealed the person who was responsible and if anything was lost, she could tell where it was. The third, Libuscha, Libussa or Lobussa was a sybil, skilled in witchcraft and vastly better at it than any other man or woman of her times. Thanks to her magic, she was able to make the

Bohemians elect Przemislaw as their leader, and then marry him. She predicted the rise of Prague and died after a long and glorious life. However, when she died, women had become so accustomed to directing affairs that they refused to submit to the rule of men again. A young maid named Wlasca, a born leader, called the women together and addressed them approximately in these words:

'Our lady Libussa governed this kingdom while she was alive. Why should not I now govern with your help? I know all her secrets; the skill in spells and the art of augury which were her sister Tecka's are mine; I also know as much medicine as Brelum did; for I was not in her service for nothing. If you will join with me and help me I believe we may get complete control over the men.'

Her ideas met with the approval of the women she had gathered together. So she gave them a potion to drink to make them loathe their husbands, brothers, lovers and the whole male sex immediately. Fortified by this, they slew nearly all the men and laid siege to Przemislaw in the castle of Diewin. The women are supposed to have ruled for seven years, and a series of rather comical laws are said to have been passed by them. However, in the end Przemislaw returned to the throne, for he too was something of a magician. Later authors retold this story and added their own particular interpretations. [37]

The Middle Ages was a great period for preserving traditions as well as for making them, and the magical processes described in the texts are monotonously repeated. Ones which are already to be found in the Vedic poems reappear in the darkest years of the Middle Ages and continue to recur even today.

The story of King Duff of Scotland, for instance, supposed to have taken place at some time between AD 967 and 972, follows a typically well-worn pattern. According to the chronicles, an illness which he caught was attributed to witchcraft. Investigations were made and some witches were eventually found cooking a waxen image of the king over a slow fire. This explained the nature of the king's illness, since he was in a continual sweat. Once the women had been condemned the king was restored to health. [38]

51

The Nature of Civil and Religious Laws

The laws of the barbarians, written in Latin and devised for the northern peoples who ruled for centuries over former provinces of the Roman Empire, abound in provisions against sorcerers and those who followed their advice.

In Book 6, subtitle 2, of the Spanish *Fuero Juzgo*, for example, one finds four laws of the Chindasvint period which condemn all the possible varieties of magic. The first of these applies to servants and simple folk who consult *ariolos*, *aruspices* and *vaticinatores*—diviners, fortune-tellers, and enchanters—about the health or death of the king. The second refers to those who give poisonous herbs to others. The third is about sorcerers and rain-makers who ruin the wine and the crops by their spells; those who disturb men's minds by invoking the Devil; and those who make nocturnal sacrifices to the Devil. The fourth condemns those who use verbal or written spells to harm the bodies, minds and property of others.[39]

These Spanish laws and others, both civil and ecclesiastical, of the same period, condemn magic in general without any specific reference to the sex of the person in question. But similar laws in old Gaul, and other countries which were also under the rule of christianised barbarians, make frequent references to the sex of the sorcerers and also make other allusions which are worth examination. Perhaps certain types of witches were more common in Gaul than in Spain under the Visigoths.

A passage in Pomponius Mela which has often been discussed seems to imply that there were women who practised magic for beneficent purposes among the ancient Gauls. Nine of them were attached to a temple, and lived under a rule of perpetual chasity.[40] Whatever the truth of this may be, it does not seem to affect the general point about the place of women in witchcraft.

We know from other sources—not wholly reliable ones however—that witches abounded in Gaul in the later period of the Roman Empire. They were occasionally consulted by people of high rank, and were equated with druids (as 'druidesses' are called in texts which relate to the third century AD).[42] These witches continued to multiply and thrive in later periods, and they were a source of worry to more than one family of high social standing at the court of the Merovingian kings. This is revealed in the works of the best-known historians of the period, who also point out that more than one woman paid dearly for her reputation as a witch.

In 578 Queen Fredegond lost a son. Suspicious individuals suggested that his death had been caused by magic and spells. A courtier accused Mummolus, one of the prefects (who was also disliked by the Queen), of instigating the crime. But those who actually committed it were said to be certain women of Paris. The latter confessed under torture to the murder of the Queen's son, and admitted killing many other people too.[42] It is not hard to imagine the fate of the prefect and the ladies in question.

This was not the only episode in the violent life of Queen Fredegond in which witches had an important role. Earlier, she accused her step-child Clovis of killing two of her sons with the aid or complicity of an old witch and her daughter. These three she also managed to kill.[43] Yet this did not stop her from making spells and consulting witches herself when she felt like it.[44]

Fredegond was no exception in the land over which she reigned. The repression of magic, which she herself practised and which she accused others of practising, was one of the major concerns of the civil and religious authorities at the time and at later periods.

Sometimes, however, there are noticeable variations in the ways in which repressive measures are carried out: a divergence of opinion between legal and ecclesiastical authorities.

It is a long time since a Frenchman called Garinet collected together the most famous laws passed by the Frankish kings and their successors against the practice of magic. This was ranked as one of the manifestations of paganism which had to be eradicated (as it was in the last laws made under the Roman Empire). More recently these laws have been studied in a more scholarly way. But Garinet's book is still useful.[45]

Superficially there is little difference between these laws and those passed by the Christian Roman Emperors and by the Visigothic and Ostrogothic rulers in their respective kingdoms. Nor do these laws differ from others known to have been passed during the same dark ages in England, Germany and Hungary. The laws are apparently so similar that books on them are invitably boring to read. But they are worth studying, even if not in great detail: for, suddenly, amongst the mass of virtually identical items, we find one that is quite different and extremely significant. As early as

AD 743, Childeric III published an edict condemning pagan and magical practices as if they were much the same thing. Amongst the former are included sacrifices to the dead, and other sacrifices which were still being made at that time not to the old gods, but to Holy Martyrs and confessors in places close to the churches themselves. Among magical practices listed, we find ligatures, fortune-telling, augury, incantations and phylacteries.[46]

Charlemagne, following in the footsteps of Childeric and other Merovingian kings, published several edicts urging his subjects to forsake their superstitious beliefs. When mere exhortation proved useless, he resorted to edicts which laid down sentences appropriate to these crimes. These edicts specifically condemned all kinds of witchcraft, such as the making of wax figures, summoning devils and using love philtres, disturbing the atmosphere and raising storms, putting curses on people and causing the fruits of the earth to wither away, drying up the milk of some people's domestic animals to give it to others, practising astrology and making talismen. The law laid down that, in future, those who practised the arts of the Devil would be dishonoured and treated like murderers, poisoners and thieves; those who consulted them and made use of them would be given a similar sentence, and in some cases that meant death.[47]

In AD 873, Charles the Bald issued a decree in Quierzy-sur-Oise, declaring that he desired to fulfil his kingly duties laid down by the saints in the proper manner. He had learnt that sorcerers and witches had appeared in various parts of his kingdom, bringing illness and even death to a number of people. And his intention was to drive out the godless, and those who made philtres and poisons: 'We therefore expressly recommend the lords of the realm to seek out and apprehend with the greatest possible diligence those who are guilty of these crimes in their respective countries. If they are convicted, whether they are men or women, they must perish, for justice and the law demand it. If they are under suspicion or accused without being convicted, and if the testimony against them is not sufficient to prove their guilt, they shall be submitted to the will of God. This shall decide whether they are to be pardoned or condemned. But the associates and accomplices of those who are really guilty, both men and women, shall be put to death, so that all knowledge of such a heinous crime may vanish from our dominions.'[48]

These three texts of three different periods may suffice to show how hard civil law was on those who were accused of crimes of witchcraft in the eighth and ninth centuries. Probably, these laws were often enforced in an arbitrary way, and people must frequently have been accused of such crimes in much the same violent and fanatical manner as Queen Fredegond accused her step-son. The danger of arraigning people who might be totally innocent had yet to be recognised.

This explains why the Church, which absolutely condemned paganism, let alone magic, from a theological point of view, promulgated a series of dispositions which would, on occasion, soften the harsh effects of the civil law. This moderation may partially have been due to propagandistic motives, aimed to attract the great mass of people who remained unconverted to Christianity in the country areas and small towns. But perhaps the more moderate dispositions of the Church also reflect the ideas of St Augustine.

J. B. Thiers in his *Traité des Superstitions* collected together a large number of references to Canon laws of Church Councils, and to other decrees which severely condemned the practice of magic, dating from the sixth, seventh and eighth centuries and later periods also.[49] Some of these emphasise the dangerous spiritual effects of magic, but others insist that sorcerers themselves are often victims of the illusions and deceits of the Devil, and deny that it is necessary to believe categorically in their powers.

Even after the promulgation of the decrees of Charlemagne which have already been mentioned, the prelates who were summoned to the Council of Tours in 813 still felt the need for priests to warn the faithful that spells could not help sick or dying persons or animals; they were nothing but illusions and tricks of the Devil.[50] In other instances the same ecclesiastical authorities disputed the validity of facts which civil law accepted, or qualified the conclusions that were drawn from them.

A good example of this is that of Agobard, Archbishop of Lyons (779–840), who, in spite of the general views held at the time, severely criticised those who believed that certain human beings were capable of bringing on rain and hail-storms. He also censured those who held Duke Grimald responsible for sending sorcerers to throw harmful magic powders into fields, forests and streams,

55

when the oxen belonging to the smallholders in the diocese were striken by an epidemic.[51]

The prelates who attended the sixth Council of Paris in 829 were in closer agreement with the civil laws and edicts. The eleventh canon of the Council expressed the following opinion:

'There are other very dangerous evils which are certainly legacies of paganism, such as magic, astrology, incantations and spells, poisoning, divination, enchantment, and the interpretation of dreams. These evils ought to be severely punished, as the laws of God ordain. But there is no doubt, as many learned men have witnessed, that there are some people capable of so perverting the minds of others with the Devil's illusions, (by giving them philtres, drugged food and phylacteries), that they become confused and insensible to the ills they are made to suffer. It is also said that these people can disturb the air with their spells, send hail-storms, predict the future, take produce and milk from one person to give to another, and do a thousand similar things. If any such be found, be they men or women, they should be severely punished, particularly since, in their malice and temerity, they fear not the Devil nor do they renounce him publicly'.[52]

There is undoubtedly a conflict between these views and Agobard's: one which is to be found time and again in later periods. It even occurs in certain civil laws, some of which put forward opinions which are flatly contradicted by other laws in the same code.

There is, for example, an act dated 789 amongst the laws of the Frankish kings; it refers to Saxony and condemns belief in *strigae* and their ability to eat men, expressing the view that they ought to be burnt for it. The same act prescribes capital punishment for all who believe such things.[53] There is clearly a connexion between this and another law to be found in the *Leges Langobardicae*, dating probably from the reign of King Rotharius. Yet although it is conceived in much the same spirit, this law holds that, from a Christian point of view, *strigae* or *mascae* cannot be capable of the acts they are believed to perform.[54]

On the other hand, the popes who were concerned with the conversion of central European and, above all, Northern peoples, gave very categorical instructions on the subject to kings and prelates of the Church. Pope Gregory II, for example, ordered Bishop Martinian and the priest called George who went with him to Bavaria, to forbid spells and enchantments, which were relics of paganism, although he makes no reference to the punishment of those involved.

On one occasion Pope Gregory VII wrote to the King of Denmark asking him to avoid, as far as possible, persecuting innocent women who were thought to have caused storms or epidemics. Earlier, Pope Leo VII had sent an instruction dated 936 to Archbishop Gerhard of Lorch, intended for the authorities of southern Germany, which again took a lenient view of those accused of witchcraft. Answering a specific enquiry he maintained that 'although, by the old law, such people were condemned to death, ecclesiastical law spared their lives so that they could repent'.

This rather ambiguous situation is typical of a period of transition like the Middle Ages. On the one hand, we have the passionate beliefs of the masses just converted to Christianity or still pagan, and on the other, the doubt and pragmatism of the ecclesiastical authorities in the face of popular beliefs and civil law. The problem of the reality of certain aspects of witchcraft was again posed in the course of the ninth century, and in a way that is of capital importance for the history of witchcraft as a whole. This needs to be discussed in another chapter.

CHAPTER 4

THE WITCHES' GODDESS

Barbarian laws concerning witches – Diana, Holda, Herodias – Satirical comments on witchcraft – More about pagan gods

Barbarian Laws concerning Witches

The history of European witchcraft is closely linked to the problem of distinguishing between objective and subjective reality.

For many country people even now everything which has a name, even everything which is expressed in words, has a physical reality and is not merely a concept. Thus if the name 'witches' exists, it is because there really are such things, and if their flights are referred to, then those flights really take place in the air around us; if tales are told of the ability of witches to change themselves into animals, it is because they have really been seen to do so, and even been wounded in their animal form. In the Basque Country—for example—the story has been told of a person living on a farm who once wounded a cat in the foot. The cat used to drink the fresh milk he put out on the window-sill each night. The moment the cat was hurt it cried out with a human voice, and the next day an old woman who lived nearby and who was said to be a witch was also found to have hurt herself in the foot.[1]

This classic 'witch's tale' has a much deeper significance historically, sociologically and psychologically speaking than might at first seem likely. For centuries Europeans have been divisible into two main groups (excluding for the moment those who are completely sceptical). First, those who believe in the reality of such occurrences, and second, those who believe them to be a figment of the imagination, possibly caused by the Devil. Augustinians and Non-Augustinians in fact.[2] This divergence of views is of considerable historical importance, and has all kinds of consequences.

In the first instance, if such things really occur, civil and religious laws must be made to deal with them; if on the other hand they do not, the laws must be altered accordingly. Many ancient civil laws held the view that metamorphoses and witches' spells were possible. But it was necessary to prove in each specific case that a witch had actually done what she was accused of doing. If the person who denounced the witch was unable to furnish this proof, he was likely to be condemned by the same law. This is a peculiar situation, because the reality of such occurrences could only be proved by methods whose validity could only be accepted by those who believed in the reality of witchcraft. Such methods have subsequently been considered absolutely unreliable.

Let us examine more carefully one of the most famous European laws—the Salic Law—which brings in witchcraft at one point and includes three short chapters on the topic.

A certain word occurs in the Salic Law which has often been connected (erroneously it appears) with the Spanish *brujo* or *bruja* (sorcerer or witch). It is found in a section which refers to a number of typical acts of witchcraft in a relatively short space.

'If one man shall call another *hereburgium* or *herburgium*, runs the wording of the law (in its ungrammatical Latin), and accuses him of having carried a cauldron (*aeneum* or *inium*) to the place where witches (*stiriae* or *striae*) meet, and shall be unable to prove it, let him be arraigned himself and condemned to pay a fine of two thousand five hundred denarii, that is sixty-two *solidi* and a half.'[3]

This is the legal position according to one of the chapters. Another runs as follows:

'If any person call a free woman *stria* (or *stiria*) or evil one, and fail to prove it, they shall themselves be arraigned and fined seven thousand five hundred *denarii*, which are sixty-two (one hundred and eighty-seven in some texts) *solidi* and a half.'

But the third passage gives us a completely different view:

'If a *stiria* or *stria* eats a man and is put on trial, she shall be sentenced and condemned to pay eight thousand *denarii*, which are two hundred *solidi*.'

This particular law seems essentially pagan in conception.[4] It also contains an extremely early allusion to witches' covens which is very different from those of classical times. Without stretching the imagination very much we can connect it with the witches' scene in Macbeth, when the three witches foretell Macbeth's career at dead of night.[5] But belief in these covens was perhaps stronger at the time of the Renaissance in Europe than in the medieval period. The beliefs of such men as Shakespeare himself and Hector Boethius,[6] who wrote about this and other Scottish legends, drawing on earlier texts, contrast with those of the bishops of the Middle Ages. It is not hard to imagine the attempts of the latter to catechise and convert the barbarians of central Europe to Christianity. In order to achieve their end they had to use similar methods to those of the early Church Fathers fighting against the paganism of the Greeks and Romans. The reality of facts which were readily accepted by the pagans had to be denied so as to weaken their beliefs. One of these facts was that witches met in covens, and were joined by a *deity* who presided over their activities when they flew through the air on dark nights, carrying out all manner of sinister deeds. Clearly this had to be disputed. If people believed in such things implicitly, it would be difficult to overcome their fear and respect for those who claimed to share the powers of this mysterious deity. In fact, the idea had to be entirely rejected with the full authority of some ancient law whose validity all would recognise. This authority was duly and inevitably invoked.

Diana, Holda, Herodias

A canon was attributed to a council celebrated in Ancyra in AD 314, which reads in translation:

'It should also be added that certain criminal women, disciples of Satan, seduced by the illusions and devices of the Devil, believe and confess that they ride through the air on certain beasts at night in company with Diana the pagan goddess (or Herodias), and a host of other women, obeying the goddess' orders as if she was their absolute mistress.'[7]

As we have already suggested, the authenticity of the text is very much in doubt. It does not appear in any collection before the ninth century. But it is to be found among the legal fragments of Charles the Bald dating from AD 872,[8] and in a treatise of Reginus, abbot of Prüm, which was written before AD 899, as well as in one or two other works of the ninth and tenth centuries.[9] There are some who believe that it is an article from an old Frankish legal work, and others who think that it was taken from a treatise erroneously attributed to St Augustine. Yet whatever its origin, the 'Canon Episcopi', as it is called, was very widely known from the eleventh century onwards. It was cited as an authority and its text was discussed throughout western Europe. It was even used as the basis for a general theory of the cult of witchcraft as we shall see.[10] One or two points relevant to it remain to be made. Burchard, Bishop of Worms from 1006 or 1008 to 1025, when he died, quotes and comments on it at the beginning of the eleventh century, in his famous *Decretales*.[11] In a series of penitential canons, he suggests that those who believe in witchcraft should do penance for two years.[12] Following St Augustine's thesis, his view was that the mass of people who believed in witches' cavalcades at that time, were returning to paganism and accepting as real what were, in fact, no more than illusions and subtleties of the Devil.[13]

In a slightly earlier section on magic in the same book, he makes a similar point when he asks, 'Do you believe that there are women who, like the one the people call Holda, ride by night on special animals in the company of devils which have been changed into women, as some people—deceived by the Devil—believe? If you do so believe, you should do penance on the appointed days for a whole year.'[14]

Critical and satirical comments on Witchcraft

It was clearly very important for this German bishop to be able to deny the reality of witches' flights. He quotes canons referring to night rides probably taken from two separate collections. And shortly after discussing the rides led by Holda, before copying the supposed canon of the Council of Ancyra, he puts the following question in support of his thesis:

'Do you believe what some women say and believe: that they can

61

enter any house they wish and bewitch small animals, killing them with a single word, or simply by looking at them? Do you believe what many women believe and declare; that in the silence of a quiet night, after going to bed, and with your husband's head on your shoulder, you can leave the house although the doors are all shut, and, journeying great distances in the company of victims of like delusions, strike men dead with no visible weapon?'[15]

Similar penances are prescribed for those who believe this to the ones given to people who continue practising pagan cults. Later on we find the same canon in the collection of Ivon of Chartres[16] and finally also in the *Decretum* of Gratian—a major legal authority—where it is given the title of 'Canon Episcopi' as we have already mentioned.[17]

All those who have written about the history of witchcraft or the history of the Inquisition (subjects which are very closely connected) have emphasised the importance of the canon;[18] they have also recognised that its character is more in keeping with modern ideas on the subject than with the canons and theological opinions of later periods.

Burchard, like Agobard, and like the author of the 'Canon Episcopi' whoever he may have been, denied what nearly everyone subsequently accepted. These and other churchmen strove to deny the more fantastic arts attributed to witches; above all, the supposition that they went about by night with a sort of evil genius, about which we shall have rather more to say later.

A number of examples were used to prove the point, which must have cropped up constantly in sermons. Here are one or two which may give some indication of what they were like.

John of Salisbury, in his *Polycraticus*, writes as follows:

'The evil spirit with God's permission uses his powers to make some people believe that things really happen to their bodies which they imagine (through their own error) to occur. These people claim that a Noctiluca or Herodiade, acting as Queen of the Night, summons nocturnal gatherings at which feasting and all kinds of riotous exercises take place. Those who attend are punished or rewarded according to their deserts. The same people also believe that children are sacrificed to *lamiae*, being cut up into small pieces and greedily devoured. Subsequently they are vomited up and the presiding deity takes pity on them and returns them to the cradles from which they were snatched.'

John of Salisbury then adds the following reflection:

'Who can be so blind as not to realise that this is the deceit of the Devil? It must be remembered that those who have such experiences are but a few poor women and ignorant men with no real faith in God.'[19]

Such were the views of a churchman of the twelfth century. The passage which follows that quoted above describes in detail the nature of the belief in witches' covens. In it there are references to banquets and rites in which human flesh is eaten, and also to a kind of tribunal which functioned at these covens punishing some and rewarding others. A high scorn is expressed for those who believe such things. Other authors who felt much the same were less open in expressing their scorn and tended to conceal it beneath a thin layer of irony. The writer responsible for the continuation of Vincent de Beauvais's *Speculum Morale*, which followed soon after the original in the fourteenth century, tells the following rather amusing story in the third book of that work. An old lady wanted the friendship of her parish priest. One day when she was in the church she said to him . . . 'You have good reason to befriend me, sir, since I have saved your life. I and other "good wives" went into your house with torches at midnight and found you naked and asleep. When I saw you like that, I covered you up so that our goodwives should not see you naked. Had they done so they would have whipped you to death.' The priest asked her how she had entered the house since the door was locked. And the old woman replied: 'No door or lock can keep us in or out of any place.' The priest made her go into the sacristy and beat her with the staff of the processional cross, saying to her 'Get out of here and fly away witch, since no door or lock can keep you in.' Naturally she was unable to leave, and the priest threw her out with the words, 'See how mad you are to believe your senseless dreams.'[20] 'Dreams': this was the answer to the whole thing; the dreams of a talkative and pretentious old woman. A nineteenth-century rationalist could not have said more.

In the *Speculum* itself there is another satirical story which ridicules belief in 'good women' or 'goodwives'. In a parish where people believed in them, one or two boisterous young men who liked a practical joke dressed up as women and went into the house of a rich farmer. They started dancing around, shouting out from time to time, 'We take away one thing and restore an hundred-fold.' At the same time they laid hands on anything that looked valuable, stripping the whole house in under an hour. The farmer, before whose very eyes all this was happening, said to his wife: 'Keep quiet and shut your eyes: we shall be rich. These are the good women and they will increase our wealth a hundredfold.'[21] The 'good women', it should be explained, are those who accompany Diana, Herodiade, Holda or Noctiluca in the texts we have already quoted. Sometimes they are known as 'Benzozia', 'Bizozia', 'Domina', 'Abundia' and 'Dame Habonde', who are similar characters in other texts.

Other echoes and criticisms of belief in witches' covens are to be found in lives of saints in medieval breviaries. A case in point is a supposed episode in the life of St Germain (390–448), bishop of Auxerre, which was often related in the later Middle Ages, although it was not mentioned in the early *Life* of the bishop by Constance of Lyon. The story is in line with earlier tales which tend to treat covens as unreal: a product of the imagination, and inspired by the devil.

This is Dom Calmet's version of it:

'It is said that St Germain, bishop of Auxerre, was once on a journey when he stopped at a village in his diocese. After dinner he saw they were preparing a second dinner for which the table was being re-laid. He asked if other visitors were expected, and was told that the preparations were for the "good women" who walk about by night. St Germain understood perfectly well what they meant and decided to watch and see what happened.

'Some time later he saw a host of devils arrive in the form of men and women and they sat down at the table before his very eyes. St Germain forbade them to leave the room and called all the people of the house to see. He asked them if they recognised any of those who had come to the feast, and they told him they did, and knew them by name. Then the bishop said to them: "Go to their houses and see if they are there." They were all found to be sleeping in their beds, so the bishop adjured the devils to confess that this was how they deceived men into believing that sorcerers and witches (*sorciers et sorcières*) exist and have their sabbaths by night. The devils did as they were told and disappeared afterwards in a state of confusion . . .'[22]

More about Pagan Gods

The 'Canon Episcopi' and the commentaries on it have an important place in the history of law and in the development of general theological and philosophical ideas. But they also pose a historical problem of which more must be said. Some years ago Margaret Murray, using them as a starting point and taking the allusion to the goddess Diana as the essential part of the canon, maintained that what we generally call witchcraft (or 'The Witch Cult' as she called it) was merely the survival of the cult of Diana in Europe, or, to be more specific, in western Europe. The covens, according to her theory, had more reality than the Church Fathers believed in medieval times. They were a straightforward manifestation of paganism of Graeco-Latin origins, with certain elements added from other eastern systems.[23] This thesis is widely known and accredited in the English-speaking world; less so outside it. Even within it there have been some voices raised in criticism.

Personally, I think it is valid up to a point. But perhaps witchcraft is not so much an example of a continuation or survival of anything, as an instance of the way in which certain basic facts of existence, to which we referred in Chapter One, can be reinterpreted at different periods. There is always the possibility, too, that the canon is not authentic, and in that case the allusion to Diana merely proves that whoever faked it was cultured enough to reproduce what he had found in Horace and other writers. Perhaps use may also have been made of popular traditions in writing the canon. There seems to have been a flourishing cult of Diana among European country people in the fifth and sixth centuries, and she was generally looked upon as the goddess of the woods and fields—except by those trying to root out the cult, who thought she was a devil.[24] Occasionally, she appeared in the company of certain spirits referred to as '*dianae*'[25]— according to texts such as that of St Martin of Braga which deal with beliefs of country-folk in the north-western regions of the Iberian peninsula. There are philological and other good reasons for believing that these spirits which superseded the classical nymphs are the direct predecessors of the *xanas* of Asturias and the *anjanas* of the Montaña region around Santander. But these are mythological beings and easily distinguished from witches[26]— even if we adopt the point of view of some ecclesiastical authorities, who think that any belief connected with magic or paganism, which they hold to be necessarily inspired by the Devil, is rooted in unreality and the dream world. However, one fact is quite clear.

Burchard referred to the Germanic Holda rather than the classical Diana in order to make his meaning plain. Since Grimm's time Holda has become well known as a character: she is the much studied 'Frau Holle', 'Frau Bert', 'Bercht', 'Perchta' etc., of folklore, the moving spirit of the 'Perchten', masked figures who appear at certain times of the year in parts of Austria and southern Germany, connected with the spirits of the dead, etc.[27] Bishops of different regions refer in their writings to similar characters with different names. Augier, bishop of Couserans, for example, writes as follows in one of his statutes, cited by Du Cange: *Nulla mulier se nocturnis equitare cum Diana dea paganorum, vel cum Herodiade seu Bensozia, et innumeram mulierum multitudinem profiteatur.*[28] It would not be difficult to quote other texts in which they are given different names. And it would even be possible to find pictures in which they are almost certainly represented. Witches riding on more or less fantastic beasts and similar characters are frequently portrayed in the decorations of churches or cathedrals, and such works of art are properly thought to have documentary value as reflections of medieval dogma, knowledge and society.[29] Thus in Lyons we find a classic case of a witch riding a male goat: elsewhere there are figures which possibly represent the central character of the Canon Episcopi, whether 'Diana', 'Holda', 'Abundia' or 'Bensozia'.[30]

The international, supranational, or (if preferred) pre-national character of the Middle Ages not only explains how styles of architecture such as the Romanic or early Gothic (and later some Schools of Painting) spread through a number of different countries, but also how many other ideas which were linked with the Church, became equally widespread. Ecclesiastical literature circulated in Latin texts and these sometimes gave rise to interesting works in the vernacular languages developing at that period. The artist, in much the same way as the troubadour minstrel, aided the propagation of certain theological ideas, and it is hardly surprising that information about witchcraft was spread in this way. However, it is possible that the beliefs about witches' covens and their night flights were reinterpreted in the course of transmission, becoming considerably modified and simplified in the process.

PART TWO

THE RISE OF WITCHCRAFT

CHAPTER 5

THE DEVIL'S PART

The Devil in the medieval cosmos - Demonolatry - Devil worshippers - Dualism

The Devil in the Medieval Cosmos

Various works on witchcraft, and particularly those influenced by the anthropological theories of the early years of this century and by certain developments in the study of psychology, have tried to find its roots in the distant past; a past so remote that it cannot be dated with any certainty.

I believe that in any research of this kind the past needs to be examined in a more specific way. However much we may wish to look for the permanent elements in things, the desires and feelings which are constant in generation after generation of men and women of different creeds, we must not lose sight of what is temporary—namely, the cultural changes in society—if serious errors of interpretation are to be avoided. There is no need to be a 'culturalist', like those who in the present century have attached an almost magical value to the word 'culture', to understand that the permanent concerns of man are reinterpreted by each succeeding generation. Just as in the history of art, Gothic and Baroque follow Renaissance, so in ideas and usage there are changes of style from one period to the next of which one needs to be aware, without falling into the abuse of terms like evolution, survival, etc. These words have a certain superficial biological and scientific force, and may be helpful if not used to excess.

In any case, if we accept the view that concepts *evolve*, and when in a state of *evolution* are *diffused*, we should also accept that they may suddenly *mutate* and go through a rapid period of change. These sudden changes are most disconcerting and require the most careful study. It is of just such a *cultural mutation* or, rather, a *change of style*, that we shall principally be talking in the next few chapters.

So far, all the details about witches, their covens and so forth to which we have drawn attention, seem to reflect concepts which are pagan in origin even though some ecclesiastical authorities looked upon them as the work of the Devil or the products of the feeble minds of one or two men and women.

The second part of the Middle Ages held rather different conceptions although they were still related to those of classical antiquity. These new conceptions of the nature of magic and witchcraft and their relation to life were not, indeed could not be, the result of a small change or partial modification of ideas. They were the result of a vast system of modifications which finds its supreme expression in the philosophy of St Thomas Aquinas and other major figures of the thirteenth and fourteenth centuries. So much has been written about the general importance of scholasticism in European culture that there is no need to deal with it here in any great detail. But it is important to emphasise the particular way in which it crystallised ideas and fixed them in new patterns.

Demonolatry

There is, in fact, a whole Christian image of the world which dates from the late Middle Ages. Vincent de Beauvais, amongst others, tried to reflect it in his *Speculum Majus*. It divided things up into various categories, relating them to 'nature', 'doctrine' (or culture as we might say today) 'morals', and 'history'. The moral aspect of things was subdivided into two clearly defined and contrasted parts: the vices and the virtues. On the one hand, there were the Christians who cultivated 'good' and 'virtue'; on the other, those people who cultivated 'evil' and 'vice'. Respectively the servants of God and of the Devil.

According to this view, therefore, it is obvious that those who pursued surviving idolatrous cults and persisted in pagan beliefs were servants of the Devil: among them sorcerers and witches. Of course, as long as paganism had some social force and as long as attempts were being made to convert people who knew nothing of Christianity, or resisted it, to the true faith, the churchmen were still prepared to debate and argue in favour of their beliefs. But once the spread of Christianity was complete and the ecclesiastical authorities were in power, their attitude changed. No longer were there merely some beliefs that were correct and others that were mistaken; now there were those which were superior and others that were inferior.

This change had untold consequences. The world order of things became much the same as that of the Gothic porches of cathedrals and churches. At the highest point and in the middle was God Himself surrounded by angels and with the saints and the blessed spirits gathered around him. Beneath came mortal men and underneath them, or looking out from the far corners, were evil spirits which were hideously or peculiarly fashioned, although they sometimes had something comical about them as well. The damned occupied the lowest place of all. But within this conception there was an obvious emphasis on the continual presence and constant activity of the Devil in the world: the Devil was a real and familiar figure, at least as familiar as the patriarchs and saints. The carvers of the Gothic period (like those of the Romanesque period before them) represented him with specific attributes, in the form of all the secondary genii of classical antiquity, or accompanied by them: harpies and sirens, centaurs, monstrous giants and terrifying dragons and serpents. Any tourist must recall having seen at one time or another Romanesque sculptures—the capitals of the columns at Vézelay for instance—in which the Devil is shown continually intervening in the life of men.

Perhaps women, however, were more subject to the attacks of the Devil than men. Woman was certainly thought to be more liable to do evil. The Bible held this view and pagan authors and the Church Fathers did so too.[2] Artists seem to have adopted a similar position.

There is ample proof of this, for example, in the series of capitals at Vézelay. Satan uses a woman as a musical instrument. Elsewhere, in the porch of the church at Moissac there is the particularly horrible detail of two serpents hanging from the pendulous and flaccid breasts of a woman. A toad sits on her sexual organs while the Devil looks on unperturbed.[3]

The art of later periods is full of similar details, and satires against women are as much a commonplace of medieval pietistic literature as of the classics.[4] In the series of Temptations of Saints we also find the Devil introducing reasonably attractive temptresses to men like St Benet[5] or St Antony, surrounded by all kinds of fantastic figures and loathsome animals. Following a more or less conscious tradition, artists tended to represent the tempter, the temptress and the horde of lower devils who look on, as burlesque figures, ridiculing them in a way which becomes almost morbidly disturbing in painters like Bosch and others of a later date.

Even in the middle of the seventeenth century the Devil is treated in the same way in pietistic literature as in medieval times. But when he is up against saintly people, he must always be humbled and made to look ridiculous in the end. An example of this is to be found in the biography of a seventeenth-century Spanish nun, Doña Micaela de Aguirre. Satan, irritated by her perfection, took to persecuting her violently. 'The servant of God was lying one night on her solitary bed,' says her biographer, 'when the Devil appeared in the shape of a well-shod horse. Getting on to the bed, he stood on Micaela and using his full weight, trampled on her, like a wild and untamed horse who kicks and tramples his rider when he has thrown him, leaving hardly a bone in his body unbroken. When the great beast from Hell had bruised her sorely he disappeared.' Sometimes several devils came and, carrying her to the well of the Convent, 'immersed her in the well with the water up to her neck and kept her there all night'; or they maltreated her in many other ways. In the end, however, the nun triumphed for 'mocking his cunning she (imperiously) bade him fetch an axe and chop wood. And this she did on one occasion (and I know not whether on others also). And the enemy could not disobey her; he took the axe and chopped the wood up with all haste (and there was a great deal of it) and departed in confusion, roaring with anger at being defeated by a young nun.'[6] Obviously this is a most suitable scene for a Gothic artist! Another nun at a later period, Sister Jacinta de Antondo, suddenly saw a large mis-shapen animal when walking with a companion, who, somewhat frightened, asked her if she saw the nasty creature. The nun's biographer continues: 'Jacinta, turning towards the animal, laughingly said to it: "What do you hope to find here, you wild thing? Wait a minute and I will give you what you deserve." Taking a small hyssop soaked with holy water she went towards the animal, which immediately turned into a toad, another creature jumping from its mouth at the same time. The nun, not in the least disturbed, chased both of them out . . .'[7] Once again we seem to be looking at some Gothic painting with its gilded background.

But let us turn to the more public acts of the Devil in the Middle Ages.

The Devil, in fact, like the pagan divinities who presided over witchcraft, was the Lord of Darkness: darkness which even in our own times is slightly awesome, and must have epitomised mystery for people living in small villages and country areas in medieval times. During the hours of darkness the most dangerous places for good Christians and honourable folk were—it was widely believed —the very cross-roads which had earlier been sacred to Hecate, places where sorcerers and witches met those who had been eternally damned, and presided over by the Devil himself.

A very popular legend of the Middle Ages gives us a clear picture of the significance of a cross-roads at night. This is the story of Theophilus, a tale of oriental origin, which Gonzalo de Berceo put into the ancient and somewhat unpolished language of early Spanish poetry.

When Theophilus was trying to find a protector after the death of a bishop who had previously looked after his interests, he consulted a Jewish sorcerer who promised him success. In the middle of the night, the sorcerer took him to a cross-roads, warning him not to cross himself while he was there. Shortly afterwards a sinister looking group of people appeared carrying candles, with their ruler in their midst. This ruler gave an audience to the sorcerer who introduced Theophilus, and the latter cursed Christ and the Virgin Mary. Subsequently, Theophilus and the King signed a pact, and by cock-crow Theophilus was back in his house, without anybody noticing that he had ever left it. From then onwards he lost his 'good colour' and even his shadow, and was only finally saved by repentance and the intercession of the Virgin Mary.[8]

Our chief interest in the tale lies less in the story itself than in the form of the pact and the nature of those who were involved.

According to the Spanish poet, the ruler's court is the *uest antigua* (the old host), that is the host of damned souls. Up to a point the group is similar to the court of an earthly king, and the Devil offers his followers precisely what kings offer their vassals: help and protection in return for complete submission. Furthermore, the pact with the Devil is very similar to the treaties which determine the relationship between rulers and subjects in civil life. It is particularly similar to the pact made by a vassal when he 'denaturalises' himself, that is to say when he considers himself outside the sovereignty of his rightful ruler, and goes into exile or becomes the subject of another ruler, as frequently happened in the Middle Ages,[9] when pacts of brotherhood were also sworn between warriors, and other comparable alliances were made.

The case of Theophilus is not unique. Historians who have been concerned with the medieval conception of the Devil have discovered details of other pacts in legends and texts of Greek rather than Roman origin; the story of Antemius, for instance, or that of Senator Proterius which is found in the life of St Basil, or later cases which are equally famous like those of Gerberto (Silvester II) and Cecco d'Ascoli.[10]

It is clear, therefore, that there were men and women who denaturalised themselves, forsaking the service of God, and seeking the allegiance of another lord, the Devil.

Leaving the imaginary world of legend and turning to the real world, let us examine cases in which people are genuinely supposed to have desired to serve the Devil. Some rather intractable material on such cases has come down to us from the Middle Ages. It is inevitably puzzling that people should have wanted to give up the service of God at that period, when so much majesty and dignity was accorded Him, in order to submit themselves to such repulsive lords as the devils who are shown making a pact with Theophilus in the Church at Souillac and in Notre-Dame at Paris, or even exercising their crude wills on bishops and kings.[11] Such behaviour has a fairly complex explanation.

Devil-Worshippers

The practice of attributing false beliefs and revolting behaviour to those who profess a religion which is not one's own, is common enough. The pagans expressed such views of Christians, the

Christians said much the same of the pagans and the Jews: the Mohammedans denigrated the Christians, and the Chinese have cast aspersions on Europeans in general and so on. A believer of one religion, in fact, will readily claim that a man who does not share his beliefs is so perverse that he will perform the most loathsome and indecent acts.

Of course, certain aberrations and inversions can occur just as frequently in other fields of human behaviour as they do in sex. They have played an important part in the history of heresy. However, it is extremely difficult to separate genuine cases of aberration from those that are merely the result of slander. It may well be that there were as many *supposed* aberrations leading to witchcraft, as there were real ones. The same can be said of the practice of those activities associated with witchcraft (some of which antedate it) that have been studied in conjunction with it. There is, incidentally, a good deal to be said in favour of *not* studying them with it, although they have been for centuries, thanks to the theologians, canon and civil lawyers of the second half of the Middle Ages. Examples of such activities can be found in Germany, a country which, as we have already seen, was destined to play a decisive role in the history of witchcraft. We shall have more to say of this later and in the meantime must content ourselves with a rapid survey of the situation there.

The people of a fertile region of Oldenburg, called Stedinger-land, were required to pay certain tithes which had been awarded by Henry IV to the Archbishop of Bremen. In 1197 some clergy-men who were sent to collect the tithes were assaulted. The Archbishop proceeded to excommunicate the inhabitants of Stedingerland, calling them heretics. They paid no attention to the Archbishop's condemnation of their activities, however, and the Pope was asked to give permission for a crusade against them. A temporary compromise was reached between the parties, but thirty years after the original revolt trouble broke out again. The Archbishop wrote to the Pope (Gregory IX) for his support, asking him to authorise a crusade, and a Papal Rule dated 1232 ordered the bishops of Lübeck, Minden and Ratzeburg to preach the crusade. In the Rule, the inhabitants of Stedingerland were accused of despising the sacraments, persecuting the faithful, being in league with the Devil, making waxen images and con-sulting witches. A further Bull, sent to the bishops of Paderborn,

Hildesheim, Verden, Munster and Osnabruck describes their crimes even more explicitly. As I believe it to be a document of prime importance in the history of witchcraft, I have translated the central passages about the 'Secret Society', which the inhabitants of Stedingerland had formed.[12]

'When a novice is to be initiated and is brought before the assembly of the wicked for the first time, a sort of frog appears to him; a toad according to some. Some bestow a foul kiss on his hind parts, others on his mouth, sucking the animal's tongue and slaver. Sometimes the toad is of a normal size, but at others it is as large as a goose or a duck. Usually it is the size of an oven's mouth. The novice comes forward and stands before a man of fearful pallor. His eyes are black and his body so thin and emaciated that he seems to have no flesh and be only skin and bone. The novice kisses him and he is as cold as ice. After kissing him every remnant of faith in the Catholic Church that lingers in the novice's heart leaves him.

'Then all sit down to a banquet and when they rise after it is finished, a black cat emerges from a kind of statue which normally stands in the place where these meetings are held. It is as large as a fair-sized dog, and enters backwards with its tail erect. First the novice kisses its hind parts, then the Master of Ceremonies proceeds to do the same and finally all the others in turn; or rather all those who deserve the honour. The rest, that is those who are not thought worthy of this favour, kiss the Master of Ceremonies. When they have returned to their places they stand in silence for a few minutes with heads turned towards the cat. Then the Master says: "Forgive us." The person standing behind him repeats this and a third adds,"Lord we know it." A fourth person ends the formula by saying, "We shall obey."

'When this ceremony is over the lights are put out and those present indulge in the most loathsome sensuality, having no regard to sex. If there are more men than women, men satisfy one another's depraved appetites. Women do the same for one another. When these horrors have taken place the lamps are lit again and everyone regains their places. Then, from a dark corner, the figure of a man emerges. The upper part of his body from the hips upward shines as brightly as the sun but below that his skin is coarse and covered with fur like a cat. The Master of Ceremonies cuts a piece from the novice's vestments and says to the shining figure: "Master, I have been given this, and I, in my turn, give it to you." To which the other replies: "You have served me well and will serve me yet more in the future. I give into your safekeeping what you have given me." And he disappears as soon as he has spoken these words. Each year at Easter when they receive the body of Christ from the priest, they keep it in their mouths and throw it in the dirt as an outrage against their Saviour. Furthermore, these most miserable of men blaspheme against the Lord of Heaven and in their madness say that the Lord has done evil in casting out Lucifer into the bottomless pit. These most unfortunate people believe in Lucifer and claim that he was the creator of the celestial bodies and will ultimately return to glory when the Lord has fallen from power. Through him and with him they hope to achieve eternal happiness. They confess that they do not believe that one should do God's will but rather what displeases Him. . . .'

From the point of view of its composition, such a group would seem to recall adepts of a mystery cult more than anything else, and many of these had sprung up in Greece and Rome at one time or another. But the real question is whether such a group is truly demonolatrous or not. Were its members really *cultores diaboli*, or was the being they worshipped some ancient and obscure local or regional divinity rather than the Christian Devil? Were their acts not really diabolical in the strict sense of the word?

Demonolatry, similar to that described in the papal document, soon came to be closely associated with acts formerly attributed to witches. But it is possible, nevertheless, to draw sharp distinctions between the nature of these and activities which resembled them, for historical reasons. Their variety can be represented as follows:

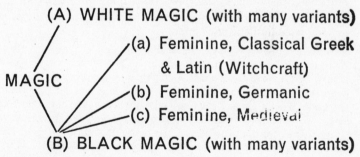

(A) WHITE MAGIC (with many variants)

(a) Feminine, Classical Greek & Latin (Witchcraft)

MAGIC

(b) Feminine, Germanic

(c) Feminine, Medieval

(B) BLACK MAGIC (with many variants)

Figure 7

Dualism

The heresy of the 'Cathars' helps to complete the picture of medieval witchcraft. It was a spiritual movement of considerable importance and most of the inquisitorial ideas about witchcraft put forward at later periods can best be understood in the light of it. The 'Cathars', spiritual offspring of the Manichees, spread through Europe remarkably swiftly, becoming singularly influential in the south of France, and causing many violent struggles there. These led to the crusade against the Albigenses (the group of 'Cathars' centred on Albi) and the creation of the first Inquisition. The interrogation of the 'Cathars' by the inquisitors, reveals very plainly the extent to which these supposed or real devil worshippers —whom we would call witches or sorcerers nowadays—were directly or indirectly influenced by the earlier dualistic theories. Either the accused themselves knew about them, or they learned of them from the inquisitors.

According to Joseph Hansen's detailed exposition of the history of European witchcraft, the great persecution began between 1230 and 1430.[13] Hansen has discussed some of the accusations which were made at an earlier date against the 'Cathars' (amongst others, that they kissed Lucifer in the form of a cat or frog, etc.). He considered that they gave a clear precedent for the point of view adopted in connexion with the deeds of sorcerers and witches.[14]

In the proceedings of the early trials, we sometimes find words which suggest that witches were linked with the Waldenses and other heretical groups whose views were communistic and contrary to the moral doctrines of the Church. We shall discuss these in greater detail in the next chapter.

CHAPTER 6

THE SABBATH

New views on magic and the works of the Devil – Notable cases of sorcery in the fourteenth century – The first 'Sabbath' – The cult of the He-goat – A general view of the 'Sabbath' – Inquisitorial practice – The 'Malleus Maleficarum'

New Views on Magic and the Works of the Devil

The thirteenth century is an immensely important period in the spiritual evolution of Europe. There are many reasons for this. Where magic and witchcraft are concerned, the real significance of the period lies in the fact that it put an end to the earlier ambiguous views on the nature of witchcraft, which cast doubt on the reality of certain acts of witchcraft and considered them to be illusions inspired by the Devil.

The authority of St Augustine was superseded by that of Aquinas. 'According to the Catholic faith,' the latter writes in a well-known passage, 'devils can cause harm by their activities and prevent sexual intercourse'. Aquinas wished to eradicate the idea that men were frightened by phantoms as a result of magic. For him such a view implied a lack of faith.[1] There could be no stronger opposition than this to the views expressed by Agobard, Burchard and John of Salisbury.

Rationalist historians have savagely attacked this view in modern times, as one might expect. However, a whole system was quickly built up around it expressing opinions that could find biblical authority in Exodus, chapter 22, verse 18, which reads *Malefica non patieris vivere*. This verse, 'Thou shalt not suffer a witch to live' (*a la hechicera no dejarás que viva* in the somewhat loose Spanish version of Cipriano de Valera),[2] had been commented on at length by the authors of the Talmud, who had frequently made statements like: 'Women are naturally inclined to witchcraft', 'the more women there are, the more witchcraft there will be', 'most women are witches' and so forth.

It is also true that the doctors of Mosaic law in the talmudic period had held that witchcraft was a crime punishable by stoning to death.[3] However, only in one or two rare instances, before or after that time, are the persecutions of witchcraft at all comparable with those carried out in Christian Europe from the fifteenth to the seventeenth centuries, persecutions which nearly always involved women. Our continent was dominated for centuries by the two criteria already mentioned. And with these as a basis, a body of doctrine in Canon Law was swiftly formulated, whereby the witch was not a person given to perverse fantasies and illusions, nor an adept of ancient idolatrous cults, but quite simply the slave of the Devil. This Devil had the same physical forms as we described in the last chapter, and appeared at legendary gatherings similar to that attended by Theophilus, or those which took place in Stedingerland.

This link between the witch and the Devil has provided so much food for thought through the centuries that to read even a small part of the studies on the subject would make one feel rather like Don Quixote after reading the Novels of Chivalry. Yet, although the witch and the Devil seem equally remote to the majority of laymen in modern society, in the past they worried everyone from popes, emperors and kings, down through humanists and scholars to the simple farm labourer.

In the light of nineteenth-century thought and as a result of the rise of rationalism, many people who believed neither in witches nor the Devil asked themselves how such an obsession could have arisen, and they gave their own fairly wild and arbitrary explanations of the phenomenon. Yet the historicist theories of the nineteenth century (and the conflicting opinions of more recent times too, for that matter) are quite as confusing as anything written at a completely credulous period. One or two instances of this will serve as examples.

Michelet, who was more of a romantic poet with a somewhat exalted imagination than a historian, assures us in *The Sorceress* that the witch of the medieval period—that age of horrors, injustices and prejudices—was a product of the communal despair felt by the mass of the people who thought that the witch was the only person who could alleviate their physical and spiritual wrongs. The witch, in her turn, brought Satan into being, and the two of them had to face the attacks of social authorities who looked upon them as a dangerous and anarchical political force. It is interesting to note that Michelet's ideas coincide with those of Malinowski on one point, since the latter continually emphasised the importance of the role of despair and frustration in magic. [4] I believe that this theory of the psychological basis of magic put forward by a romantic historian and an Anglo-Polish anthropologist is a valid one for the interpretation of certain aspects of witchcraft. It is certainly true that the practice of witchcraft increases, as we frequently find in the fourteenth, fifteenth and following centuries, when a general state of anxiety exists or catastrophes occur; at moments, in fact, when collective misery is a stronger force than individual passions.

But this is not the only theory that has been put forward to explain this striking historical fact.

Canon Döllinger, having established his reputation as a cleric within the Catholic Church, but finding that his beliefs would not permit him to accept certain dogmas which Pope Pius IX sought to propound, assembled a whole arsenal of learned arguments to denounce abuses of the papacy. Included amongst these abuses was the alleged papal responsibility for the invention of satanism and the repression of witchcraft by methods which came into existence at precisely the period of the Middle Ages now under discussion. [5]

Thus, on the one hand, we have a romantic historian who considers the witch to be a real person, a product of despair: the priestess of a cult formed by outcasts and unprotected members of society; and on the other hand, we have a theologian, in disagreement with his superiors, who looks upon the witch as a monstrous product of the imagination dreamed up by small-minded lawyers and theologians in the service of a temporal authority.

A contradiction is still present but the conflicting views are rather different from those expressed in earlier periods. The reality or unreality of witches' actions has ceased to be a theological problem and has become a historical one.

The controversy has, in fact, continued right down to the present day between, on the one hand, those who support the view that actions attributed to witches, and more particularly their covens, really took place, and on the other those who think that everything, or nearly everything, believed about witches is nothing but a gigantic falsification. Personally, I think that this last view goes too far. But to clear up the question we must first make a distinction between sorcery and witchcraft; differentiating between Black Magic of an *individualistic* nature, which we shall call sorcery, and a more complex and *collective* kind which is apparently connected with a specific *cult* and which is properly called *witchcraft*.

Notable Cases of Sorcery in the Fourteenth Century

We need not spend much time on medieval sorcery as practised by women. Cases brought against women for this crime are to be found in great numbers and in a variety of places; legal depositions, penitential canons. There are a number of Spanish texts like Section 1, Article 35 of the Second Book of the *Fuero* of Cuenca which says categorically: 'a woman who is a witch or a sorceress shall either be burnt or saved by iron.'[6] In this case, the context makes it clear that this was an individual and not a group problem.

According to jurists like the famous Bartolus,[7] the legal authorities of the later Middle Ages seem to have favoured death by burning as a punishment for sorcerers. Yet, regardless of this and other penalties, the sorceress continued to frequent nobles' castles, bishops' palaces and royal fortresses much as she had in previous centuries. There can have been few persons in France, Germany, England or Spain at that period who were not tempted to use sorcery at one time or another in spite of the penalties which could be incurred. What is more, there are, surprisingly enough, legal documents of the thirteenth century which show that enchantment practised with good intentions could be considered respectable and even praiseworthy at that date. This was certainly the view of Alfonso X of Castile who doubtless had recourse to enchantment on some occasion in a life that was so full of unfulfilled aims and projects.[8] It was normal, however, to condemn out of hand not only magical practices as a whole but also those who were accused of employing them. One need hardly say that such condemnations were amongst the first to appear in the famous collections of *causes célèbres* which were so popular in the eighteenth and nineteenth centuries. Between 1308 and 1318, for instance, there were several cases brought against people of some standing in France, alleging witchcraft. Bishops, soldiers and women of noble birth, had to defend themselves, with varying measures of success, against accusations of practising witchcraft, usually with the aid of women who were experts in the black arts. In 1315 Enguerrand de Marigny was condemned for the spells cast by his wife and his sister-in-law with the aid of a sorcerer and a witch, who had helped these ladies to make figures of wax to kill the king.[9]

Earlier, between 1308 and 1313, Guichard, Bishop of Troyes, was put on trial. He was not a very moral prelate perhaps and was thought by some to be the son of the Devil. He was accused above all of killing no less a person than Joan of Navarre, queen of France and the daughter of Blanche d'Artois (the queen of Navarre), by means of spells. It was also thought that he killed her mother but by poison rather than sorcery.

In the course of his trial, which has been studied in detail,[10] witnesses declared that the bishop had indeed practised magic in secret, helped by two monks and two women, in the chapel of Saint Flavit. Following the advice of the Devil, he had made a waxen figure, baptising it formally and giving it the queen's name —there were even god-parents for the ceremony—before sticking a spike through the head and other parts of the figure. The queen died as a result of these and other actions.[11]

In 1317 the Countess of Artois, Mahaut, who had been judged innocent at the trial, was accused of manufacturing philtres and poisons by a witch from Hesdin.[12] Other examples could be quoted *ad nauseam.* Later we shall see how this type of witchcraft recurred at the time of the Renaissance with certain classic characteristics. In the period under consideration it can be seen that the female assistant involved is still a frustrated woman; old, ugly and without social status, fulfilling other people's desires, including people of considerable importance in society. Such is and remains the paradoxical situation of the witch. There is little or no variety in what she does, nor in the people who make use of her or persecute her. As a whole there is no reason to think that the reactions to this ancient figure vary very much.

83

The feelings of terror the witch inspired were not unmixed in the Middle Ages any more than they had been in classical antiquity. Sometimes the reaction was one of mockery. Perhaps, indeed, terror and laughter are more often found side by side in medieval art than anywhere else. Whereas the sculpted or painted images of saints and biblical characters seem full of dignity and reality, images of witches are lacking in these qualities and tend to provoke terror or ridicule.

More specific material about witchcraft is to be found in the bulls of Pope John XXII, which stand out amongst the great mass of orders and instructions of Church Councils. These condemned magic in all its forms in the early years of the fourteenth century. They urged the inquisitors to keep a careful watch on such activities. Particularly notorious is the bull *super illius specula* of 1320 which seems to mark the beginning of a new era in witch-craft.[13] Many historians have considered the effects of this bull to have been decisive.[14]

The First 'Sabbath'

The 'Sabbath' appears for *the first time* in inquisitorial trials in the Carcassonne and Toulouse regions shortly after the trials of Guichard, Enguerrand de Marigny and the Countess Mahaut; shortly, also, after the promulgation of the bull, between 1330 and 1340.[15] From the very beginning, the 'Sabbath' always took the same form. Here is a description of it from depositions attributed to certain witches of Toulouse in the fourteenth century.

'Anne Marie de Georgel and Catherine, the wife of Delort, both from Toulouse and advanced in years, have declared in their con-fessions to the legal authorities that they have been members of the numberless hosts of Satan for about twenty years, and have given themselves to him for this life and the next. Frequently on Friday nights they have attended the Sabbath which is held sometimes in one place, sometimes in another. There, in company with other men and women who are equally sacrilegious, they commit all manner of excesses, whose details are horrible to tell. Each of them has been interrogated separately and they have given explanations which have entirely convinced us of their guilt.

'Anne Marie de Georgel declares that one morning when she was washing clothes near Pech-David above the town, she saw a man of huge stature coming towards her across the water. He was dark-skinned and his eyes burned like living coals; he was dressed in the hides of beasts. This monster asked her if she would give herself to him and she said yes. Then he blew into her mouth and from the Saturday following she was borne to the Sabbath, simply because it was his will. There she found a huge he-goat and after greeting him she submitted to his pleasure. The he-goat in return taught her all kinds of secret spells; he explained poisonous plants to her and she learned from him words for incantations and how to cast spells during the night of the vigil of St John's day, Christmas Eve, and the first Friday in every month. He advised her to make sacrilegious communion if she could, offending God and honouring the Devil. And she carried out these impious suggestions.

'Anne Marie de Georgel then admitted that she had not ceased to do evil, practising all manner of filthiness during the years which passed from the time of her initiation to that of her imprisonment. The fear of Our Lord did not stay her hand. She boiled together in a cauldron, over an accursed fire, poisonous herbs and substances taken from the bodies of animals or humans which she had sacrilegiously and foully taken from the consecrated ground of cemeteries to use for her spells; she frequented the gallows-trees by night stealing shreds of clothing from the hanged, or taking the rope by which they were hanging, or laying hold of their hair, their nails or flesh. Like a true daughter of Satan, in answer to questions about the symbols of the Apostles and the faith which true believers had in our Holy Religion, she averred that God and the Devil were completely equal, the former reigning over the *sky* and the latter the *earth*; all souls which the Devil managed to seduce were lost to the Most High God and lived perpetually on earth or in the air, going every night to visit the houses in which they had lived and trying to inspire in their children and relatives a desire to serve the Devil rather than God.

'She also told us that the struggle between God and the Devil had gone on since eternity and would have no end. Sometimes one is victorious, sometimes the other, and at this time the situation was such that Satan was sure to triumph. At first, after she had been taken prisoner, having been denounced by respectable persons who had good reason to complain of her spells, she denied the abominable pact she had made and would not confess in spite of the requests of others as well as ourselves. But when she had been justly forced to give an account of herself, she finally admitted a series of crimes which deserved the most horrible punishment. She has sworn she repents, and has asked for reconciliation with the Church which

85

has been granted her. Nevertheless, she must still be handed over to the secular arm which will realise the penalties she must pay.

'Catherine, the wife of Pierre Delort of Toulouse, stands convicted on her own declarations and on the evidence of trustworthy persons, of meeting a shepherd in the field of the Parish of Quint and having a relationship with him contrary to the law. He, abusing his power over her, obliged her to make a pact with the Devil. This loathsome ceremony took place at midnight at the edge of a wood at a place where two roads meet. She let some blood from her left arm and allowed it to flow on to a fire made of human bones which had been stolen from the parish cemetery. She pronounced certain strange words which she no longer remembers and the Devil Berit appeared to her in the form of a violet flame. Since then she has made certain harmful concoctions and potions which cause men and beasts to die.

'Every Friday night she fell into a strange sleep during which she was carried to the Sabbath. Asked where this took place she answered: on the slopes of Pech-David in the wood at Bouconne, in the middle of the open country between Toulouse and Montauban. Sometimes further away still, on the top of the Black Mountains or the Pyrenees, and in countries quite unknown to her. There she worshipped the he-goat and served his pleasure and that of all those who were present at that loathsome feast. The corpses of newly-born children were eaten by them; they had been stolen from their nurses during the night; all manner of revolting liquids were drunk and there was no savour in any of the food.

'Asked whether she had seen any of those of her acquaintance at the Sabbath she replied that she had frequently. She did not name them; some of them had died in their wickedness, others have been taken into custody thanks to our vigilance; a few have escaped, but the vengeance of the Lord will be upon them.

'Catherine, forced to confess by the means we have power to use to make people speak the truth, was convicted of all the crimes we suspected her of committing, although she protested her innocence for a long time and made several false declarations. She made hail fall on the fields of her enemies, caused their wheat to rot by means of a pestilential fog, and damaged the vineyards with frost. She caused the oxen and sheep of her neighbours to sicken and die for the advantages this might bring her. For the same motives she caused her aunts, whose heir she was, to die, by heating waxen figures dressed in one of their blouses over a slow fire, so that their unfortunate lives wasted away as the waxen figures melted in the brazier.'[10]

The antiquity of the text and its nearness in date to others written from a radically different point of view, which we have discussed in earlier chapters, merit some reflection. In this case everything *is real*.

H. C. Lea, following the line of thought which had earlier led Döllinger to affirm that the witch trials resulted in wholesale miscarriages of justice, held the view that the methods of the inquisitors were largely responsible for the accused's admissions of guilt. Awareness of the legal falsifications involved, the physical and mental torture, the way in which evidence was elicited and the scant respect shown for the defence, is certainly vital to the understanding of the problem[17] and a considerable help in assessing the nature of the *reality* which the judges accepted. It is quite true that the extracts from the above trials provide clear evidence of the extent to which torture was responsible for the confessions of the accused. But it must be remembered that while torture may often explain the confessions of innocent persons, it can never explain away the crimes themselves. Torture is not, in fact, responsible for the nature of the accusation, as one sees when one examines the trials of the Spanish Jews and other persons denounced to the Inquisition.

What are we to think, then, of the nature of the actions attributed to these women and to many others who were put on trial at the same period?

The Cult of the He-goat

The only thing that strikes one as new in these depositions are the references to the Sabbath and to the theory of witchcraft. All the rest we have seen before: the activities carried on, and the evils associated with magic which are described. Even the Sabbath is not unlike the earlier meetings of the 'Stedinger' to judge from the available documentary evidence. And, finally, the witches echo the dualistic doctrine. Information about it piles up with extraordinary rapidity in various places from the middle of the fourteenth century onwards.

At the beginning of the fifteenth century people were still being tried for Black Magic and Devil worship in Carcassonne and Toulouse as well as other centres—Dauphiné, Savoy, Lyons and Vivarais. As we shall see, the trouble spread through Switzerland, the Tyrol and the Po Valley towards Italy. In the Lyons region the sorcerers called their meetings *le Fait* (the Fact) and the Devil was referred to as *le Martinet*. The ordinary people called these strange gatherings 'a synagogue',[18] doubtless identifying them with the meeting-place of another ostracised group in their society.

The Jews, in fact, may well have provided other parallels. For example, there have been many learned theories about the origin of the word 'Sabbath'. These have tried to find subtle links with other terms which would reflect some connexion between the witch cult and pagan cults like that of Dionysus for example: *Sabazius* or Σαβάξιος etc.[19] But I see no reason for looking any further for the origin of the name than the Hebrew Sabbath, since the rites and beliefs of the Jews were considered the height of perversion at this point in the Middle Ages. To call something the 'sabbath' or 'synagogue' was to condemn it out of hand as something essentially vile. But we must return to the depositions already quoted, since they require more comment.

We have already suggested that the system of beliefs attributed to witches in these documents might have been influenced, in part at least, by the dualistic religious systems of an earlier period. This need not really be so surprising since both the judges and the accused might well have known something of the views preached earlier by the 'Cathars' or Albigenses in the same part of southern France.[20] The witches seem wholly demonolatrous. Without making the slightest mention of female divinities like Diana, who were formerly supposed to be the patrons of spells and incantations, they declare themselves to be worshippers of the Devil; a devil who appears in a variety of forms, but at the height of the ceremony appears in the shape of a he-goat. It is surely not irrelevant that this animal has always been associated with perverted rituals of a sexual nature.[21]

A General View of the 'Sabbath'

The fact that the Devil should be given this particular form, although he is sometimes given more human traits, would seem to be the result of classical inspiration: satyrs, sylphs and fauns come immediately to mind. It must also be admitted that the picture could have been largely suggested by representations of the Devil in art.[22] It is probably more worthwhile to examine some of the characteristics of the manifestations of witchcraft than to try to follow up the views of those who have seen a possible link between the Devil's image and a horned deity of prehistoric times.[27]

The dualism of God and the Devil to which witches in the south of France seem to refer, as do others who were tried elsewhere at a later date, can be closely linked with the characteristically medieval system of factions and blood-ties.[24] There were numerous reflections of this in different parts of Europe. The view was that the whole of society could be divided into two groups, which were constantly fighting one another in everyday life, representing two opposing factions with different interests. The sorcerers, both according to themselves and to their inquisitors, which is beside the point, belonged to one particular side. And no quarter was given in the war between the two sides on a spiritual any more than on a physical plane.[25]

This would explain why members of the strongest party or band—in this case the civil and ecclesiastical judges—should go to such lengths to exterminate sorcerers and witches, who were no longer merely slightly dangerous or ridiculous women, but a group of *men and women* in league with one another and bound by the closest ties. The *witch*, however, was always the more typical figure of the two in the opinion of the masses.

In 1435 Jean Duprat, the Inquisitor of Carcassonne, examined eight men and women who had banded together under a woman called Mabille de Marnac.

Paul Viguier, Armande Robert, Matheline Figuier and Pienille Roland boasted of the Sabbath they had attended in the mountains at Alaric, and André Ciceron, a shepherd from the Black Mountains, had parodied the mass in order to cast a spell. Two other shepherds, Catala and Paul Rodier, were accused of being poisoners and magicians. They had summoned the Devil by night, at a cross-roads, by sacrificing a black hen, in order to promote strife in the district.[26]

The inquisitors, then, were faced with a variety of different cases. Yet poets and the common people continued to fit them all into a stereotyped pattern. One of the characters in Martin le Franc's *Champion des Dames* (Le Franc died c. 1460) gives the following description of their activities:

'Je te dy avoir veu en chartre
Vielle, laquelle confessoit
Aprez qu'escript estoit en chartre,
Comment, dès le temps qu'elle estoit
De 16 ans ou poy s'en faloit
Certaines nuis de la Valpute
sur ung bastonnet s'en aloit
Veoir la synagogue pute.
Dis mille vielles en un fouch
Y avoit il communement,
En fourme de chat ou de bouch
Veans le dyable proprement
Auquel baisoient franchement
Le cul en signe d'obéissance
Reneyant Dieu tout plainement
Et toute sa haute puissance.'[27]

(I tell you I have seen an old woman in prison who confessed, after it had been recorded in a document, how, from the age of sixteen or nearly, she had gone on a stick on certain Walpurgis nights to attend the obscene synagogue. Usually there was a crowd of about ten thousand old women present, gazing upon the devil himself in the form of a cat or a he-goat. They kissed his hind-parts as a sign of obedience, and openly renounced God and His omnipotence.)

This portrait is a typical one—the same that led to witches being called *scobaces* or 'women with brooms' in Normandy because of their supposed practice of flying about on broomsticks[28]—which had come to be widely accepted.

Already at an earlier period Jean de Meung in the *Roman de la Rose* (1277) had said that *lamiae* or *mascae* who flew under cover of darkness committing all kinds of atrocities, constituted a third of the population of France.[29] But the lawyers needed more concrete conclusions than these and tried to systematise the material which the trials were bringing to light. Furthermore, the inquisitors were able to produce new information about the orgies at the Sabbath which were, subsequently, accepted as part of their established pattern.

Here, for example, is what the Inquisitor Pierre le Broussard had to say when he was summing up the crimes attributed to sorcerers in Arras:

'When they want to go to the *vauderie*,[30] they spread an ointment, which the Devil has given them, on a wooden stick and rub it on their palms and all over their hands also; then they put the stick between their legs and fly off over towns, woods and stretches of water, being led by the Devil himself to the place where their assembly is to be held. There they meet together and there also they find tables loaded with wines and things to eat, and there the Devil appears to them, sometimes in the form of a he-goat, sometimes as a dog or a monkey; never in human form. They make oblations and pay homage to the Devil, worshipping him. Many of them give him their souls or at least part of their bodies. Then with candles in their hands they kiss the hind parts of the goat that is the Devil . . .'

The writer goes on to say:

'And the *Abbé de peu de sens* we have already mentioned (that is, one of the principal people involved in the trial) was the man responsible for the neophytes, and the master of ceremonies. When the paying of homage was over, they all walked over a cross spitting on it, scorning Christ and the Holy Trinity. Then they exposed their hinder parts to the sky and the heavens above as a sign of their disregard for God, and, after eating and drinking their fill, they all had sexual intercourse; and the Devil appeared both in the form of a man and of a woman, and the men had intercourse with him in the form of a woman and the women in the form of a man. They also committed sodomy and practised homosexuality and other vile and monstrous crimes against God and nature.'[31]

Graphic representations of this kind of Sabbath are to be found in French miniatures as early as the fifteenth century. And this view of the Sabbath subsequently became popular although with certain modifications at times.[32] However, the artists who painted these scenes always reproduced them with scrupulous care and remarkable objectivity. There is none of the mixture of terror and grotesqueness in their works which we find in artists of openly sceptical periods such as Goya.

Inquisitorial Practice

As early as the first quarter of the fourteenth century Bernard Gui, an inquisitor of Toulouse, was setting out methods for dealing with sorcerers and witches in his *Practica Inquisitionis Haereticae Pravitatis*. The number of trials taking place at the time made it possible for a skilled lawyer to attempt a systematically doctrinaire approach to the subject. But in Gui's work (which has been reprinted in the present century) the major concern was with heretics like the Cathars, Waldenses, Beguines and so on, rather than with witches as such.[33]

The famous *Directorium Inquisitorum* of the Catalan Dominican, Nicolàs Eymerich or Eymeric (1320–1399), was written rather later, around 1376, after many more years of experience, and reprinted several times in the sixteenth and seventeenth centuries.[34] Eymerich pointed out the existence of three sorts of witchcraft.

1. The witchcraft of those who practise Devil-worship, making sacrifices, prostrating themselves, singing prayers, lighting candles and burning incense, etc.

2. The witchcraft of those who merely respect the devils and mention them in litanies along with the saints, asking for their intercession with God.

3. The witchcraft of those who summon up devils by tracing magical signs, by placing a child in the middle of a circle, by using a sword or a mirror.

The inquisitor, however, made one point that is worth remembering when generalising about magic. If the Devil is only asked to do what is in his power, to tempt a woman with sexual desires, for example, and if, when he is asked to do this, he is given commands in the form, 'I order you', 'I adjure you', 'I require you', there is nothing seriously heretical about it. On the other hand, if the Devil is addressed in more respectful terms, 'I ask you', 'I beg you', for instance, then it is a case of clear heresy, since the words are a kind of prayer and imply worship. Like other scholastics, Eymerich was quite capable of careful reasoning, although the consequences of his reasoning are no better and no worse than they would have been had he been illogical.

The work of the judges of Toulouse and Carcassonne was the basis for the body of doctrine formulated in treatises written down in the course of the fourteenth century. Similar work in different parts of Europe helped to modify and extend these doctrines, and the evolutionary process culminated in a book which was the judges' guide for a long period, although it was severely criticised from the moment it first appeared, namely, the *Malleus Maleficarum*.

The Swiss persecutions, organised by Peter of Berne, found an able theorist in the theologian Johannes Nider, who died between 1438 and 1440. Between 1435 and 1437 he wrote a rather muddled book which usually goes by the name of *Formicarius*, the ant-heap, and is often published with the *Malleus*.[35]

Its twelve chapters take the form of dialogues between a theologian (Nider himself) and an idle individual who wants to find out without too much effort the proper attitude to take to sorcery and spells. The theologian gives examples to illustrate his basic assumptions, derived from authorities of various periods, with illustrations from recent cases.[36] It is difficult to see after reading the book, however, why the author uses ants as an image for human society in condemning the excesses of sorcerers in the same way as Peter of Berne.

It seems that three men were particularly troublesome from the latter's point of view: Stadelein, Scasio and Hoppo. But this did not stop him from having many others burnt as well, including a number of women,[37] particularly in the diocese of Lausanne. Many fled from territories which were under his jurisdiction. The Swiss sorcerers seem to have engaged in all the usual practices. They brought on tempests, sterility in men and animals, and madness; they travelled through the air to distant places; they plagued those responsible for persecuting them with foul smells and made them feel intense and uncontrollable fear. They also had the gift of prophecy.[38] Their close relations with the Devil were obvious. To create a storm, Stadelein first asked the Prince of all Devils to appoint an executor, who appeared on the spot. Then he sacrificed a live black chicken and threw it into the air. The Devil, having caught it, threw a correspondingly black cloud over the place the sorcerer wanted to damage, unless God happened to forestall him.[39]

Women were thought to be responsible for making love potions —out of beans and cock's testicles amongst other things[40]—and they were also believed to eat human flesh and steal children. They cooked the latter in cauldrons, making the solid parts into ointments and filling bottles and other vessels with the liquid which was left. Places of authority within the group were obtained by drinking this liquid.[41]

Amongst other things Nider tells us that a sect of sorcerers was believed to exist. To join it, the suppliant had formally to renounce the Christian faith on a Sunday, when all the leaders of the sect would go to church with him. After his renunciation, he paid homage to the *Magisterulo*: the Devil himself. Subsequently, he would have to drink the liquid we have just mentioned.[42]

The 'Malleus Maleficarum'

The witch-hunts organised by Peter of Berne were no more successful in putting an end to witchcraft in Switzerland than were similar persecutions in different parts of Germany. Witches were burnt at Heidelberg in 1446 and at Cologne in 1456 even before others were similarly treated by the authors of the *Malleus*. Eugene IV gave orders for such repressive measures in 1437 and 1445, Calixtus II in 1457 and Pius IV in 1459. These were later followed by Alexander VI in 1494, Julius II and Leo X in 1521, Hadrian VI in 1523 and Clement VII in 1524.⁴³ In fact, the popes from John XXII onwards have often been criticised for their actions. But it is difficult to imagine today what it was like to live in an age which believed in magic, in countries where violence was accepted as a common and everyday occurrence.

The most famous of all the papal dispositions and the one to which both civil and ecclesiastical judges appealed as the supreme authority for a long time, was the Bull *Summis desiderantes affectibus* of Pope Innocent VIII, promulgated on December 9th, 1484.⁴⁴ It was addressed to a number of German prelates in whose dioceses witchcraft was rife, and it laid down the powers of the Inquisition to be used for its suppression. But the most curious part of the Bull is the description of the sorcerer's activities.

'Recently', it says, 'it has come to our notice, much to our regret, that in some parts of Upper Germany, in the provinces, towns, territories, localities and sees of Mainz, Cologne, Treves, Salzburg and Bremen, a number of persons of both sexes, forgetful of their own salvation and contrary to their belief in the Catholic Faith, have given themselves up to devils in the form of incubi and succubi. By their incantations, spells, crimes and infamous acts they destroy the fruit of the womb in women, in cattle and various other animals; they destroy crops, vines, orchards, meadows and pastures, wheat, corn and other plants and vegetables; they bring pain and affliction, great suffering and appalling disease (both external and internal) upon men, women and beasts, flocks and other animals; they prevent men from engendering and women from conceiving; they render both wives and husbands impotent; they sacrilegiously deny the faith they received in Holy Baptism; and they do not abstain from committing other fearful excesses and foul crimes, endangering their souls, mocking God and causing a serious scandal, at the instigation of the Enemy.'⁴⁵

Two preaching friars, who were sent as inquisitors to the

areas concerned, found that there was a certain amount of hostility between clergy and people. In view of this, they made representations to the Pope, who requested the Archbishop of Strasburg to provide the necessary facilities for them to carry out the work for which they already had plenary powers from Rome.[46] The practical work of these two friars was memorable. Still more memorable, however, were the resultant theories. The two collaborated in writing the *Malleus Maleficarum*, a lengthy legal work specially concerned with crimes of witchcraft. First printed in 1486 and frequently reprinted from then onwards until the end of the sixteenth century, it has been published again in recent times by German and English scholars for its curiosity value.[47]

The theory of the *Malleus*, or rather of its two authors, Henry Institor (Kraemer) and Jacob Sprenger, was the culmination of belief in the genuine reality of magical actions: violently opposed to the point of view held by Burchard and others.

In the first part, which is divided into seventeen chapters, the work stresses the need to accept the actions of witches (as opposed to sorcerers) and their collaboration with the Devil who is himself capable of witchery. The existence of incubi and succubi is defended, and the possibility is advanced that they are in part responsible for the existence of those who practise witchcraft. These can be divided into different categories beginning with an inferior grade and working upwards. Celestial bodies also play a part in the multiplication of spells which are, moreover, more often the work of women than men. An enormous number of these spells are inevitably, therefore, connected with sexual activity. Through the activities of witches, the Devil is able to inspire hate or love; he can render people impotent or incapable of sexual intercourse and even cause them to believe they have been castrated. Freudian theories about castration complexes would indeed find strange documentary support for their views in Part I, Chapter IX of the *Malleus*. In that chapter there is some discussion of the possibility that such an illusion can be entertained; *membra virilia quasi sint a corporibus evulsa auferre soleant*.[48] Witches, who are mostly midwifes, are equally capable of changing men into animals.[49] Although Chapters XXII to the end discuss sorcery on a more generalised and theoretical level, its seriousness and reality is constantly affirmed and backed by references to numerous authorities.[50]

The second part of the *Malleus* contains rather more narrative and casuistical material. Two separate topics are considered. In the first sixteen chapters the extent of the witches' power is outlined. Then in the next, methods of combating witches and destroying their evil work are described. The greater part of the cases are the fruits of the writers' own experiences, though some are taken from Nider and other German and Austrian inquisitors.

Sprenger and Institor also look on sorcerers and witches as members of a sect. They refer to various initiation ceremonies. One of them is the same as the one described by Nider; others are rather more solemn. The Devil receives the homage of the initiate in person, after he has made his renunciation. There is even a private form of service for initiation. The evidence of a girl from the Diocese of Basle is the source of their description of the formal renunciation which is part of the real 'Sabbath'.[51] The Devil is said to use three methods to win disciples and more particularly women. He either makes them feel tired of life, or tempts them, or corrupts them.[52]

Once members of the sect had learned the Black Arts, they behaved in the usual manner: flying through the air on broomsticks or rakes, making various sorts of pacts—physical, amatory, some of them almost comical—changing men into animals, possessing them with devils, making them sicken or die, causing rain and hail storms.[53] The list becomes monotonous.

Fortunately, the two judges seem to have been relatively untroubled by such phenomena in the course of their investigations, and they soon discovered that witches had no power over them. They were disturbed, nevertheless, by voices, insults and foul language from time to time, and those under investigation sometimes appeared to them at high windows or out of murky corners in the shape of monkeys, dogs and goats.[54] All very much like a Gothic carving.

Some of the narratives in the *Malleus* are like fables—'tales' in the strict sense of the word. One such is the story of an old witch of Baldshut in the Diocese of Constance who was so annoyed with her neighbours for not inviting her to a wedding that she asked the Devil to bring on a hail-storm at the height of the celebrations. The Devil obligingly carried her through the air to a nearby mountain so that she could achieve her object. There some shepherds saw her make a hole and urinate in it, stirring the liquid with her finger when she had finished. Then the Devil carried it all up into the sky and showered hail down on the wedding guests when they were dancing. The evidence of the shepherds and the suspicions of the guests were enough to put the old woman on trial and have her condemned to be burnt.[55]

This case and other similar ones raise a question of considerable importance in the evolution of theories on witchcraft and magic in general. What kind of evidence was needed to establish the fact that an event really took place, and how was guilt proved? But this is a subject which will be discussed later.

The third part of the *Malleus*—the part which most interested the authors, Institor and Sprenger—deals with their methods and central ideas. They can be summarised in the following way.

An accusation levelled by an individual or the unproved denunciation of some zealous person normally starts the proceedings. But often a vague rumour can cause the judge to open a case. A child's evidence is considered adequate, and even statements made by personal enemies of the accused are accepted. The sentence ought to be straightforward, brief and final. The judge's powers are absolute. He it is who decides whether the accused has the right to defend himself; he also appoints counsel for the defence and hedges him about with so many conditions that he is virtually just another counsel for the prosecution. Torture may be freely employed; and if the 'guilty' party cannot be made to confess, even under duress, his failure to do so can always be attributed to the Devil's power over him. Trial by fire or water is rejected, but the accused cannot escape the sentence. Retraction and repentance are no way of avoiding the death penalty. Those under sentence are simply handed over to the secular arm—if the secular arm is not responsible for the conviction in the first place—since witchcraft is a civil as well as a religious offence.[56]

The *Malleus Maleficarum* is, in fact, an enormously interesting and disturbing work. Sprenger and Institor appear to have had certain obsessions. But it is as well to remember that theologians and scholastic philosophers were not the people responsible for putting their obsessions into practice. From the time of the book's first publication down to the middle of the eighteenth century, it was the law and lawyers (frequently Protestant ones at that) who made the greatest use of it. And the doctors, philosophers and even progressive theologians opposed it.

The battle lasted for two whole centuries: the sixteenth and the seventeenth. It seems to have been won in the eighteenth by those who in the name of radical ideas or moderation restricted the reality of acts of magic and witchcraft. But while the battle lasted it was a violent one, as we shall see in the next few chapters.

CHAPTER 7

THE RENAISSANCE CRISIS

Witchcraft in Italy – The Celestina as an archetype – Doubts entertained by some Spanish theologians – Views of some Italian intellectuals – The reaction in Germany

Witchcraft in Italy

Burckhardt, in his work on the civilisation of Italy during the Renaissance, devotes several fascinating pages to the study of magic and the superstitions of the period. His analysis of the subject leads him to the conclusion that a strange mixture of ancient and modern superstitions was then widely accepted. The ancient superstitions which survived were, obviously enough, linked with those of classical times. Often enough, however, the connexion was the result of the scholarly pursuits of the Renaissance. There was, for example, a widespread belief in astrology amongst the cultured classes. The observation of omens and presages, belief in the ability of certain people to call up devils, and fear of ghosts, were all common at this period.

The primitive and popular way in which the magic arts survived from Roman times, was in the *streghe* with many of their classical characteristics intact, according to Burckhardt. These *streghe* mostly lived by fortune-telling or divining. But, according to popular belief, they frequently used their knowledge to make men and women hate or love one another, and to bring on sickness or death—particularly in young children. The women of Gaeta were notorious for being *streghe*. And Nursia was a veritable hotbed of witches—worthy successors of Horace's Canidia. Aeneas Silvius refers to them in one of his finest letters which Burckhardt quotes.[1]

Not satisfied with merely giving details about witchcraft, Burckhardt also evolves a theory about it. He compares the classical witch, about whom he was able to find quite a lot of material in original texts, with the witches hunted and brought to trial by followers of Institor and Sprenger in the north of Italy, in regions close to Switzerland and the Tyrol. And he does not hesitate to assert that the real source of the findings of witch-hunters in those parts was the fertile imagination of mendicant friars. He maintains, in fact, that the *Malleus* and a hundred years of witch-trials conditioned people to believe in the possibility of the practices which these had condemned. Witchcraft, therefore, as described in the inquisitorial treatises, was of German origin.

'The Italian witch', he says in conclusion, 'has a job and wants to earn money. Above all she must have a good deal of sang-froid and act rationally. Not for her the hysterical visions of the witches of the North, belief in long rides through the air and so forth.'

The *stregha* is simply an aider and abettor of pleasure, a servant of the God Eros.[2] She finds her proper place in the works of Aretinus who describes not only witches themselves but also the objects used by courtesans to attract their lovers. He gives lists of practices employed to bind people together, setting out one or two of the spells which were part of the secret science of the *stregha*.

Two great cities—Papal Rome and Naples—gave these women a home.[3]

Burckhardt's observations make a useful distinction between two types of witch found in Europe at the time of the Renaissance and perhaps also before as well as after that period. However, his *racial* theories of witchcraft, if we can call them that, do not deserve too much attention. The Italian witch is much the same as those described by the German inquisitors in the earlier trials at Toulouse and Carcassonne in the south of France.

The real difference between these witches and the sorceress described by Burckhardt needs to be worked out on a sociological rather than ethnic basis. The typical witch is above all found in *country* areas; the sorceress of classical extraction, however, is more usually found in *urban* districts, or in areas where an urban-type culture exists. The same difference which Burckhardt found between the witches of Northern Italy, in Como or in Val Camonica for example,[4] and the sorceresses of the Gaeta or Nursia area, can be found in Renaissance Spain between the witches of the Basque provinces—the *sorguiña* for example, about whom I shall have more to say shortly—and the Castilian or Andalusian witch whose archetype is the Celestina of Fernando de Rojas' *Tragicomedy of Calisto and Melibea* (1499?).

The Celestina as an Archetype

An enormous quantity of material from a variety of documentary sources is available on both witches and sorceresses. In a work which I published on *Magic in Castile in the Sixteenth and Seventeenth Centuries*[5] in 1944, I collected together numerous references in literature to the Celestina type of witch. These allusions, to which others could be added, show that in spite of the fact that Fernando de Rojas made use of literary sources in delineating the figure of the witch Celestina (Ovid, Horace and others), the character was so close to the real thing to be found in cities like Toledo, Salamanca and Seville in the fifteenth and sixteenth centuries, that the work became a model for realistic writers. Celestina, and all her disciples and children—legitimate and illegitimate offspring—is a woman of ill repute, who has passed her youth giving love for money, and becomes a procuress or go-between in her old age. She acts as adviser to a series of prostitutes and ruffians; is a skilful maker of perfume, cosmetics and other beauty products. But she also indulges in sorcery; erotic sorcery in particular. She is good at conjuring devils and her laboratory is extensive.[6] She mixes together plants which have genuine properties (both medicinal and poisonous) with the very same ingredients which so repelled Latin poets, although they had no real ideas about their effect. Celestina too, like Canidia and other witches of Esquilinus before her, goes in search of the fat of the dead, and of children when necessary, in order to make her spells.

Novelists and poets who imitated Rojas gave detailed lists of these mysterious and repulsive ingredients. And it should be stressed that, if the materials were the same as those of classical antiquity, they were also identical with those listed by the inquisitorial tribunals who tried Castilian witches at this period. A large number of files on persons who came under the jurisdiction of the Inquisition at Cuenca and Toledo have been preserved and are models of precision in questions of detail. Several Spanish scholars have studied them, but there is still much useful work to be done on them.[7]

But this is not the place for a lengthy discussion of small technical details. What I wish to emphasise above all is that Celestina herself, the women who work for her, the men who make use of her as a go-between, and the girls who claim to have been seduced as a result of her spells, are all city-dwellers living in a pleasure-loving society, similar to that of Renaissance Italy according to Burckhardt, which favoured the activities of the *stregha*.

Serving-maids, keepers of hostelries, female hermits, prostitutes, young gipsies and girls of Moorish descent were at the command of these evil old women. Rogues and bandits at one end of the social scale and knights at the other made use of her real or imaginary services. There is a link here between Horace's Rome and the Graeco-Roman cities of the south of Italy, the scene of Petronius's *Satyricon*, and the Salamanca of the fifteenth century or the Seville of the sixteenth. Celestina is a *low-born* daughter of an *urban* area, an intelligent and evil offspring of the city. She provoked protests from moralists of the old school like the misogynistic Archpriest of Talavera long before she interested those whose concern was purely literary, like Rojas.

'In how many ways do they sunder husband and wife,' writes the Archpriest. 'How many bonds do they make and break with their spells and curses! They cause husbands to leave their wives and go off with other women: and by the same token they cause wives to leave their husbands and live with their lovers; they cause the daughters of the good to do evil; they cause young women, widows and wives to lose their reason. Yet men and women run panting after these hags for their spells, as if they were beasts.'[8]

The preacher's misogyny served as an example to other sections of society—including women themselves. The civil courts punished these half-witches, half-procuresses as much, if not more, than the ecclesiastical courts. But the authorities in Renaissance Spain or Italy rarely doubted the success of their spells, although many distinguished men could soon not accept as true the facts described by the authors of the *Malleus* or given as evidence in cases against witches, who flew, and attended the 'Sabbath' or similar meetings.

Doubts Entertained by some Spanish Theologians

Whilst the Celestina type of sorceress cropped up time and again in central and southern cities in Spain, witches, who had already appeared in the south of France, also began to put in an appearance in the Spanish valleys close to the Pyrenees.

Catalonian documents of the fifteenth century refer to men and women of the Aneu region paying homage to the 'Biterna he-goat', and thus becoming sorcerers and witches. The references to the activities of these sorcerers are similar to those described in the Carcassonne trials already mentioned.[9] The first documented cases of witchcraft in the Basque provinces of Spain also date from the fifteenth century as we shall see. The witches of the Amboto mountain of Vizcaya were particularly famous in the early sixteenth century and their trials had considerable repercussions.[10] It is worth noting, however, that several Spanish theologians of the period still did not believe that the flight of witches and other acts, which were already accepted in France, really took place. Fray Lope de Barrientos, the Bishop of Cuenca, for example, followed the same line in the fifteenth century as the earlier 'Canon Episcopi', wholeheartedly denying the reality of such events[11]— like many a theologian of the eleventh or twelfth centuries or a rationalist of more recent times. Other writers were less consistent, however, like the Bishop of Avila, Alonso de Madrigal, nicknamed *el Tostado* (the "Dark-skinned"), who on one occasion maintained that the 'Sabbath' was pure imagination induced by drugs, while, on another, he attacked the 'Canon Episcopi'.[12]

We find echoes of the dispute as late as the middle of the sixteenth century in Francisco de Vitoria, who held the view that devils were *sometimes* capable of metamorphoses, flights through the air, etc., which the 'Canon Episcopi' considered mere illusions, although he did not deny the possibility that witches were at times the victims of dreams and visions.[13]

But the dispute at that period, and even slightly earlier, had its most far-reaching effects in the very countries in which the *Malleus* had its origins. There the argument came very much out into the open, for the book, which was so momentous from a legal point of view, was almost immediately after its publication examined in the light of the new philosophical and scientific ideas of the Renaissance and the theological attitudes of the Protestant or Reformed churches.

Views of some Italian Intellectuals

It should not be assumed that there was a united reaction against the *Malleus*. Far from it. One must remember that men like Ficino and his disciples, deeply imbued with neoplatonic ideas, were well disposed to be fairly credulous, more so perhaps than their masters, Plotinus himself, for example. But thinkers like Pietro Pomponazzi (1462–1524) were already beginning to show in some of their works that they did not wholly believe all that was said at that period about spells and magic. In consequence they were even accused of being atheists and heretics by Protestants and Catholics. Yet Pomponazzi's work is so largely speculative that it gives very few concrete examples of what was said and done at specific periods. The assertions and refutations that we find in it are largely based on the analysis of Greek and Latin texts and some theoretical works of Arabic doctors like Avicenna.[14] Probably few people would have been able to make much use of it when discussing the problems of their own times.

Much more specific than Pomponazzi's lucubrations is the attack on the *Malleus* written by a jurist called Gian Francesco Ponzinibio. This work expressly denied that witches flew through the air or did other equally fantastic things. Its point of departure was once again the much used and abused 'Canon Episcopi'.[15]

Ponzinibio in his turn was attacked by Bartolommeo de Spina who held inquisitorial posts and was an official at the Papal court. He ended his book by demanding that Ponzinibio be put on trial on suspicion of heresy. But it seems that Spina's descriptions of the repressive measures against witchcraft in northern Italy[16] caused something of a scandal themselves.

In fact, as Hansen has already shown, there were a number of Italian ecclesiastics in the early sixteenth century who flatly denied the existence of the very acts of which the witches were accused. They also felt that the inquisitors had acted in a seriously sinful manner. This was the view of Samuel Casinensis, for instance, as expressed in a short work written in Milan about 1505,[17] to which Vicente Dodo, a Dominican from Pavia, replied the following year (1506),[18] defending, one need hardly add, the inquisitorial point of view.

A book on similar lines to that of Dodo was Paulus Grillandus's treatise on spells, heresy and sexual intercourse. Grillandus acted as judge in many trials, mostly in the south of Italy however, and later authors who wrote on witchcraft from a credulous point of view, made great use of the cases and opinions he quoted.[19] It was Grillandus, for example, who gave the most detailed accounts of witches' covens, popularly believed to have taken place in Benevento (*ludis beneventanis*).[20] Yet his accounts were based on sheer old wives' tales.

Grillandus tells how a noble from the Duchy of Spoletto sent for him in 1525 and asked him to go to the Castle of St Paul to examine three witches he had imprisoned there. One of these confessed that an old witch had taken her to a coven (presided over by the Devil) before she was fifteen years old. She had renounced God, her faith and religion in the Devil's presence and had sworn an oath, putting her hand on a book written in a very dark lettering, to obey his commands and go to covens, taking with her as many people as she could. She confessed that subsequently she had taken four men with her to the 'Sabbath' and had wreaked havoc on animals and plants.

The Devil, for his part, had promised his faithful followers endless happiness and pleasure. If on any occasion the witch failed to go to the coven without good reason she had been unable to sleep or rest at all during the night. As soon as she set out she had heard the voice of a man—whom she called *parvum dominum Martinettum*, presumably her familiar spirit[21]—calling her. But before leaving, she had had to anoint herself with a special ointment and she had ridden to the place where the coven was being held (normally under the great walnut tree at Benevento) on a he-goat, which was waiting for her at the door. Once there, having paid homage to the chief Devil, the witches had danced and copulated with their familiar spirits. After that, there had still been time to return to their homes with their familiars and give further proofs of willing adoration.

The fate of the woman who told this story was the usual one. In spite of promises that she would be freed, she was burnt to death, together with her ointments and spell-binding powders, in the company of others implicated by her evidence.[22]

Grillandus tells the story of another event that occurred in 1526 which proves that the walnut tree was notorious in the whole of southern Italy from Rome downwards. A peasant who lived near Rome noticed that his wife, after getting undressed one night, left the house. The next day he beat her until she told him the truth: she went to witches' gatherings. Subsequently, he asked her to take him with her as soon as she could, and later, after doing what was necessary, the two were borne swiftly to such a meeting on the backs of he-goats. The wife warned her husband that he must not mention God while he was there, not even in jest. And the man watched all those present pay homage to the Devil-Prince who was dressed in magnificent garments and surrounded by the most important people there. After this ceremony was over, the Devil gave orders for dancing to begin. And all those who took part in the dance had to form a ring facing outwards so that they could not see each other's faces, as they can in country dances. This was done—Grillandus suggests—so that they should not betray one another later. After the dance, feasting took place, although prior to this the wife told her husband to pay his respects to the Prince. The food that was served at the feast was unsalted. The man asked for salt, and when he thought that it had been brought he exclaimed: 'Thank God the salt has come!' Immediately the Devil, men and women, tables and food, all disappeared. And the good peasant found himself naked and alone, terribly cold and in the dark. When day broke, he met some shepherds and asked them where he was. They told him that he was in the County of Benevento; and he realised that the whole affair had taken place a hundred miles from Rome. At first with the help of the shepherds and then by begging his way, the man reached his house thin and exhausted. Shortly afterwards he denounced his wife, who was naturally burnt alive after she had confessed and been convicted.[23]

Grillandus was so lacking in critical spirit that he unquestioningly accepted a common tale about witches as if it was a factual account of something that really took place at a specific time and place. He even gives another version of the same story himself! According to this version, a girl, thirteen years old, was taken by an old woman from the same Duchy of Spoletto to a witches' coven in 1535. Surprised to see such a large gathering of people, the girl exclaimed, 'Good God, what is this?' As soon as the words were out of her mouth, the assembled company vanished and the poor girl was found at dawn by a peasant to whom she told the whole story. The old woman, who was denounced by the girl, was also burned.[24]

Even in books published some time later, we find many instances of tales about the famous walnut tree, describing similar events which took place there. According to a work by a seventeenth-century doctor called Pietro Piperno, for example, it was under a walnut tree that a Devil and several witches removed the hump from an unfortunate hunchback who had caught their fancy when he had witnessed one of their orgies. This is, in fact, a well-known European folktale.[23]

But such stories, which nowadays only interest fairly inoffensive and perhaps rather boring people (like those of us who collect old wives' tales) were in the sixteenth century the subject for serious deliberations by lawyers. They produced terror in those who read them, as some literary works of the period clearly attest, even if they seemed comic to a few others.[26] It must be recognised, however, that Grillandus and those like him were criticised by men of far superior intellectual powers like Andreas Alciatus, Hieronimus Cardan, Andreas Caesalpinus of Arezzo and Gianbatista Porta, amongst others.

Andreas Caesalpinus was a radical after the manner of Pomponazzi.[27] And Cardan and Porta, for their part, recognised, as did the Spanish doctor Andrés Laguna, that stupefying drugs could sometimes have a decisive influence on the evidence given by witches. They based a general theory on this observation. Cardan gives analytical details about the composition of an ointment which he claims could induce a state of hypnosis and cause those who used it to see visions.[28] Porta refers to the case of a witch whom he saw under the influence of such an ointment.[29]

This reaction of a small group of intellectuals, largely Italian, could not have had much of an impact at a period when Benvenuto Cellini could talk about his dabblings in necromancy, and believe implicitly in the reality of the supposed results.[30] This is borne out by a famous experiment conducted by the Spanish doctor, Laguna. Laguna was in Metz around 1545 in the service of the Duke of Lorraine, who was seriously ill. At about that time, an elderly couple were imprisoned, and confessed under torture to having practised witchcraft and, amongst other things, causing the Duke's illness. Laguna denied that this was possible but his view failed to impress the magistrates who were convinced of the couple's power. Had they not claimed to be able to cure the Duke in the same way as they had made him fall ill, they would have been immediately condemned to be burnt.

When the Duke interviewed the supposed sorcerer, the latter explained his reasons for hating the Duke and described how he had caused him to waste away. The judges postponed passing sentence and, in the meantime, Laguna took charge of a green-coloured and evil-smelling ointment which had been discovered in the hermitage of the two accused sorcerers. He tried it on a patient, the wife of the city-executioner, who was so consumed with jealousy that she had considerable difficulty in sleeping. As soon as Laguna had rubbed it all over her body, she fell into a deep stupor during which she dreamed of a thousand extraordinary things. This led Laguna, who was studying Dioscorides at the time, and had been fascinated by the passage referring to a plant which sent people to sleep and made them see fantastic visions, to reach the conclusion that witches, in general, do not really move, and only fly and attend covens in their dreams. But these observations were of little value in the circumstances. The old witch was burnt in the end and her husband was set free on condition that he saved the Duke. Shortly afterwards he died in peculiar circumstances however; then the Duke also died, and Laguna left Metz. The whole tragedy became a footnote to the Greek text of Dioscorides which Laguna translated and annotated admirably.[31]

The Reaction in Germany

In France and Germany personal opinions were as conflicting as they were in Italy. But, in general, legal action continued to be extremely harsh.

Shortly after the publication of the *Malleus*, a Swiss lawyer, Ulric Molitor, brought out a book entitled *De lamiis et phitonicis* (*sic*, for *pithonicis*) *mulieribus*, which examines the activities attributed to the witches who had been tried by Sprenger, Institor and others. Although the author admits the power and efficacy of some spells, he follows early medieval thought in rejecting the view that witches really fly through the air. The book went through several editions and the first ones are much sought after for their woodcuts, which illustrate the supposed activities of witches in a way which must have inspired many later artists.[32]

Molitor, who practised in Constance, must have had some connexion with the Archduke Sigmund of Austria, since the work is dedicated to him. The book itself is short and takes the form of a conversation between the Archduke himself, Molitor and another lawyer called Konrad Schatz. The conversation ranges over fourteen topics, each of which has a chapter to itself. Amongst other points, they conclude that witches cannot really bring on rain or hail-storms, cause illnesses or impotence, change themselves or other people into something else, fly to attend the 'Sabbath' as they are supposed to do, have relations with the Devil and have offspring by him, or foretell the future. In this way, the Devil's influence on human actions is thought to be restricted, but the power of the imagination is openly recognised. Molitor is even in favour of the early dream theories to explain what is supposed to occur at the 'Sabbath', and he maintains that the divinations of sorcerers are sheer invention. . . .

In spite of all this, nothing could ultimately prevent the lawyer from thinking that witches ought to be harshly punished in civil law for their sinfulness and lack of faith.[33] So let us examine more notable personalities than Molitor. Although he could defend his case, apparently a good one, with a minimum of argument, he was incapable of drawing the obvious conclusions.

Luther was one of those who firmly believed in the power of spells. In the third chapter of his commentary on the *Epistle to the Galatians*, he speaks significantly about the Devil's power in the world. Everything we eat and drink, the clothes we wear and the air we breathe are in his power. He can, through witches, seriously harm men, children and animals, cause storms and so on.[34] The same reformer gave proof of his credulity elsewhere too, when he admitted, for instance, that his own mother had had a quarrel with a witch.[35] Both Melanchton and he defended the earlier view of flights through the air and metamorphoses, as did other theologians who became Protestants.[36]

However, the most interesting views in the parts of Europe where belief in witchcraft was strongest, are to be found in men who were scientists rather than theologians.

A man who won considerable fame as a miracle-worker, for instance, Henry Cornelius Agrippa, spoke out against the immorality of judges and inquisitors in certain cases. In northern Italy these men had filled the minds of weak and simple folk with the fear of torture and bloodshed. They had extorted money from women of distinguished families, which inevitably provoked relatives to action.[37]

A disciple of Agrippa, a doctor of German origin called Jean de Wier, wrote a book in French summarising the arguments which disputed the reality of activities attributed to witches and devils.[38] In the third part of the book, which is divided into forty-one chapters, Wier pays particular attention to witches, although he sometimes digresses,[39] as was customary at that period.

It is undeniable—he asserts—that there are unfortunate people who seek to work miracles by making a pact with the Devil. But he denies that the Devil puts his power at the service of such people and, consequently, he denies also that their intentions can really be carried out or that the pact is really agreed to by both parties. All the Devil does is to deceive such people, by getting power over their minds. And it is obvious that to do this he must choose the most suitable people for his purpose: the weak, the melancholy, the ignorant and the malicious. As these types of people are more frequently to be found among women than men, it is only natural that more women should have fallen victim to the Devil.

Starting from this view, and making the necessary exceptions for biblical cases, Wier rejected not only the idea of the flight of witches, but also their supposed ability to cause illnesses and atmospheric disturbances, have intercourse with the Devil and so forth. When he admists that they can do harm on occasion, he points out that this is the result of natural causes.

This, however, should not lead us to assume that the doctor is virtually a nineteenth-century scientist. For at times he pays tribute to the Devil himself in spite of imposing limitations on his activities. He maintains, for instance, that the Devil frequently forewarns witches of the approach of a storm so that they can make the spells which they believe are responsible for the bad weather. This is like shutting the door to keep out the cold and leaving the windows open.[40]

At the same period one of the greatest of French writers, Montaigne, seemed to be almost totally incredulous about anything connected with witchcraft.[41]

But the polemics on the subject did not end until long after this, and for nearly a whole century more witches were burnt here and there, while the presses groaned under the weight of books for and against the realist thesis. In spite of this, there continued to be a dozen books, which readily accepted the activities of witches, for every one which had some doubts on the subject—

110

however subdued the doubts might be for the sake of prudence.

I cannot discuss in detail all those who wrote on the subject. But most writers on witchcraft in the middle of the sixteenth century, at the height of the Renaissance, fall into one of three main groups.

1. Those who share the views on witches' covens of the 'Canon Episcopi' and other works of the early medieval period: believing them to be rituals presided over by a pagan divinity.

2. Those who accept that the 'Sabbath' genuinely takes place in the presence of Satan, complete with pacts, etc.

3. Those who dispute both the previous views of the nature of the meeting, and find natural causes to explain the evidence, as either (a) the mere consequence of judicial procedure, torture, etc.; or (b) the effect of stupefying drugs; or (c) the result of the mental deficiency of the person giving evidence.

There are grounds for a separate study of urban, individualistic, and erotic sorcery, on the one hand, and rural, collective, and rather more mysterious witchcraft, on the other. The two fields are extensive, and the division between them is not always clear.

CHAPTER 8

THE DEFINITIVE FORM OF THE CRIME OF WITCHCRAFT

The contribution of French judges to the theory of witchcraft – Daneau and Bodin – Pierre Grégoire and Rémy – Boguet and Martín del Río

The contribution of French Judges to the theory of Witchcraft

There is a Spanish proverb which says—Every little teacher has his little book—a saying which hardly needs an explanation in this age of manuals and handbooks. With reference to the sixteenth century, one might equally well say—every little judge has his little book. But the most frequent subject matter of the judges' little—or large—books at the period is no laughing matter; many of them relate how hundreds of people in different places were put to death for reasons which seem absurd to us today, and which seemed absurd to many people even then.

By a typical paradox of history, France, the home of reason and critical sense, seems to have been plagued more than the rest of Europe by this kind of book, often written by secular judges, and even by men who in other spheres of life were very distinguished. No parcel of fair French soil was free from investigations of crimes of witchcraft, and it is hard to distinguish, such is their apparent similarity, between the witch of the north and that of the south, east or west. Thanks to men such as Bodin, Grégoire, Rémy, Boguet, de Lancre, and others less well known, the crime of witchcraft was taking on a more uniform appearance.

112

The work begun by the inquisitors of Toulouse and Carcassonne in the fourteenth century, had the approval of men such as Bernard Basin in the fifteenth. His *Tractatus exquisitissimus de magicis artibus et magorum maleficis* (Paris 1483), which became a standard work, upheld the thesis that in certain cases the 'Sabbath' was a reality even though, in others, only an illusion of reality conjured up by the Devil. This theory seems to have been popular among Spanish theologians.[1] The books of Nicolas Jacquier,[2] Jean Vinet, Pierre Mamor and Jean Vincent of the same period contain equally credulous views.

The fact that these writings proliferated in the time of Louis XI, a monarch still in conflict with medieval society, is less difficult to explain than their success during the reign of a king like François I. But the reigns of his immediate predecessor and his descendants were, like his own, punctuated by the persecutions of witches and wizards, who were almost always accused of attending 'Sabbaths' by a variety of unnatural means. In 1521 for example, Jean Boin, prior of the Dominicans at Poligny, passed sentence on a certain Pierre Burgot, alias Grand-Pierre, and on Michel Verdung, whose evidence Jean de Wier transcribed in his book in order to dispute it. The case was that around 1502 on a feast day, there was a storm and heavy rain in Poligny. Pierre Burgot was tending a flock of sheep at the time. But the amount of rain was such that both shepherd and sheep took fright; the animals ran away and were lost. Once the storm was over, Burgot and his fellow shepherds searched for their respective flocks, and the former, finding himself alone for a moment, was met by three dark men on horseback dressed in black. One of them, the third one, asked the shepherd where he was going and what the trouble was. Pierre Burgot told him what had happened. Then the horseman, telling him he was a worthy man, said that he could introduce him to a master in whose service he would learn many things and never be disappointed. He also promised money, and the quick recovery of his sheep. The shepherd accepted the offer and promised to return to the same place four or five days later for further discussion. This he did, and met the gentleman in question, who asked him if he was willing to give his services. Pierre in his turn asked the gentleman who he was: *Je suis serviteur du grand diable d'enfer*, came the reply. The deal was clinched immediately. The Devil, for it was no other, forbade him in the usual way to pronounce the name of God, the saints or the sacraments, and gave his cold, dark, corpse-like hand to be kissed. Pierre was in his service for two years yet hardly received anything that he had been promised. He obeyed instructions about not touching holy water, being late for Mass, and so on. But after two years he gave up being a shepherd, and bearing in mind how little the Devil had helped him, decided to forget all about him and began to lead the life of a practising Catholic. About eight or nine years later, Michel Verdung entered his life, urging him to re-swear allegiance to his old master at the place of their first encounter. Pierre agreed, on the condition that the Devil gave him money, as he had previously promised. Back once again in the diabolic fold, he was given a rendezvous close to Chastel Charbou, which he subsequently kept one evening. He saw people he did not know dancing, each one carrying a green torch which cast a blue light. On another occasion Michel told him that if he wished he could be made to run at a great speed. Pierre agreed, with the usual proviso that he must be given the promised money, and Michel told him he could have all he wanted. So he made the experiment. He undressed, rubbed his body with an ointment and saw with growing terror that he was turning into a wolf and was running in this guise at high speed by the side of his companion, who was similarly transformed. Afterwards, their familiar devils anointed them to restore their human form. From then onwards they committed various atrocities such as killing children and eating them, having intercourse with she-wolves, etc. The prior of Poligny condemned them to be burnt,[3] failing to realise that this slow-witted shepherd, obsessed by money, might easily be a sick man. This is, of course, a rather specialised case of bestiality which has been made to look like sorcery.

Other cases heard in south-east France show sorcerers acting along more liturgical lines. On October 9th, 1519, a certain Catherine Peyretonne, widow of Montou Eyraud, was burnt alive in Montpezat for attending a 'Sabbath' riding on a broomstick given her by the demon Barrabam. The 'Sabbath' took place in the 'suc de Beauzon' and in 'Rocha-Alba' and was attended by various local people named by the accused. It consisted of the customary Devil-worship, dances and feasting. But in the case for the prosecution there is an untranslatable paragraph which is in some ways curious:

Ipsa delata fuit plerumque in synagoga diabolica cujusdam sectae Jovis, de nocte, ubi per diabolum se cognosci carnaliter per indebitum sexum, posteriori, per anum, peccatum sodomiticum commisit, et hoc est verum.[4]

What made the judge, clerk, or suspected witch, bring Jupiter into the Devil's affairs?

The accusations abound with this sort of suspect material. But from 1570 until well into the seventeenth century, writers on magic filled their books with every possible learned allusion, so that they contained the maximum information about sacred and profane law, and the minimum of common sense.

Daneau and Bodin

The first edition of a treatise on sorcerers by Lambert Daneau, a fairly well-known Protestant theologian (1530–1595) was probably the one published in Geneva in 1574. Soon afterwards, in 1579, it was reprinted, together with a treatise on card games.[5] In the section on sorcerers Daneau drew extensively on material from the case of the witches of Valery in Savoy, in which the Sabbath took what was fast becoming its definitive form.

In 1580 Bodin's famous book *Demonamie* appeared. Speaking of the earlier work and of the case cited in it, Bodin reached the conclusion that the Devil is one and the same everywhere and that the Sabbath, too, is everywhere identical.[6] It is rather surprising, therefore, to find such a renowned lawyer and political writer finally establishing that sorcerers are guilty of as many as fifteen crimes, neither more nor less:

1. Denial of God.
2. Cursing God and blaspheming.
3. Giving honour to the Devil by worshipping him and making sacrifices.
4. Dedication of children to the Devil.
5. Murdering children before they have been baptised.
6. Pledging to Satan children yet in the womb.
7. Spreading propaganda about the cult.
8. Honouring oaths sworn in the name of the Devil.
9. Incest.
10. Murdering men and little children to make broth.
11. Disinterring the dead, eating human flesh and drinking blood.

12. Killing by means of poisons and spells.
13. Killing cattle.
14. Causing famine on the land and infertility in the fields.
15. Having sexual intercourse with the Devil.[7]

To arrive at this catalogue of crimes Bodin made use of a great deal of material and followed the classic method of many treatises on the same subject. The first part of the work is of a theological nature, dealing with the Devil, his power and its limitations. This is followed by a second part containing an exposition and analysis of the deeds of sorcerers and witches, the various types of magic, etc. And in the third and last part ways of eliciting statements are enumerated and the penalties corresponding to each crime are listed together with the opinions of various authors including Bodin himself.

One must remember that Bodin had a great gift for analysing the legal and political structure of societies, even if he was only mediocre as a physicist and a very dubious theologian, as is frequently only too obvious.[8] (New and unusual proof of the fact that men of political ability are no more competent at grasping fundamentals than the average man!) Bodin, as a man of law, never doubted that magic was within the proper scope of the law. Yet this scholar, who condemned Jean de Wier as a 'foul sorcerer',[9] was in his turn accused of being a sorcerer, an atheist, a Jew, and countless other things, by men who considered the charge too lenient. It is clear that such ideas were common among those colleagues of Bodin who did not achieve his eminence in other fields. They had probably picked them up at the university. Not everything that one learns at those institutions is really worthwhile.

Pierre Grégoire and Rémy

Soon after the publication of the *Demonomanie* . . . there appeared a Latin treatise by a certain lawyer of Toulouse, named Pierre Grégoire, which summarised the civil and ecclesiastical laws on witchcraft and gave some curious details of specific cases. Pierre Grégoire mentions in passing that in the year 1577 the Parlement of Languedoc burned four hundred sorcerers accused of 'classic' crimes of witchcraft, and all had the Devil's mark on them:[10] a purge that can only be compared with the endless repressive measures employed in Lorraine.

The secular, almost middle-class character of the Lorraine persecutions has been emphasised by nearly every writer who has dealt with the subject, notably Albert Denis and Emile Gebhardt. But the latter was wrong to claim that the laymen involved were not motivated by theological doctrines and scholastic ideas in their pursuit of the Devil. In this respect they were relics of the Middle Ages.[11] But at least there was one judge who had theories about witchcraft in Lorraine, and of him we must now speak.

Nicolas Rémy's book, printed at Lyons in 1595, was, in fact, even broader in scope than Grégoire's. The writer, who lived from 1554 to 1600, was yet another instance of a magistrate put in charge of a witch-hunt in Lorraine, a district which had been particularly prone to such activities throughout the sixteenth century.[12] It is, nevertheless, worth remarking that Nicolas Rémy had studied at Toulouse. This meant that he had acquired his legal training in a district where the crime of witchcraft had long since been clearly defined. It was only natural, therefore, that he should have had set ideas on the subject before starting on his witch-hunt. In the fifteen years between 1576 and 1591, he condemned to death about nine hundred people.

Subsequently he wrote his book,[13] which contains very little new theoretical material although one might say that it set a good many precedents in practical matters. Depositions made before this rather formidable judge, held that devils, with the help of sorcerers, laid waste crops, meadows and farmland by means of clouds of insects (which were in reality evil spirits); they froze the vapour on the clouds to produce hail; and witches flew up to them on broomsticks or ploughshares. The accused also gained access to houses by mysterious means, perpetrating evil; and they were punctual in attending the 'Sabbath'.

What shocked Rémy most was the positive desire for death openly expressed by many sorcerers. This is a tendency which should perhaps be investigated in the light of modern theories about the contagious nature of suicide.[14] In any case, it is an indication of the wretchedness of life in those days that men were so willing to die. Rémy was one of a trinity of French judges who were as violent as they were erudite. None of them was above embellishing the legal proceedings with a line from the classics or a choice learned quotation. The other two were Boguet and Pierre de Lancre.

Boguet and Martin del Río

Henri Boguet *grand juge de la ville de Saint Claude, natif de Pierre Court, baillage de Gray en Franche-Comté* has left an account of his judicial proceedings in a book first published in 1602, and reprinted in 1603, 1606 and 1608.[15] This chiefly relates to his activities in the Jura. Boguet's system was largely based on that of the inquisitors.

Suspicion alone was enough to warrant arrest. Not to shed tears while making a confession; looking at the ground, speaking as if in asides or blaspheming was a sign of a witch. In order to spare the accused embarrassment, on the other hand, the judge heard them alone and the clerks remained hidden. Although ordeal by water was not used, the accused had to be shaved in order to reveal any significant marks, and it was desirable for a doctor, expert at finding the marks, to be present at the inspection. Were the accused unwilling to confess, he would be put on the rack and tortured as many times as the judge considered necessary. Sons could denounce fathers, and discrepancies of detail on the part of witnesses was no indication that the accused was innocent so long as there was general agreement that he was guilty. Children's accusations were of special importance. And men convicted of sorcery were to be burnt alive. This, in brief, was Boguet's system as far as procedure was concerned.[16]

With regard to the behaviour of sorcerers he was equally dogmatic. He said nothing very new about 'Sabbaths', metamorphoses, spells, etc., but supported existing views from his own experience. Boguet ended by declaring he had seen demons coming out of the body of a bewitched child in the form of balls, in spittle from an exorcised witch and so on.[17] Witchcraft as interpreted by this judge was frequently complicated by cases of demoniacal possession and lycanthropy. The trials of Françoise Secrétain and Guillaume Villermoz, which Boguet recounts with a terrifying lack of feeling, would be enough today to bring a magistrate into the blackest disrepute.[18] But a long time had still to pass before the people of Franche Comté, whether Protestant or Catholic, were rid of this blight.

One of the latest known trials is that which took place in Quengey in 1657. It began with the arrest of Renobert Bardel, his children and his mother, and has been studied recently by

Francis Bavoux.[19] The accused in every case seem to confess under torture in a wild and contradictory way, but in line with the wishes of their judges. The bitterness of family feuds often makes itself clearly felt in the evidence taken down by the clerks. And to accuse a person of witchcraft was the best way of ruining his reputation, although it was always claimed that the accused was known to cast spells. But in sixteenth-century Europe, how many could be entirely free from this suspicion?

At this stage, the next judge to be discussed should be Pierre de Lancre. But for various reasons it is better to leave him till later. Writers of treatises from other countries must be mentioned for the contribution they made to the general theory of witchcraft and sorcery. Within a short time of one another there appeared at the end of the sixteenth century two treatises in Latin which became standard works—one by the Fleming, Binsfeld, and the other by Martín del Río. Binsfeld, who died in 1598, published his *Tractatus de confessionibus maleficorum et sagarum* in 1591,[20] and del Río his famous *Disquisitionum magicarum libri sex* in 1599.[21] Binsfeld seems more familiar with his subject than del Río, and is more scholarly and better known as a humanist. But the interest of the latter's work lies precisely in the fact that he makes a synthesis of the versions of the 'Sabbath', taking elements from various sources, and quoting Rémy, Binsfeld, the earlier French and Italian inquisitors. Here is his description, translated from the Latin:

'So it is that the witches, once they have anointed themselves with their ointments, generally go to the Sabbath on poles, gallows or pieces of wood (sometimes balancing on one foot), also astride broomsticks or canes, or on the backs of their respective bulls, goats or dogs (all these modes of transport are given as examples by Rémy in Book I, Chapter 14 of his work). They arrive at the Games or *Ludus* of the Good Society (as it is called in Italy) where, illuminated by the fire, the Devil presides, evil and menacing, sitting on a throne, generally in the terrifying guise of a goat or dog. They draw near to worship him, but not all in the same manner; some approach him on their knees, some on their backs, others walking on the hands but managing to keep their faces upturned. Then, with an offering of tapers made from pitch and umbilical cords, they kiss his hind parts in homage. And to render the sacrilege absolute, they proceed to a travesty of the sacrifice of the Mass, using holy water and following the Catholic rite closely, as is proved by the account given in the third book of senator Raimundus.

119

Then they offer up two children to the Devil. In former years this had been done by mothers—frequently, according to Binsfeld—and in 1458 a mother sacrificed three of her children, according to Jacquier in the seventh chapter of his book. Other authorities say that they make a sordid sacrifice to the idol Moloch; offering to the Devil and killing in his honour with great cruelty and malice both their own children and those of strangers. Even ejaculated semen is offered up, as in the case of the sorcerer who had sexual intercourse with a woman in a church and mingled his semen with the holy oil, as Jacquier relates in the 58th Folio of his *Scourge of Fascinators*. Finally, when they communicate they keep the Host in their mouths and afterwards remove it and offer it to the Devil, subsequently to be trampled on by the company. This much many witches confessed to Jacquier himself, as he indicates in the eighth chapter.

Once these and other ignominious and execrable abominations have been performed, they sit down to table and help themselves to the victuals which either the Devil provides, or they bring themselves. They dance, sometimes before and sometimes after the banquet. There are usually several tables with three or four sorts of foods, some very fine indeed, others tasteless and unpleasant, meted out to each of the diners according to his rank and ability. Sometimes a diner's familiar demon will sit beside him, sometimes opposite him. And as one may suppose the meal is not complete without a "grace" suited to the occasion composed of blasphemous words which attribute to Beelzebub himself the part of Creator, Giver and Preserver of all; the same is said at the end as a grace after meat, when the diners rise. I have read the formulae for these occasions as written out by a notorious sorcerer. They appear at the banquet sometimes with the face uncovered, sometimes covered by a veil, cloth or even a mask. Frequently the familiar demons take their respective masked pupils by the hand and all those who are able perform together a grotesque rite; they arrange themselves back to back in a circle, hand in hand, and dance around tossing their heads in a frenzy. Sometimes they hold lighted tapers in their hands, used for the ceremonial adoration of the Devil, and kiss him in the same way as before, singing obscene verses in his honour and dancing to pipes and drums played by musicians under a tree. The devils intermingle with their disciples to such an extent that all kinds of ridiculous and unnatural acts take place. The sacrifices are usually preceded by an act of adoration, and they are sometimes made at a distance from the coven.

Lastly, everyone present tells of the exploits they have performed since the last meeting, and the most outrageous and worthy of condemnation by normal moral standards are most applauded by the assembly. If a sorcerer or witch has done nothing at all, or nothing quite bad enough, the Devil or one of the older and more respected sorcerers whips him or her savagely for some time. Finally, snuff is distributed—the ashes of the he-goat whose form the Devil has taken during the ceremony, according to some, consumed by the flames which had surrounded his figure—and other poisons also. Then the idea of doing harm is obliquely expressed in the following instruction from the Demon Pseudo-god: "Let us take our revenge, so that you may know the law that is opposed to the law of charity; for if we do not we shall die." This done, all present return to their homes. They usually travel during the silent hours of the middle of the night, when the powers of darkness reign, or at midday, as the Psalmist implies when he refers to the "Devil that walketh by noon-day". Ibn Ezra also speaks of the special hours and days that sorcerers keep for their operations.

In various regions it is apparent that the witches have set days for their meetings. In Italy they attend on the night preceding the sixth feast, as Comanus says in his *Lucerna*, and at about twelve o'clock, according to Michaelis in his seventh commentary. The witches of Lorraine meet on the eve of the fifth feast and on Sunday itself, according to Remigius (Rémy), Book I, chapter fourteen. In other authors I have read that meetings were held on the eve of the third feast.[22]

Martín del Río's book is better known than most others. But it cannot be said to be the fruit of direct experience, as can possibly be claimed for works mentioned earlier. In the same category may be placed the *Compendium Maleficarum* of F. M. Guazzo (Guaccius), a Milanese. The book contained unusual illustrations,[23] and still had its imitators and partisans well on into the seventeenth century. The enthusiasm for the study of witchcraft up to that time was immense; but later, and with an amazing rapidity, it began to fall into disrepute and to be treated with scant respect. The period at the end of the sixteenth century and the beginning of the seventeenth is, in my opinion, the most interesting in the history of West-European witchcraft.[24] It was then that all kinds of information, theories and experiences came to be known, which led to an absolute reversal of ideas and the overthrow of virtually all existing conceptions of magic in the minds of cultivated Europeans. This is a revolution which has still not taken place, as is well known, in vast sections of Africa, Asia, America, and the Pacific, where people continue to believe in the power of sorcerers, enchanters and witches, and even the law is subject to the workings of magic.

CHAPTER 9

THE SPIRIT BEHIND THE DECLARATIONS

German witches and Walpurgis night – Witches in the British Isles – New discussions

German Witches and Walpurgis Night

Although some theologians of the sixteenth century continued to quote the 'Canon Episcopi' and look upon Diana as the patron goddess of witches, most books and trials of the period regarded the Devil as their Lord: the Devil, that is, with very specific physical characteristics. There was, in fact, at the end of the Middle Ages and the beginning of modern times a real cult of the Devil in Europe, or something very similar, as numerous documents attest. The problem is to distinguish one kind of demonolatry from another. For the term 'Devil' might legitimately have been used to describe pagan divinities from a theological point of view, although, historically speaking, this would have been misleading. One specific case will serve to illustrate my point. A *conquistador* called Pascual de Andagoya (1495–1548), in the process of exploring the Darien region, claimed to have found many sorcerers and witches among the native population. According to him they caused harm to many animals and elderly people 'at the Devil's command', and also used ointments given them by the Devil himself. Continuing his account, Andagoya says that:

'When questions were asked about the form in which the Devil appeared to them, it was discovered that he took the shape of a beautiful child in order not to frighten these simple-minded people but to win their confidence. Whenever the witches caused harm to others, the Devil went with them and entered the houses of those they wished to hurt in their company. It was also revealed that a witch, who was in a certain town one night with many other women, was seen the very same hour in a room a league-and-a-half distant from that place, where other servants of her Master were gathered.'[1]

This text could equally well have been alluding to any group of witches in Andagoya's own country Alava, in the Basque provinces. But American scholars would, no doubt, know which particular divinity is referred to as the 'Devil' in this instance, and could give more specific details of witchcraft in Darien.

Is it possible to find some other force behind the Devil, if we base our conclusions on the evidence of trials which took place in the sixteenth century? Certainly not, if we confine ourselves to them and to the material provided by theologians of the period. But other sources of information may enable us to go a little further.

The folklore of a number of countries makes it clear that belief in an ancient deity who presided over witches was very widespread in Europe; and indeed, this belief has been passed down to our own times. According to popular tradition, meetings of witches have sometimes been confused with meetings of mythical beings. Godelmann, for example, who wrote extensively on witchcraft in Germany early in the seventeenth century and who has frequently been quoted on the subject, has the following point to make. After explaining that witches (or *lamiae* as he calls them in his Renaissance Latin) are referred to as *Zauberinnen*, *Unholden*, *Heren*, *Wahrsagerin* and *Wettermacherin*[2] in Germany, he goes on to say that:

On the subject of the supposed activities of witches, it is said that after anointing themselves with the fat of cats or wolves, asses' milk and I know not what else besides, they can fly out of their houses riding on broomsticks (either going out by the usual way or even passing through some narrow hole) and go to the place where their banquets and feastings with devils are held. It is widely believed that all German witches are carried, on the night of the first of May, in the shortest time imaginable, to the mountain called Blocksberg and Heinberg, in the Bructeri region, having first anointed themselves. Some are borne along by their familiar spirits which take the form of he-goats, pigs, lambs and other similar animals; others fly on gallows-trees or sticks. They spend the whole night in feasting and jollity, dancing with their lovers.'[3]

Blocksberg is the ancient name for the highest peak in the Harz mountains. It is usually called Brocken on maps and lies to the east of Altenau, which is 1,147 metres high, and other mountains of northern and central Germany. The date of the meeting is a particularly significant one in German mythology and folklore. Early specialists in the field, like Grimm and Karl Simrock, had already discovered numerous coincidences which seemed to indicate a connexion between the mountain meetings of witches on the night of the first of May and meetings of the Valkyries.[4] But even if this view of mythologists is correct, it did not prevent many men and women from being burnt in the sixteenth century for confessing— as did a villager to whom Godelmann himself refers—that they had been to witches' covens on the first of May over a long period of years—and this despite the fact that the man's wife maintained he had not left their bed on that or any other night.[5] The witches— according to Godelmann's treatise—left their houses and formed a procession (*Das wütende Heer*),[6] shouting *Oben aus unndnirgent an*.[7] This cry also recalls certain myths according to which, on certain nights of the year, the sounds of mysterious armies can be heard—the procession of souls and departed spirits which takes place more particularly at about the time of the winter solstice.

In Prussia, Livonia and Lithuania people also believed that at that time of the year, on Christmas Day to be precise, sorceresses automatically forsook their human shape for that of wolves in order to enter country houses and kill animals, drink beer and so on. This belief in lycanthropy is also slightly at odds with the official view of the authorities, as expressed in legal documents.[8]

Other cases cited by Godelmann, which received severe sentences, also have a mythological flavour about them. Take the following, for example, which occurs in Camerarius. A certain butcher was walking one night through a wood, when he heard sounds of love and laughter coming from some bushes. More curious than frightened at this, he went towards the place from which the sounds appeared to be coming and saw several male and female figures. The latter vanished at once, leaving behind them tables laid for a banquet with glasses for wine and among them one or two silver goblets. To prove that what he had seen was real, he picked up two of the goblets before leaving the place and took them to the local magistrate, telling him what had occurred. The magistrate was soon able to identify the owners of the goblets who declared they had been stolen from them. The magistrate, therefore, began to entertain certain suspicions about the wives of the people in question and, when these had been thrown into prison, they were convicted of unimaginable crimes. Some time later, the butcher was riding past the same place in the wood, where he had seen the nocturnal feast, when he was overtaken by a rider of fearful aspect who attacked him violently and hurt him so much that he had to stay in bed for several days. Furthermore, a prominent tree at that place was soon cursed by the witches who had changed themselves into animals so as to be able to continue their activities. These witches were disciples of the ancient goddess Holda—'Unholden', in fact.[9]

Witches' banquets inspired paintings by a number of artists of the Flemish and German schools, who often treated them satirically and produced various comic versions of the scene. Yet in spite of this, the current ideas of satanism and demonolatry continued to be accepted. Even as late as the end of the sixteenth century, the ancient central European districts from Alsace to the Polish frontier still witnessed burnings of large numbers of women who had been accused of this sort of activity. And scholars have, from an early period, studied these persecutions in detail.

In the Tyrol and other parts of Austria, on the other hand, the witch-trials went on describing the 'Sabbath' in much the same terms as the fourteenth and fifteenth centuries in the south of France and the Alpine district.[10] In fact, the only difference was that satanism was being substituted for pagan myths.

Witches in the British Isles

The trials of sorcerers and witches living in Nordic territory in the sixteenth century, in Celtic rather than Germanic areas, suggest that here too witchcraft was at that time more readily linked with mythological beliefs than with straightforward satanism.[11] Take Scotland, for instance, where the well-known trial of Bessie Dunlop before Protestant judges is a case in point. This woman, born in Lyne near Dalry in Ayrshire, was condemned to be burnt on November 8th, 1576. Like so many others who paid the same penalty, she was a mid-wife and quack by profession.

According to her evidence, on a number of occasions since 1547, she had seen the ghost of a neighbour of hers called Thome Reid who had died at the battle of Pinkie. The ghost had given her medical advice and encouraged her to do good works. When he had first appeared to her the mid-wife was for a time profoundly disturbed. The second time he had come, he had urged her to become a Catholic, and the third time he had appeared when she was with her family, although no one else had seen him. He had led her out to a place near the kitchens warning her not to make any noise. Four knights and eight elegant ladies had appeared to her there and had invited her to go off with them. Bessie had said not a word and the figures had disappeared in a gust of wind. The ghost, who had hidden during this interview, had come out as soon as they had gone and had explained that the ladies were 'good fairies' who lived at 'the Elfin court'. Bessie had still not accepted their invitation and the ghost had been slightly annoyed. Yet in spite of this, he had continued to help her. Ultimately however, after failing on a number of occasions to cure people and divine correctly, she was cast into prison and after a trial at which she denied all knowledge of Reid, she was burnt.

A similar case is that of Alison Peirsoun of Byrehill. Like Bessie, Alison was visited by the ghost of a dead relative, William Sympsoune. The latter took her to see the good fairies and the kingdom of the elves. Alison was a quack and the fairies thought so highly of her that they allowed her to help them make ointments; she went out with them picking herbs at break of day. Her prestige was such that Patrick Adamson, Archbishop of Saint Andrews, sent for her when he was ill. By chance, or thanks to the woman's skill, the archbishop recovered. Later, however, he repented and, attributing his cure to the power of the Devil, not only failed to pay Alison but had her taken into custody and charged instead. Alison accused many people of attending the gatherings of the elves and she too was burnt, after the usual confession and conviction.

These examples will serve to show how close was the relationship in Scotland between witchcraft and belief in beings of the nether world (*elfydd*) before the association with satanism was established. When King James and Princess Ann of Denmark made their voyage to Scotland from 1589 to 1591, there were so many storms that the boats could not cross the North Sea. Some superstitious or malicious individual suggested that interested parties had caused the storms and the King followed up the insinuation. Investigations were carried out, and the most important person to be accused was the head of the Catholics, the Count of Bothwell. He was taken prisoner but managed to escape to the mountains of the North, where many of his supporters lived.

However, many people of humble birth were arraigned before he was. An assistant magistrate from the town of Tranent, for instance, accused his serving girl, Geillis Duncan, of being a diabolical witch, because of the cures she was able to perform. Making use of his position and powers he had her tortured, but to no avail. Subsequently, following a practice which was new in Scotland, he ordered her body to be searched for the witches' mark, so often cited on the continent, and it was found. This action was followed by others, and in the end Geillis denounced no less than thirty persons of the County of Lothian as witches, after first confessing her own guilt. Amongst those whom she denounced were a certain Doctor Fian also called John Cunningham, Agnes Sampsoun, Euphame Mackalzeane and Barbe Napier. When the interrogations—another new practice in Scotland—were over, it was taken as proved that the Count of Bothwell had asked the witches for information about the possibility of procuring the death of the King, and that he was guilty of even fouler crimes.

Cunningham, after being brutally tortured, also confessed to having made a pact with the Devil, who always appeared to him dressed in white. The latter marked him with a special mark and carried him to distant lands, at least *in the spirit*. He also confessed to having attended the 'Sabbath' as the secretary of the Devil himself. On the first occasion this was held in the church at North Berwick, some fourteen miles or so from Prestonpans. Those who were present processed round the church counter-clockwise. The Devil sat on a throne and urged everyone to do evil. He was worshipped in a revolting manner. In the dance that followed some two hundred people took part. Cunningham was master of ceremonies and Geillis Duncan played on an instrument. Agnes Sampsoun, Euphame Mackalzeane and Barbe Napier, who were women of some status, admitted having cast various spells. In many instances they corroborated Cunningham's evidence, in others they added to what he had said. The storms which had caused the King so much trouble were generally produced by throwing a cat into water. The trial lasted all through 1590. And the following year the majority of the accused were burnt or strangled. The Count of Bothwell put up a fight in the mountains and subsequently recovered his influential place in society. But that is another story.

In spite of the innovations in the conduct of these trials there are still details in them which are traceable to early folklore. One of the places at which the sorcerers met, apart from North Berwick church, was called 'The fairies' hole', between Prestonpans and Musselburgh. And the idea of processing round the church at the meeting also recalls pagan rites: the women went round six times and the men (who were far fewer in number) nine.

The Scottish trials bring us into contact with a world where the old myths are still very relevant. The English trials of the same period, on the other hand, reflect a puritanical society in which hysteria could cause violent and dramatic action. Throughout the sixteenth century there were sporadic trials of witches in England. In 1584 Bishop Jewell, in preaching before the Queen, claimed witchery had increased enormously over the previous four years. He thought Queen Elizabeth's subjects 'looked pale and thin; stammered and acted in a confused manner. . . .'

Essex was the scene of a large number of trials at the period, but it was in Huntingdon that the trial of the Warboys witch, which was one of the more significant, took place.[12] In 1589 there was a much respected gentleman living in Huntingdon called Robert Throgmorton. He had a wife and five daughters, Jane, Elizabeth, Mary, Grace and Joan, all of them young. Even Joan, the eldest, was hardly a grown woman. There were a large number of maid-servants in the house, as there always were in those days. The master of the house must have felt rather isolated, surrounded by women. Mr Throgmorton helped to support several poor families in the neighbourhood, amongst them a family called Samuel consisting of an elderly husband and wife and their daughter Agnes.

The wife in particular often used to visit the Throgmorton household. Suddenly one day, the youngest of the Throgmorton girls had a fit of convulsions, and shouted in her delirium that Mother or Aunt Samuel had bewitched her. Soon the other sisters were taken in the same way and made similar accusations. The eldest spoke deliriously of being carried through the air and so forth.

The parents were perplexed at first. The doctors they called in maintained that the case was unnatural. And at this stage an old friend of the family, a certain Lady Cromwell, who seems to have been a rather fierce individual, stepped in to cause trouble. The girls' uncle, Mr Pickering, joined in the general hysteria. And shortly afterwards some of the serving-girls began to have fits and to be delirious, as the eldest daughter had said they would.

The unfortunate old lady, Mrs Samuel, was in an awkward predicament. Her house was swarming with people who cursed her, urging and begging her to put matters right. She, her husband and her daughter felt powerless to do anything.

Then came a time when the delirious girls themselves begged help from the old woman and, though they had previously fallen into fits at the very sight of her, they were now comforted by her. Yet even this did not cure them. In the end Mother Samuel herself went mad after three years of persecution and confessed to Mr Throgmorton, begging his forgiveness, that she really was a witch and had made a pact with the Devil. Throgmorton, who must have been a kindly individual, although perhaps rather weak-willed, forgave her. But then the old woman tried to take it all back, and the girls took to speaking with the evil spirits. Lady Cromwell went on with her meddling and finally, in 1592, the Samuel family was hanged. This case seems like material for a nineteenth-century novel. The kindly Throgmorton with his five demented daughters; Lady Cromwell and Mr Pickering wanting everything done and undone in their own particular and supposedly public-spirited way; the servants full of silly superstitions; the local doctors and priest hiding their helplessness by keeping quiet or making solemn gestures, and, finally, old Samuel and his daughter protesting their innocence, with poor Mrs Samuel bemused amidst all the conflicting opinions. It is a surprisingly real collection of characters by comparison with the wooden caricatures of the *Malleus* and Grillandus. Small wonder that when the historical novel was at the height of its vogue in England several authors used the old trial as a plot.

New Discussions

In about 1584, a clerk called Reginald Scot published a book called *Discoverie of Witchcraft*, which made quite a stir. This book, and one or two others which appealed for moderation, so irritated James I that he felt obliged to answer them, condemning the particularly harmful opinions put forward by Scot who maintained that evil spirits only had intercourse with men in very exceptional circumstances, and certainly not the kind of intercourse which was then believed to be common. In spite of the fact that Scot's book was burnt by the public executioner, it did not go unread and was republished some time afterwards in a fairly mutilated version.

At the beginning of the present century James I's *Demoniologia* was usually an object of scorn, while the works of Scot, Giffard and others were well thought of. But times have changed and it has been seriously claimed that Scot's book was 'a blatantly sceptical work' and James I more than justified in denouncing the 'damnable opinions' it contained.[13] Such a fact should not be overlooked. There is a dangerous tendency to accept magic, which needs to be strongly countered. For a world which accepts magic is, above all, a world which accepts slander as we shall show in the next chapter when we examine a number of specific cases.

CHAPTER 10

WITCHCRAFT AND POSSESSION
BY DEVILS

The production of spells by material means – Possessed persons, the Devil and those who induce possession – Towards new interpretations

The Production of Spells by Material Means

Possession is a religious phenomenon which crops up in a large number of societies with very different spiritual beliefs. It was studied at length by a Professor of Tubingen, and the fruit of his labours was quite well known some years ago.[1] There is no point in going into the subject in great detail here, nor in discussing the theories of theologians and psychologists about the state of the possessed. This can be considered from a subjective or objective point of view, and need not be confined to possession by the Devil. Our aim is to describe some of the characteristics of possession in specific cases of magic and witchcraft.

According to the most usually accepted view, the man or woman who is 'possessed by the Devil' feels 'possessed' by an evil or foul spirit which makes him or her act as *it* wants and not as he or she wants. The outward signs of possession are nearly always the same; the individual's personality vanishes and a different and devilish personality takes its place for a while, almost as in a fit. The person possessed is, then, a victim, when possession is not self-induced. In fact, there are two ways in which an individual can become possessed: either the Devil passes straight into his body, or another person, working in conjunction with the Devil

131

himself, decides to bewitch him, because he bears him ill-will
or for some other reason. Thus we saw in the last chapter how the
Throgmorton girls accused a woman of bewitching them by spells.
During the seventeenth century, and particularly during the first
half of it, there were other cases of possession by devils induced
by witches and, more especially, by sorceresses. Some of these
were highly sensational. We shall look at these in detail. But first
we must make a few observations on the belief that the basic personality of a human being can be altered, or at least be rendered incapable of controlling the acts which it nevertheless performs, by the
intervention of spirits or substances within the body of that person.

For a start, it is well known that there is a deep-rooted belief
in various parts of Europe in the existence of people who quite
involuntarily bring 'bad luck', *mal fario, cenizo* (literally, the plant
called white-goose's foot) or have the 'evil eye'. For this reason
several Spanish writers of the sixteenth and seventeenth centuries
worked out theories to show that the 'evil eye' was the result of the
presence of certain harmful properties in the eye or in other parts
of the body of certain types of people. It could not always be
considered a result of ill-will on their part. [2]

A sixteenth-century Spanish author Fray Martín de Castañega
wrote a whole chapter (the fourteenth) of his book on witchcraft
to prove that the 'evil eye' is a natural phenomenon and the result
of the foul thoughts and evil designs which shine through certain
people's eyes—more particularly through those of elderly spinsters,
cripples and certain types of sick people. Years later, Miguel
Sabuco in his *Nueva filosofía* and other doctors took the same view. [3]
In our own times, the word *gafe* has become widely used in Spain
to signify belief in certain people's ability to attract evil and cause
harm as a result of some mysterious quality within them. There is
no point in giving examples of this: *gafes* abound in all sections of
society, particularly whenever there is a strong feeling of tension.

This belief is slightly reminiscent of one which Professor Evans
Pritchard studied in the Azande tribe. In their society it is commonly believed that the ability to cause harm to others (which
sorcerers, witches and 'gafes', too, are believed to be able to do
in Europe), is the result of a certain substance within the body
of the person concerned. The substance grows as the body grows
and it can be inherited. It is more virulent in older people than in
young. [4] Those who possess this substance are feared and perse-

cuted because of it, since it is believed that the power of the substance can sometimes be used deliberately.

But leaving aside the Azande, who are some distance away from our own world, let us remember that there is or has been a second type of individual who is thought to be capable of doing evil without being wholly responsible for his or her actions. According to the evidence given at the trials—and also according to popular beliefs which have been documented in some countries—a witch can transfer her witchcraft to another by passing on some material object which contains forces of evil. This object, which is generally handed over *in articulo mortis*, makes the person to whom it is given a witch.[5]

In the same way (that is by handing more or less common objects to another person), sorcerers or witches bent on doing evil are believed to be capable of bewitching others or causing them to be *possessed* by the Devil. People possessed by the Devil in ancient Greece were said to have been in the power of πνεύματα but those possessed in more modern times at the command of sorcerers seem to have had something rather more physical and corporeal than πνεῦμα in them. This is why substances with a strong smell or flavour are used for the purpose of exorcism to drive out the spirits within the body, as one would drive out or kill pests with insecticides or by fumigation.

A rapid glance at Mengus's *Flagellum daemonum* is enough to show the importance of salt and water in the ceremonial blessings aimed at alleviating the situation of those possessed of the Devil; of wine in fighting spells with a physical effect; and of gold, incense and myrrh in dealing with incubi and succubi. The same book gives whole recipes against spells with white hellebore, attar of roses, and rue as some of the ingredients.[6]

It is quite possible that the wide circulation of some of the neo-platonists in the sixteenth and seventeenth centuries may have led to the belief in devils as *other beings* who had to be reckoned with. Their books contain long catalogues of 'devils' with details of their background, place in the hierarchy and characteristics.[7] It was possible to take this approach to extremes as did Fray la Peña or Fuentelapeña. In the latter half of the seventeenth century he wrote a fat volume to prove the existence of 'irrational and invisible animals', which must have been the traditional *duendes* (familiar spirits) or spirits of some other type.[8]

133

So the devils, who had been the object of *psychological* and ethical speculations amongst authors of classical times, who had constituted a *social* problem for the Middle Ages, finally ended up as beings which had to be defined *physically* and *materially*. And, in fact, books like the work of Padre la Peña are not so much the result of theological aberrations as of a monstrous and sterile marriage of theological ideas and natural sciences. But to return to our starting point.

The material aspect of spells has frequently been described. A list of them will wear down any scholar who takes on the un-enviable task of studying them. There is little difference between the spells which Celestina[9] knew and used, and those enumerated in Latin texts ... and this is not simply due to the classical erudition and scholarly background of her creator, Fernando de Rojas. Similar lists and recipes can be found in inquisitorial documents.[10]

It cannot be too often repeated that the sorcerer puts a devil into another person's body by using a material object. Time and again, in fact, what we might call materialist conceptions arise in connexion with the nature of evil and devilish actions. And it is hardly surprising that feelings and reasons of a thoroughly *carnal* nature should be involved in cases where a man is accused of causing others to be possessed—as they clearly were in many of the seventeenth-century trials referred to at the beginning of this chapter. We must now make one further observation about these trials to complete the picture.

Possessed Persons, the Devil and those who induce Possession

In the history of many religious movements, particularly those which have to struggle against an Established Church, an import-ant part is played by men who have a physical and sexual power over groups of slightly unbalanced women in addition to strong spiritual powers. The classical example of this in modern times is Rasputin. But it would not be difficult to quote other examples where a man with this same combination of spiritual strength and sexual powers of suggestion acts in a different way. There are yet other instances where friends and enemies of this kind of personal-ity have attributed more powers to that person than he really had.

This kind of spiritual leader comes into his own in movements like that of the illuminist *alumbrados* in Spain in the sixteenth and seventeenth centuries, the *fraticelli* of an earlier period, and the *khlystovskie korabli* in the Russian church at the beginning of this century.

In the reign of Philip II, Fray Alonso de la Fuente, a friar from Estremadura, who was against the *alumbrados*, claimed (in a document that reflects the author's inability to understand this group and his willingness to adopt popular criteria) that the leaders of the sect, 'great sorcerers and magicians',

> 'Win women and enjoy their bodies with the aid of magic, the Devil also helping them considerably. The Devil comes to these women and arouses such burning carnal desires in them that they go running to their masters in a frenzy asking them for medicine to cure their ailments since no one else can do it. And these masters remedy their ills with no regard for chastity, telling them that it is no sin, and calling sensuality the joy of all spiritual people, since it is no offence to God to satisfy spiritual needs in this way.'[11]

Whether the accusation was true or false, many men lost their reputations as a result of it, and other eminent people very nearly lost theirs. But there is no point in discussing this here.

At a later stage we find such people formally accused of being sorcerers and magicians (for seducing those who were in their care or whose spiritual directors they were) and causing the women they had abused to be possessed by the Devil. But the history of these men and women has led to a great deal of casuistry in spite of the fact that the general outlines of their stories are always much the same.

In 1610, for instance, the case of Gauffridi occurred. He was the spiritual director of the Ursuline convent at Aix and was accused of witchcraft for abusing the nuns who confessed to him and causing them to be possessed by the Devil. If the man was, in fact, guilty of some sexual crime, this was certainly exaggerated into something more. His accusers and judges made him out to be something he clearly was not: a great magician or satanist.[12]

Some time later and again in France, a young clergyman who was attractive, something of a libertine, smooth-tongued, vain, and a great favourite with his parishioners, was accused by a hysterical nun (with who knows what strange and conflicting feelings towards him), by several families who also thought he had offended them, and by the officious agents of no less a person than Cardinal Richelieu. As a result of this, he has been passed down to posterity as a major sorcerer, having been burnt at the stake, for making a pact with the Devil, causing a whole convent to be possessed by the Devil, and more besides. Many contradictory views have been expressed about the case of Urbain Grandier. According to earliest opinions he was naturally guilty. The Protestants were the first to look upon his case in a different light, and nowadays it is plain that this unfortunate priest was far from being the terrible person he was made out to be. His flesh was weak and his moral and physical vanity were the cause of his downfall.[13] Grandier worked from a distance. His accuser, the Mother Superior of the convent at Loudun, had never been very intimate with him in spite of what has been said. Nevertheless, his case was, largely for political reasons, one of the most notorious of its times, and new things are still written about it from time to time.

He was not, of course, the last person of his calling to be accused of these crimes. And ultimately Barbey d'Aurévilly in his story *L'ensorcelée* made a beautiful character-sketch of this kind of priest. He depicted Jéhoël de la Croix-Jugan as a man of strong and slightly enigmatic character, fascinating to women, and ultimately believed to bewitch them. And his epic of *Chouannerie* has inspired a number of French and Spanish writers fond of discussing traditionalist societies.[14]

At all events the seventeenth century was a good time for religious crises—and witchcraft, demoniacal possession, 'abandonment', etc., were involved in them. The consequences were numerous cases like those of the nuns of the Order of St Brigitte in Lille, the bewitched nuns of Louviers, Chinon, and Nîmes, and others of less importance which occurred in France during the reign of Louis XIV and, in Spain, under Charles II *el hechizado* (the Bewitched).

Let us now look at one of the better-known Spanish cases. Unlike the events at Aix and Loudun, there were one or two clergy in Spain who really were guilty parties, whilst the nuns who were implicated with them—possessed by the Devil, damned by popular opinion and then even condemned by the authorities—seem to have been entirely blameless. A rather brief study of the affair of the nuns in the convent of St Placidus in Madrid which was contemporary with the Loudun business, may be appropriate here. There are three versions of the story: 1. That of the inquisitors, which led to the condemnation of several nuns together with their spiritual director; 2. The popular version; 3. The version of Doña Teresa Valle de la Cerda, Mother Superior in the convent, who after being condemned asked for her case to be reviewed since she had acted out of pure obedience. Later she was granted complete absolution by the Inquisition.

According to the inquisitorial version, the Benedictine Father Confessor of the nuns, Fray Francisco García Calderón, was a heretic and *alumbrado*, a lascivious and dominating personality who seriously harmed the women in his charge—they were possessed by the Devil after being seduced by their confessor. The case was investigated by inquisitors who were predisposed to condemn, and the Father Confessor was found guilty on serious suspicion of heresy while the nuns were punished in various minor ways (*de levi*). But, in fact, the sentence against the friar was highly irregular since it was largely based on charges which were probably false, making him out to be a repository of all kinds of heresy and ambition.[15]

A popular version of the story, which is later in date, describes the convent's patron, Don Jerónimo de Villanueva, as a sorcerer, claiming that he allowed all kinds of irregularities to go on; this version confuses the 'possession' part of the affair with a later case in which Philip IV and the Conde-Duque de Olivares were involved. It states that while the king made love to a nun, the Conde-Duque and Don Jerónimo, the chief notary of Aragon, performed sacrilegious rites. . . .[16] On the other hand, Doña Teresa Valle de la Cerda, when she asked for the sentence on the convent she had founded to be quashed, did not hesitate to admit that she had been possessed by a devil called Peregrine, and that some twenty-five other nuns were also possessed by devils. She rejected entirely, however, the assertion that they had professed opinions similar to those of the *alumbrados*.

'As for the charge that is made against me that I learned dogmas and doctrines of the *alumbrado* sect from Fray Francisco, such as that lascivious contact between people and kisses were not a sin, I deny it entirely, for I swear on my oath that I never heard him say such things.'[17]

She made no reference to sorcery at all.

Towards New Interpretations

The above case gave rise to three quite different interpretations of the same basic fact: possession by the Devil. With the lapse of time the guilt of the parties appears to grow and the hostility of the interpreters increases. The most hostile version comes from people who had nothing whatever to do with the affair and who were mixing it up with their own worries and political anxieties.

Similar cases recurred in Europe at a much later date. Even in the middle of the eighteenth century there were memorable instances of possession for which sorcerers and witches were held to be to blame. Even protestant countries were not entirely free from such cases; like that of the witches of Salem, for instance, which dates from late in the seventeenth century. This particular case has recently achieved some notoriety as a result of a famous play, which uses it to criticise certain judicial practices in modern states. It must be emphasised that the cases of possession which repeatedly occurred between 1688 and 1693 were, without doubt, provoked to some extent by too much reading of books on witchcraft and demoniacal possession written by influential theologians. The latter played a great part in the trials and were ultimately responsible for the death of many innocent people. The hysteria of those who were possessed by devils in Salem is even attested by the theologians themselves.[18] They were so obsessed by the idea of their own purity (they were not Puritans for nothing) and by their belief in the tangible physical reality of devils that they were wide open to subsequent severe criticism.

These incidents and theories in North America cropped up at a time when experimental science in Europe was just beginning to develop. With this went a cold, objective approach and a concern for evolving *methods* rather than fixed beliefs. It is only natural, therefore, that men who tended to reduce even philosophy to a geometrical system should remain somewhat sceptical when faced with possession and witchery, and with a mass of mystical phenomena like trances, visions, and divinations. And it is hardly surprising that ultimately they should adopt an attitude of complete derision. As soon as a 'scientific method' (that is to say a mechanical and mathematical method) is used to throw light on reality, such phenomena seem tedious and monotonous fictions. Thanks to this materialist view of spirits, spells and so forth, and thanks to

rationalistic, mathematical and empirical methods, these phenomena soon came to be dismissed en bloc as sheer invention. Nowadays, when we look on emotional states in a different way, we may
think that these critics went too far. There can be no doubt that
the war declared on superstitions, both old and new, in the
seventeenth and eighteenth centuries was a valuable one. But it
ended up with quite a few vacuous ideas being accepted as if they
had been proved by scientific investigations and experiments. We
are still paying dearly for one or two of these ill-conceived opinions.

Ultimately, it was not the rationalists, with what Pascal might
call their 'geometric spirit' who went furthest, but other thinkers
more inclined to the 'spirit of finesse'. In other words, it was a
humanistic approach rather than a scientific one (and I use
'scientific' here to mean physical and mathematical) that finally
broke down the structure which societies had erected year by year
for centuries, to protect themselves against their *angst*, against
evils they did not know how to fight and desires they were unable
to satisfy. By a strange paradox Spain was quicker than any other
country to exchange judicial error for a more sane idea of the
reality of witchcraft. In the next five chapters I shall show how
this came about.

PART THREE

THE CRISIS OF WITCHCRAFT IN
THE BASQUE COUNTRY

CHAPTER 11

WITCHCRAFT AMONG THE BASQUES IN THE SIXTEENTH CENTURY

Witchcraft in the Basque country from 1466 to 1527 – Witchcraft in the Basque country from 1527 to 1596

Witchcraft in the Basque country from 1466 to 1527

So far we have followed the general outlines of the history of witchcraft and must now examine in greater detail its development in some of the regions particularly plagued by witches and their judges. The aim will be to give answers to the more polemical questions involved in each specific case, or rather to show how radically interpretations of basic facts can change over relatively short periods of time.

I have already explained at the outset why I have chosen the Basque Provinces for this detailed analysis. I believe that apart from any personal inclinations on my part, the documents[1] which are available on witchcraft in that region are of considerable historical importance, even if they are less well known than those of other regions.

In 1466 the province of Guipúzcoa sent a petition to Henry IV of Castile complaining about the damage done by witches in that area and asking for them to be stamped out immediately.[2] The document in question also admitted that the local mayors did not pay enough attention to the problem and were not strict enough in dealing with the accused. Some were inhibited, others afraid of witches, and yet others refrained from treating them hastily because their own relatives, friends or social connexions were involved. Furthermore, the local regulations governing the forces of law and order made no reference at all to witches, their crimes or appropriate punishments, so that it was impossible to take any action against them without appealing to a higher authority.

The province, therefore, asked the king to give local mayors the power to pass sentence and execute it in cases of witchcraft, without allowing the accused the right of appeal. Henry IV duly granted this in a Royal Charter dated at Valladolid on August 15th the same year.

It is no less significant that thirty-four years later, in 1500, there are references to a case being brought against witches in the mountainous region of Amboto in Vizcaya.[3] For this region is still famous today as the haunt of some sort of divinity, frequently referred to by local people as the 'Lady of Amboto', a figure not unlike 'Frau Holle', and 'Bona Sozia' in the folk traditions of other parts of Europe. She is sometimes called by other names and interesting research has been carried out into her by the Basque ethnographer and prehistorian, José Miguel de Barandiarán. We shall be referring to this divinity later.

The important point to remember for the moment is that the witches of Amboto had from the start all the characteristics of Devil-worshippers, and they were also experts in the Magic Arts. There are references to their worshipping the Devil in the form of a he-goat, mule or man. But whatever the form he took, there was always some obvious symbol of wickedness by which to recognise him, like a horn on his head or forehead, or projecting teeth. . . .[4] It is also relevant to note that the Durango region to which we are referring (some texts even speak of the witches as 'Durangas', women from Durango[5]) had earlier been the home of a religious movement rather like the *fraticelli*,[6] which was held to be pagan or idolatrous by contemporary scholars living relatively near the area, such as Fray Alonso de Cartagena, the famous bishop of Burgos, for instance.[7] It is clear, then, that witchcraft in the Basque Provinces was closely linked from the start to the special social structure of the region. Its pagan traditions also played their part—so much so that in the fifteenth century some people could even refer to the Basques as *Gentiles*[8]—which may seem rather surprising in view of their strongly catholic traditions today. In 1507 another unspecified centre of witchcraft was discovered in the Basque regions and the Inquisition burnt quite a number of women—more than thirty according to Llorente and Lea, and twenty-nine according to Menéndez y Pelayo.[9]

Meanwhile in Navarre, a canon of Pamplona called Martín de Arles wrote a treatise on superstition in which he implied that witches were common in that Pyrenean kingdom; he accepted the existence of their spells, and the harm they could do to men and agricultural land. He held that witches acted on the guidance of the Devil, but did not believe, however, that they flew through the air, and he quoted the 'Canon Episcopi' in support of his views.[10]

The canon's book, which is wholly based on authorities earlier than the *Malleus*, must have been written at about the time the province of Guipúzcoa was demanding new action. It was published in 1517.[11] Ten years later, the history of witchcraft in Navarre entered a new phase and the people who figured as judges were quite as credulous as those in Italy at that time, like Grillandus.

It was in 1527 that two girls, one nine and the other eleven, appeared before the counsellors in Pamplona. They promised to make all kinds of revelations providing their own crimes and sorcery were pardoned. The counsellors were prepared to do this in view of the age of the girls, and the latter made the following declaration:

'Sirs, the truth is that we are witches like many others, who do much evil. And if you want to punish them we will point them out to you, for we have only to look at their left eyes to be able to recognise them, since we are of their kind. Anyone not of their kind could not do it.'

The counsellors decided to see justice done and nominated one of their number to investigate. The individual appointed duly set out with the two girls and fifty soldiers. In every town he entered, he followed the same procedure. He shut up one of the girls in a house and put the other one somewhere else; then summoned the local authorities to find out who was under suspicion. These he took into custody, made them change their clothes, covered them with blankets and cloths so that they could not be recognised, and then lined them up in the sun. The town justice uncovered their left eyes and one of the girls said whether they were witches or not. Then the other girl had her turn. There was absolute agreement between the two, and thanks to this one hundred and fifty sorcerers and witches were put in prison according to Fray Prudencio de Sandoval, who later became bishop of Pamplona.[12]

We know more about the person in charge of the investigations from another source. He was an inquisitor called Avellaneda, who is said to have written a letter to the Constable of Castile, Iñigo de Velasco, giving a rather more extraordinary account of the remarkable affair. This letter appears to have been written from a valley in the Pyrenees some six months after the inquisitor had started his sensational work, which kept him busy in and around the Salazar valley most of the time.[13]

Avellaneda declares that at first he was not inclined to believe what the girls said about the witches attending their covens, leaving their houses by doors and chimneys in an incredible manner. But while he was still in a state of doubt, which important texts and authorities required him to be, a remarkable thing happened. Both he and Fray Prudencio de Sandoval tell the following story about it. A witch was to be tortured. . . .

. . . . and so one Friday, just before midnight, I went to the inn, where she was, with the secretary Vergara and the constable Pero Díaz de Término and the corporal Sancho de Amiçaray and nearly twenty more soldiers and local men. She anointed and prepared herself before them all, and I and the secretary with me and another man put her in an inner chamber; and she anointed herself in her usual way with a poisonous ointment which is also used to kill people, and she went to a window which was in a high place with a great rock beneath it on which a cat would be broken in pieces if it fell from one to the other. And then she called on the Devil for help, and he came as was his wont and took her and carried her nearly to the ground. And to be more sure of what happened, I had with me the corporal with one of his soldiers and a local man [and we were] outside the house and below the window, and one of the men, terrified to see such a thing, began to cross himself and call on Jesus Christ by name, and at this the Devil disappeared and so they both escaped. And the next Monday three leagues from that place I found her, and seven others with her, at a harbour town, in a hut where the snow lay very deep around.'[14]

This and other equally well attested experiences enabled the lawyers of the Council of Navarre to resolve their obligatory doubts and conclude that witches really did fly through the air and attend covens. The witch's sentence was as usual very severe; she was condemned to death.

In the course of his investigations Avellaneda found as many as three covens of sorcerers and witches: one of them attended by one hundred and twenty people in the very valley from which he was writing his letter—almost certainly the Roncal valley. There was another in the Salazar valley which over a hundred witches attended, more than eighty of whom were tried and sentenced; and a third in the region lying between the valley of the Aézcoa river, Roncesvalles, and the district just north of Pamplona itself, consisting of over two hundred. . . .[15] The whole area was infested according to Avellaneda, who, after this sensational preamble, went on to describe in outline the conduct of sorcerers and witches. The tone of his assertions is much the same as that of the *Malleus*, but he includes some new details which are worthwhile bearing in mind.

Sorcerers and witches renounce God and his laws, the Blessed Virgin and the saints in return for the offer of great riches and pleasures which the Devil, or Satan, makes to them. Sometimes, however, he uses force to make them follow him, and they fear that he will destroy them if they fail to do so.[16]

The process of anointing, the journey to the coven and the adoration of the Devil are described in much the same terms as in other writers we have quoted. The Devil appears once again in the form of a he-goat, *akerra* in Basque.[17] The meeting he attends is, therefore, properly an *akelarre* (*aquelarre* is the equivalent spelling of the word in Castilian, meaning a witches' sabbath) although the word is not used in this instance. However, this 'Sabbath' has not quite the same repulsive character which it is given in other descriptions. It is merely a sexual orgy at which men and women have intercourse with devils of both sexes, who corrupt virgins and even young girls. Those taking part, however, form an evil sect, sworn to do harm to men, animals and crops, and those who commit the most evil deeds are rewarded, while those who fail to do evil are punished.[18]

Friday (as in Italy) is the appointed day for the meetings, or rather the night between Friday and Saturday, for reasons closely related with Christian beliefs: in memory of the day when Christ was crucified. Because of this, Holy Thursday is also an important day for their celebrations in commemoration of the Passion. The reason that witches have to fly away at cock-crow is also connected with the bible and St Peter's denials of Christ,

147

for only after the cock had crowed the third time did the Devil leave him.[19]

In witchcraft, Christian symbols and values are always used in an inverted form. Whereas in Christian ritual the blessing is given with the right-hand, witches use the left hand when making their spells. The Devil guides them in the form of a dog, fox, or even a man to places where there are unsanctified animals or where no Cross, or images of the Virgin and Holy Water exist; places, in fact, which are suitable for witchcraft because of the very absence of Christian symbols, since at the mere mention of the name of Jesus all spells lose their power.[20]

Once people have become sorcerers or witches they cannot receive the Sacrament and are given the mark mentioned by the two girls. This was placed 'in the left eye above the pupil and was the sign of a frog's foot'.[21] The emphasis which Avellaneda, in his letter to the Constable of Castile, placed on the evil that was done by large bands and assemblies of sorcerers, together with the fact that the investigations were carried out at a critical historical moment, when Charles I was annexing the kingdom of Navarre, suggests that there may have been some political motives behind what is usually considered to be a religious question. The accused may well have been supporters of the ancient kings of Navarre, that is, *agramonteses*. The inquisitor urged Don Iñigo de Velasco to use all his influence in the good cause, and finally pointed out the ways of telling whether or not there were witches in a district.

You must accept, Sire, that this evil has spread through the world, and in order to discover whether there are sorcerers or witches in these parts you should seek information as to whether any crops of wheat have been ruined when the grain was ripe, and whether there is a grain like pepper in the ears of corn that are left, and whether this turns to powder when it is touched, and if there are any drowned animals or bodies of toads near where this is found. You may rest assured that when this is the case there are sorcerers and witches about.[22]

The inquisitor Avellaneda, like many others, declared himself to be very willing to learn from personal experience and he went so far as to describe in his letter, in much the same way as the authors of the *Malleus*, his violent struggles with the Devil, who had ordered his disciples to kill him. Yet he was right in thinking that his investigations were concerned with 'the most serious case of the century'.[23]

That it achieved notoriety in Spain is proved by the number of literary works of the period which refer to it. A passage of Villalón's *El Crotalón*, for example, a work full of reminiscences of Lucian, relates the story of how in 1522 a young and vicious soldier went to fight in Navarre, serving, in fact, under Don Iñigo de Velasco.[24] While there he fell into the hands of some women, whom he describes in the following way:

'Sir, they command the sun and it obeys them, they change the stars in their courses, and they take away the light from the moon and restore it again at their will. They cause clouds to form in the air, and make it possible to tread on them, and they travel about the country. They cause fire to grow cold and water to burn. They turn themselves into young girls and in the twinkling of an eye into old women, or sticks, stones or beasts. If a man pleases them they have the power to enjoy him at will; and to make him more willing they can change him into various animals dulling his senses and his better nature. They have such power by reason of their arts that they have only to command and men must obey or lose their lives. For they like to move freely by day and night along roads and valleys and over mountains about their business, which is to cast spells, gather herbs and stones and make pacts and agreements.'

But Villalón's account is hardly a factual one and it is full of classical reminiscences. The whole work is cast in the mould of Lucian's dialogues, and the author claims that the women he describes were more like the direct descendants of the sorceresses of Thessaly than Basque witches. Gonzalo Fernández de Oviedo, in Stanza XLII of *Las Quinquagenas*, is another writer who refers to the large numbers of witches in the kingdom of Navarre. He recalls an earlier work written against them by Fray Martín de Castañega, about which something should now be said.[25] In actual fact, it was the book which made the most use of Avellaneda's investigations and legal cases.

Fray Martín's book came out in 1529 and it has been reprinted more recently. The first edition was published in Logroño and the work was dedicated to the Bishop of Calahorra, Alonso de Castilla. It may be taken as a fair reflection of the views of many inquisitors on the subject.[26] If any work makes witchcraft out to be a complete *inversion* of Catholicism, it is this one. In Chapter III it claims that whereas there are sacraments in the Catholic Church there are 'excrements' in the Devil's Church; the communion service is parodied by the Black Mass, which Castañega considers common practice amongst witches. These 'excrements' are not only different from the sacraments on a spiritual plane but also on a material one. The equivalents of bread and wine in the 'excrements' are wholly disgusting. Nevertheless the form of service used by witches closely follows the rites of the Church.[27]

Speaking of the various kinds of pact which are made with the Devil—those which are made 'expressly', as a result of direct contact with Devil, or those made 'explicitly', as a result of agreements with the Devil's ministers—the book refers to enchanters, sorcerers and *bruxos* (witches) as people wholly dedicated to the Devil. Some of the words used have a distinctly local flavour, however, (*megos* and *xorguinos*, for example, the latter obviously connected with the Basque word *sorguin*). Castañega explains that *sorguioñ*, which is wrongly written *xorguino*, is derived from the word *sortilego*. It is derived from the Latin *sors—sortis* (French *sort*, Spanish *suerte*, and English 'fate') with the addition of the Basque suffix *guiñ*, *eguiñ* (or *egin*) which means somebody who does or makes something. (There are other words in Basque with this suffix like *arguiñ*, a builder; *zurguiñ*, a carpenter, and so forth.)[28]

The most familiar and popular figure amongst the Basques is the *sorguiña*, the witch. (The word is found in Spanish too). Castañega is following a medieval Christian tradition when he says in Chapter V that 'there are more women than men amongst the Devil's ministers'. Women are sinks of iniquity and the old and impoverished among them more so, if anything, than the young. So far as the actions carried out by the witches are concerned, they are ones with which we are already familiar: the causing of storms, the ability to change themselves, or others, into something else, vampirism and the eating of human flesh, and Devil-worship. . . . But in order to have something original to say, Castañega claims that although witches can leave any place in the shape of a bird, cat or fox, or even by making themselves invisible, yet they cannot pass through a door or window which is not large enough for the animal whose shape they have taken. What he has to say about inheriting familiarity with the Devil in Chapter X is particularly interesting. Again he finds a perfect parallel between the practices of the Church and those of the Devil:

'Just as a Jew or a Moor who does not believe in Baptism yet accepts it, or receives Baptism as Christians do without protest, is baptised and becomes a Christian indeed, and so far so that when he finally comes to believe, it is not necessary to baptise him again, so also any person who receives anything from their mother or grandmother or any other person who is a witch, as a sign that their familiarity with the Devil has been left to them, and accepts the token, even though they do not believe in it, without protesting against the evil that is in it, then do they allow and give leave to the Devil thereby to use them in the same way as he had used the person from whom they accepted and inherited it.'

Yet in the middle of all this credulity, Castañega admits in Chapter XXII that sometimes those who are said to be bewitched or possessed by the Devil, are really ill and need to be treated with normal remedies and medicines.

At the same period, a more famous character in Spanish scientific history, Pedro Ciruelo, was studying all the magical arts in detail in his *Reprovación de las supersticiones y hechizerías* (*A reproof of superstitions and witchery*). He gives several lines in that work to the *brujas xorguinas* (spell-casting witches) and admits the possibility of two different views about their flights through the air and other activities. These are the two we have already come across, according to which the witches really do sometimes leave their houses although at others they merely dream everything they subsequently relate.[29]

Witchcraft in Navarre from 1527 to 1596

It is clear that the investigations carried out by the inquisitor Avellaneda in Navarre had far-reaching consequences for the study of the theory and practice of witchcraft. At much the same time there was a campaign against witches in Vizcaya in which several famous preachers took part, and Fray Juan de Zumárraga was appointed as inquisitor in charge—a job which he was in a better position to perform than some since he had been born in Durango and spoke fluent Basque.[30] Perhaps, however, the fact that he had been born and bred there made him more lenient than the authorities thought proper. In 1528 Avellaneda himself was sent to the area, and on February 22nd that year the Inquisitor-General, Manrique, ordered Sancho de Carranza de Miranda, who was an inquisitor at Calahorra and the brother of the famous archbishop, to conduct a full investigation in the whole region.,

The civil authorities (like those in Guipúzcoa in 1466) were apprehensive about the extent of the damage done by witches,[31] and so were those who attended a General Council in Fuenterrabía in 1530 and appointed three lawyers to consult the vicar-general of the diocese about methods of stamping out witchcraft. This consultation was probably responsible for the dispatch of an inquisitor called Ugarte whom we know to have been in Guipúzcoa the following year and who, according to a tradition which was recorded at the beginning of the seventeenth century, died of poison at the hands of witches.[32] There were new outbreaks of witchcraft in Navarre around 1538, and in 1539 the prisons were full of people accused of it.[33]

In 1555 several towns in Guipúzcoa once again asked for witches to be punished. But the Supreme Inquisition—the highest tribunal in the organisation—decided that there were not enough grounds in the cases which had been submitted to them for arresting the accused, as had been done in the past, and in March 1556 they ruled that the cases were totally unproven.[34]

It looks, then, as if the Spanish Inquisition, which has so often been criticised for its activities, was much less hasty than other tribunals of the period. There is further proof of this in other cases which occurred in the Basque Provinces at this time. On a number of occasions the civil authorities, obsessed by the belief that witchcraft was a powerful force of evil, chose to act on their own initiative without taking any notice of the Inquisition, which had always proceeded with extreme caution in the North and in those regions which had *fueros* (local rights).

A good example of a civil case is that of the witches of Ceberio which was heard between 1555 and 1558. The files of the case are in the archives of the Royal Chancery at Valladolid.[35] This case involved two opposing groups of local people, one of which accused the other of practising witchcraft, or rather, one of which induced some young girls to make the accusation mentioning all kinds of horrors. One of the principal, if not *the* principal, accusers, Catalina de Guesala, was eight years old when she made her first declaration. She was the daughter of Juan de Guesala and lived in the parish of Santo Tomás de Olabarrieta. According to her evidence both parties used force to make her take their side. The centre of witchcraft activities was the house referred to as 'Hereinoça' or 'Bereinoça'. All the members of the family who lived there were sorcerers or witches: the master—Juan—his wife, his mother (who had the strange name 'Puturu') and his sister, not to mention a lady referred to as 'Bastiana de Herenoça', Mariachea, the wife of Min de Ameçola, Marina de Barbachano and her daughter, Juan de Ysasi and several others including Diego de Guinea and Mari Ochoa de Guesala, the girl's mother. At one of the meetings, Juan de Hereinoça, took out the usual ointment and when they had anointed the soles of their feet, the palms of their hands, their left breasts, shoulders, chins and foreheads, they all went out on to a balcony and flew to meet the Devil, at a place called Pretelanda, where there were great rocks, a cross, a chapel and a small house. Beelzebub himself appeared at the meeting in the shape of a pitch black nag with horns, sitting on a seat. After the usual dances they pretended to eat, and the Devil gave his own, bitter urine in a silver cup to his disciples to drink. Then they all took part in a sexual orgy.[36]

The second witness, Marinacho de Unzueta, who first gave evidence in Areilza on August 7th, 1555, thoroughly compromised the previous witness whom she described as a hardened witch. She had seen her in peculiar circumstances, and Catalina herself had told her of her extraordinary experiences.[37]

The third witness was one 'Hurtuno de Areylça e Torreçar', who lived in Durango. He described how Diego de Guinea, who seems to have been generally disliked, had opened his veins and sucked his blood when only four years old and had carried him off to the house of the real sorcerer, Goicoechea. Later his wounds were rubbed with some ointment.[38] A priest, called Don Iñigo, who also gave evidence, being Vicar of Arandia and Curate of Santo Tomás de Olabarrieta, declared that he had heard one of his servants say that he had seen a man and two women in a grove of chestnut trees by the weaver's house in the parish of Santo Tomás. They were apparently preparing a spell, and the man was up a chestnut tree with a sheet into which he was scattering powder, while the women stood below. One of the women had become a witch because of the powder the other had given her; the powder was also the kind used to ruin crops.[39]

On this evidence the judges who were hearing the case ordered twenty-one persons of one family (only four of them men) to be

153

thrown into the prison at Bilbao. On August 31st, 1555, when the seventeen women were in custody in the 'house of the Naja' Hernando de Gastaza with Juan de Zuazo found that two witches, María de Gorocito and 'Marina, freyla de San Bartolomé' had bruise-marks on their knees as well as wounds which had been made for the sucking of blood.[40]

However, the judges made further investigations and took more evidence. Some of it was quite fantastic, like that given by María de Zubiaur, an assiduous congregant of a church called Nuestra Señora de Ceberio. She declared that she had been picking apples one day on her property when the Devil appeared to her 'and made a wry face at her' because she was not a witch. She was one of those who had tried hardest to discover who was. . . .[41]

The person who seems to have been destined for strange things from the very start is the first witness, Catalina or Catalinche de Guesala. At the time of her birth, her mother had said that the Devil had conceived the child, who was to be the anti-Christ. Catalina later made a second deposition in which she described a gathering of witches and emphasised the sexual perversions that took place. But the sentence was not finally a very severe one, since the judge decided that Diego de Guinea, and the others who had been implicated, should be given ordeal by water and beaten with whips as he thought fit.[42]

The trial of the witches at Ceberio, conducted by civil judges, is particularly interesting since the latter took the view that covens of witches and sorcerers were almost a family matter, with nothing grandiose about them. They merely consisted of people with bad reputations and close family ties who could easily pass on the cult of witchcraft from one generation to the next. The bulk of the evidence, however, came from individuals who were not of age, and who seem to have suffered neuroses or been motivated by personal animosities. The same is true of other cases later on.

There do not seem to have been any other important cases for some twenty years. But there was one in 1575, in Navarre again, which led to the arrest of a number of men and women on the instructions of the Council of Navarre. Once again the Inquisition seems to have been very restrained in its actions. The secular arm demanded that an example be made of the sorcerers and witches, but the ecclesiastical authorities refused to act with excessive severity.

On this occasion one of the major problems of the whole business cropped up once more: the language difficulty. The inquisitors could not understand the prisoners, who doubtless spoke nothing but Basque.[43] Their restraint is in marked contrast to the readiness of the provincial authorities to arraign people of ill repute. As late as 1595, the elected representatives of Tolosa at the meeting of the General Council of Guipúzcoa, stated that there were too many witches in their district and they felt that the Inquisition should be asked to take some action. The result of this declaration is not known.[44] However, the Supreme Tribunal must have made some investigations, since an inquisitor called Don Alonso de Salazar y Frías, in a document to which we shall refer later, says that there were nine cases involving witches and sorcerers in the Basque Provinces between 1526 and 1596. All of these apparently followed the same pattern, according to the inquisitorial archives.[45] They were soon eclipsed, however, by the new cases which came up early in the seventeenth century, and it was Salazar's comments on these which were to be particularly interesting.

CHAPTER 12

THE GREAT TRIALS OF THE EARLY SEVENTEENTH CENTURY IN THE BASQUE COUNTRY

Pierre de Lancre - Satan's regal position at coven - The Church as model for the 'Sabbath' - Credulity and lack of critical approach

Pierre de Lancre

Witchcraft in the Basque country is well known and frequently cited in books for the following two reasons only: Firstly the notoriety of the witch trials in Zugarramurdi which ended in 1610; and secondly the writings of Pierre de Lancre, a witch trial judge in the Labourd region, who was responsible for repressing witchcraft in a brutal way in the area at that time.

The works of this French judge, who followed in the footsteps of Rémy and Boguet, were soon published, but were not subjected to any criticism by other judges. The trials of sorcerers and witches from the north of Navarre before the Inquisition at Logroño on the other hand, had far-reaching consequences for the history of Spanish law. And the account of the trials, which is quite as absurd as anything de Lancre wrote, though slightly less pretentious, came in for serious criticism. The first attack came, in fact, from one of the three judges responsible for the conduct of the trials; he had disagreed with the opinions of the other two and was subsequently asked to review the sentences. But first let us look at the repression of witches in Labourd and the character of de Lancre and his works.

De Lancre was born in Bordeaux of a well-known legal family

in the middle of the sixteenth century (probably between 1550 and 1560). He himself tells us that he acted as companion to Pietro de Medici in 1577 when the latter was staying in the capital of south-western France, since he knew Italian at the time and was fond of dancing and society life. He must have been proud of his Gascon background in spite of his Basque ancestors, and he was a pious individual who always recalled his Jesuit education with pleasure. Some of those who have written about him describe him as a mystic,[1] others as a kind and humorous person, spiritually sound and deeply concerned with religion. This is Michelet's view.[2] My own is that de Lancre was a typical lawyer, obsessed with the desire to uncover criminal activities, who accepted religion as the basis for the penal code. I feel he had an essentially repressive concept of law, and, therefore, a rather primitive approach to justice.

There is no doubt that he was talented and something of a scholar. But all his qualities pale into insignificance beside his personality as a judge, and a harsh judge at that, on questions which required more skill and perception than the Parlement of Bordeaux could have taught him. Henry IV commissioned him to go to Labourd in 1609, and when he had finished his bloodthirsty work in that relatively quiet region, he began his career as a writer. The years, and his experiences of one particular kind of judicial problem, increased his outward piety. We know that he went on a pilgrimage to Our Lady of Loretto and he may have made others. In 1610, at the end of his legal tour, he asked for leave of absence, spent some time in Rome and Naples and visited Lombardy.

As a reward for his services he was made a State Counsellor in Paris sometime between 1612 and 1622, and he died in the French capital about 1630.[3] The life and fame of Pierre de Lancre would have been quite insignificant had he not been involved in witch trials. As a result of them, he has a certain reputation, though perhaps not a very enviable one, as a judge and writer. Two of his works give us numerous details of his role in the trials and investigations. The first and most important of these is his *Tableau de l'inconstance des mauvais anges et demons*,[4] printed in 1612. The second book that is relevant to our work is *L'incredulité et mescréance du sortilège plainement convaincue*, which was published in 1622.[5] Let us examine some of the contents of these books.

In 1609 the Labourd region empowered two gentlemen, d'Amou and d'Urtubie (Dortobie), to ask Henry IV to appoint judges to deal with crimes of witchcraft; sorcerers and witches were apparently plaguing the district.[6] The King agreed and appointed as his commissioners a counsellor of the Parlement of Bordeaux and its president—de Lancre and one d'Espaignet. D'Espaignet, or Espagnet as he is sometimes called, whose studies on hermetic philosophy were well known, was a scholar without a very sharp mind, and he took little part in the investigations. He was soon diverted to other matters. The actual carrying out of the repressive measures was, therefore, left to de Lancre and he wrote the *Tableau* with all the files and documents on the cases in front of him.[7]

Labourd seems to have had a bad effect on the judge from the outset. His general remarks about the character of the Basque people are comparable with the wild statements of Aymeric Picaud or those of other detractors. But his remarks need to be borne in mind because they help to explain a number of things. Pierre de Lancre was a member of one of the most typical social classes of his period, the legal *parlement*. As a lawyer he had a profound respect for the monarchy and was always willing to leap to its defence. To his way of thinking there were plenty of geographical, moral and 'folk' reasons why Satan should have chosen the Basque region for his foul machinations and made it the hot-bed of witchcraft in Europe.[8] Labourd was a populous area, but its population spoke a language—Basque—that helped to cut it off from other people to a large extent. Besides, its geographical position on the borders of the ancient kingdom of Navarre and close to other Spanish territories, together with the fact that its partition into dioceses bore no relation to its political divisions, only served to facilitate the meetings of the Devil and his disciples.[9] In spite of its high population, it was not a fertile region and the people of Labourd preferred 'the inconstant labours of the sea' to tilling the ground. The sea, of course, had always been a symbol of inconstancy, treachery and the unexpected and it was not surprising that seamen should be treacherous, inconstant and unpredictable. The people of Labourd, bad tillers of the ground and worse craftsmen, had little love for their country, their wives and children, and since they were neither French nor Spanish they had no established pattern of behaviour to follow.[10]

Seamen returning home for the winter from Canada or New-foundland would spend the money they had saved on having a good time with their families—eating and drinking their earnings away. Poor once more, they would go back to fishing, leaving their wives and children totally unsupported behind them. This would, in turn, lead to the break-up of marriages, immorality and generally godless existence.[11]

De Lancre's book, therefore, starts out from an almost political viewpoint. But his explanation of the growing forces of evil in his time soon becomes a truly fantastic hodge-podge of religion, politics and political geography. He speaks of the emigration of devils from America, Japan and other parts where missionary work had been successful, for instance, and claims that the outcasts had settled happily in the much neglected Labourd region, winning over the souls of women, children and even priests. He was able to assure his readers that a number of English and Scottish travellers who had come to Bordeaux by sea had actually seen great hordes of devils making for France[12]—doubtless in search of more living space, and better accommodation.

In spite of the fact that the Basques in Labourd were a restless and turbulent people, fond of magic and wild dancing, they did not lack good qualities. If they were inclined to be vengeful, they also reacted strongly against treachery and thieving.[13] But what was there to be said for their womenfolk, who ran the country in the absence of their husbands, fiancés and sons? Pierre de Lancre was probably fond of women since he was a man of the world, and this in itself would have made him aware of the dangers of their sex. But we shall not go into his comments on those of Labourd, nor discuss the various local customs which he found extremely distasteful, such as, for instance, the way in which people loved the houses they lived in (even giving up their surnames to take the name of their house instead); the aristocratic spirit of the Basques who always considered themselves lords of their houses, however small they were;[15] and the corruption of the clergy. One point that particularly irritated de Lancre is, however, worth mentioning. The fact that Labourd women acted as sacristans in the churches seemed especially shocking to him in view of their notorious reputation for loose living, unfaithfulness and immorality.[16]

The overture ends and the opera begins. The arrival of the commissioners thoroughly frightened the inhabitants; whole families streamed south towards Lower Navarre, swarming over the Spanish frontier. Some of the fugitives swore that they wanted to make a pilgrimage to Monserrat or Santiago de Compostella, others fled to Newfoundland and elsewhere overseas. The inquisitors on the Spanish side were not quick to identify the fugitives. But the majority stayed behind to be condemned to death, exiled or sentenced in some other way.[17] There was hardly a family which was not implicated, and members of each family accused one another. De Lancre and his assistants took down the evidence as usual without any regard for the age, six, or mentality of those who gave it. Here is a summary of the conclusions he thought he could draw.

Satan's Regal Position at Coven

The meetings of witches and sorcerers were much more frequent in Labourd than anywhere else. Not only were they held on Mondays, which was the usual day for the meetings, but on other days of the week too, and at all hours: at midday, for instance, or during Mass. There were special meetings, however, on the four major festivals of the year, and more than two thousand people were said to have attended one of these, which took place on the coast at Hendaye.[18] In the town named Azcaín meetings were held in the main square itself, and elsewhere at cross-roads or in deserted places such as the *landes* region. According to de Lancre the meeting place was called *lane de Aquelarre*, which means *lane de Bouc*.[19] In fact, *akelarre* itself means the field or plain of the he-goat (from *akerr*: he-goat, and *larre*, *larra*: a field).

The principal meeting places were the region around the La Rhune mountain, the chapel of Saint Esprit and its environs, the parish church of Saint Esprit, the church at Urdax, and a number of private houses. Meetings were even held in the judge's house at Saint Pe which was called 'Barbarenena'.[20]

The Devil usually appeared at these meetings in the form of a he-goat (which is why *aquelarre* is a more appropriate term than the Jewish word *Sabbath*), but the following evidence suggests that he sometimes took other shapes:

1. María de Aguerre, who was thirteen years old, claimed to have seen the Devil as a he-goat, emerging from a great jar and increasing in size once he was out of it.

2. Others said that he took the form of a dark tree trunk, without arms or legs. He had the face of a man but much larger and more frightening, and sat on a seat.

3. Some asserted that they had seen him in the shape of a man with dark clothing and a red and fiery face. But four horns on his head made his general appearance less human; and in some instances, he appeared with two faces like fawns.

4. In one place, de Lancre said, he appeared in the shape of a large black hound, or as an ox or a bronze ox in a recumbent posture.[21]

President Espaignet wrote a Latin poem on the 'Sabbath' for the first edition of his companion's book and this appeared again in the second edition with a French translation. But a wood-cut of the 'Sabbath' illustrating the fourth discourse of Book Two of the *Tableau* must have made a greater impact on readers than Espaignet's poetry or de Lancre's prose. The plate has been torn out of many copies but we reproduce it here (Plate 9). The following analysis of the picture explains the various figures depicted.

(a) Satan, in the form of a he-goat, is sitting on a golden throne. He has five horns, one of them alight, used for lighting all the fires at the meeting.

(b) On his right is the queen of the coven, elegantly dressed and wearing a crown on her head. She has long hair and also sits on a throne; in her hand she holds some snakes. On the left of Satan, on another throne, sits a nun also holding snakes in her hand. Several toads decorate the latter's throne.

(c) A witch and a lesser demon stand before the Devil's throne with a child they have stolen.

(d) (The right-hand foreground of the plate)—Around a rectangular table five devils and five witches prepare to enjoy a banquet of carrion flesh, bodies of hanged men, hearts of unbaptised children, and animals of a repulsive nature.

(e) Lesser witches and sorcerers, who have not taken part in the important ceremonies, stand around in isolated positions.

(f) *Après la pance vient la danse:* witches and devils, having dined well dance around a tree in a disgusting and indecent manner. The devils face outwards and the witches inwards as they dance in a ring, holding hands.

(g) (Upper left-hand corner)—Five witches, in a group under a

161

tree, play different instruments; a bagpipe, a double flute, a violin, a lyre and a lute.

(h) Beneath these six others are dancing, stark naked and facing away from the centre.

(i) Three old witches, skilled in the Black Arts, are preparing philtres and poisons. One of them uses a bellows to brighten up a bonfire in which bones and skulls are burning. The other two are cutting up a frog with a sickle. The one in the middle of the group has snakes in her hand which she is going to skin before throwing them into the great cauldron to make poisons.

(j) Meanwhile some witches are arriving, mostly on sticks and brooms, but some ride on the back of a he-goat (accompanied by two children they have stolen or lured away to offer to Satan) or on a dragon. Snakes and monsters are also flying through the air.

(k) The rich and influential persons who attend the meeting to decide what is going to be done stand on one side in a group: *Les femmes avec des masques pour se tenir toujours à couvert et incognues.*

(l) A group of children, with sticks, stand beside a pool far from the main ceremonies, looking after collections of toads.

Each of the above scenes is discussed at lengthy by de Lancre, who quotes all kinds of depositions and evidence. It is plain that the judge does not doubt the reality of witches' flights and movements for a moment, and he supports his case against those who do by quoting the evidence of a woman called Necato, who had carried a girl of fourteen called Marie de Gastagnalde, Christoval d'Aspilcueta and many others to a 'little sabbath' on the coast at Hendaye.[23]

As if this were not enough, there are also a large number of depositions which allude to the fines to be paid by those who failed to attend the meetings, whether large or small, and whether presided over by the Devil or by a confederate. In connexion with this, de Lancre describes how, when he reached the parish of Urrugne with the commission, the local sorcerers asked the Devil for special protection against the bonfires which they saw being lit all over the country for burning witches. The Devil, when he heard their appeal, stopped going to the covens from June 20th, 1605, to the 22nd. He convinced his followers that he had spent the time arguing with God (whom he referred to scathingly as *Ianicot*; little John). It transpired that he had won the battle, so

1. BC 400 Cabeiric cup with a scene representing Circe offering a potion to Ulysses. The element of caricature illustrates the readiness of artists to express sceptical views about witchcraft subjects.

2. Witches' banquet. Flemish painting of the sixteenth century in Bilbao Museum.

3. Proof state of a print in which a witch is riding to a Sabbath on a monster. The engraving was executed by Bernard Picart in Amsterdam in 1732 after a sixteenth-century drawing by Francesco Mazzola ('il Parmigianino') (1503–1540). The he-goat representing the devil seems to be controlling the witch. Another witch, with spindles in her hair, is carrying a child, whose innocent look contrasts with the evil around it, to the Sabbath.

4

7

5

8

6

4. Baptism by the Devil at the Sabbath. One of the woodcut illustrations to Guazzo's *Compendium maleficarum* (1609).

5. Homage being paid to the Devil, who sits enthroned as King at the Sabbath (Guazzo).

6. Devils, witches and sorcerers dancing (Guazzo).

7. Witch producing a storm (Guazzo).

8. Sorcerers changed into animals cast their spells (Guazzo).

9. The Polish engraver Jan Ziarnko's plate for De Lancre's *Tableau de l'inconstance* (1612). Ziarnko lived and worked in Paris from 1605 to 1629.

10. The second of two engravings made by Jacques Callot of *The temptation of St. Antony*. Callot engraved the scene in 1634 and it was published in the present form the following year. The horned beast with wings symbolising the devil dominates the scene, and goats, toads and serpents also play their inevitable part. But the general atmosphere is theatrical, even humorous, rather than horrifying.

11. David Teniers the younger (1610–1694?) painted several witchcraft scenes, and the present print is based on one of them. It has been ascribed to the artist himself, but the evidence is not conclusive. Another engraving after the same Teniers painting was made by Jean-Jacques Aliamet in the eighteenth century. It has one or two details which do not appear in the present plate, and the witches are less motherly in appearance. But if we cannot be certain what Teniers himself felt about witches in this instance, it is evident that he rejected the horned devil in favour of the winged figure found in some of Dürer's wood-cuts. In following Dürer for his image of the devil, Teniers was doing much the same thing as the judges, witnesses, and perhaps even the witches themselves, at the trials, who often seem to have derived their conception of witchcraft from earlier accounts of it.

12. The witch in Jan van de Velde's illustration of a sorceress casting spells is a graceful figure. Elements in the scene suggest that the artist felt witchcraft to be a comical rather than terrifying subject: a pretext for dramatic light effects and curving lines. In spite of its almost Blake-like quality the print was made in 1624.

13. The plate illustrating the Sabbath from Chapter XI of Laurent Bordelon's *L'histoire des imaginations extravagantes de Monsieur Oufle* in the Amsterdam edition (1710). It is virtually a copy of one of Crespy's plates for the Paris edition of the same year. Crespy, however, made the enthroned he-goat almost cross-eyed: more palpably satirical. Monsieur Oufle himself can be seen in the bottom left-hand corner of the plate. The fool accompanies him in all the illustrations.

14. Goya's *Capricho* 60 'Ensayos' ('Practice'). Witches rehearsing flying techniques, with the traditional he-goat in the background, and distaffs, cats and skulls in the foreground.

15. Goya's *Capricho* 67 'Aguarda que te unten' ('Wait until they've anointed you'). The irony of the artist is evident in the caption. The goat is over-anxious to take to the air.

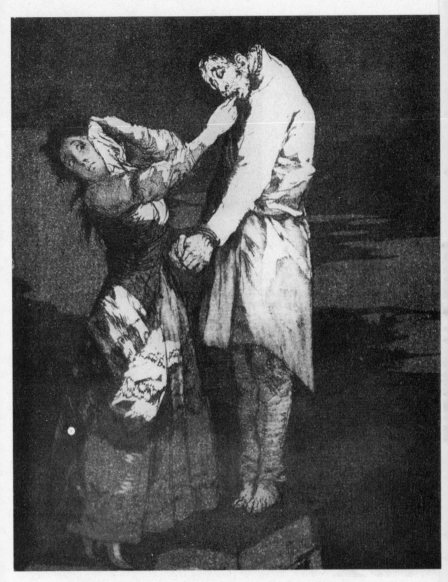

16. Goya's *Capricho* 12 'A caza de dientes' ('Hunting for teeth'). One of the prints inspired by Leandro Fernández de Moratín's satirical commentary on the *Auto de Logroño*. The teeth and fat of the hanged were commonly used as materials for spells.

17. Goya's *Capricho* 68 'Linda maestra' ('Attractive teacher'). The artist again mocks the witches on the way to the Sabbath in his caption.

18. The image of the witch in popular woodcuts probably dating from the early nineteenth century in England.

the sorcerers and witches would not be harmed. This very interesting piece of legal information was made known by two witches skilled in the Black Arts, one of whom was executed—Marissans de Tartas and Marierchiquerra de Machinena.[24]

In all written accounts of witchcraft there is a striking tendency to mix realistic and fantastic detail. Some of the accused say that the 'Sabbath' will disappear if certain words are spoken or that one can avoid going by acting in a religious way. Marie de La Ralde (or rather, Larralde) claimed that this was the case, and she had been taken to the meetings ever since she was ten years old, albeit on foot, by Marissans de Tartas. Jannete d'Abadie from Ciboure made similar assertions. To avoid going, she stayed in the church and kept vigil with other girls; however, the Devil robbed her of a fig, which she wore to keep him off, and she was at his mercy once more.[25]

The Basque country is a land of seafaring people; it rains a great deal and there are violent storms in the autumn. Its inhabitants would, therefore, be only too willing to believe that the majority of disasters, caused by storms on land or sea, were due to witches. Jannete d'Abadie claimed that her instructress, Graciane, had carried her to Newfoundland, where she had seen many people from Labourd. The witches there had caused a ship belonging to Miguel Chorena (more correctly Miguelchorena) from Ciboure to founder. Its owner was also a sorcerer and he had contributed to its shipwreck, for reasons which remain unexplained.[26]

Adolescent girls, and girls and boys between five and twelve years old, agreed that they had attended meetings and had flown through the air. The details they gave were corroborated by the evidence of old women accused of witchcraft, taken down under threat of torture or while they were being subjected to it.[27]

Even when in prison the witches managed to go to the 'Sabbath', as a girl of fifteen or sixteen called 'Dojartzabal' from Azcaín revealed.[28] The same girl declared that when the Devil wanted to take young girls to the 'Sabbath' he placed an image of them in their mother's arms as a substitute. This had happened in the girl's own case since she had found her double with her mother when she had returned on one occasion.[29]

The master of the house of Ioanissena who suspected his serving-girl of being a witch and attending meetings, decided one night to tie her to a table-leg and stay up all night, preventing her from going to sleep. . . . Yet in spite of all this, it was proved that she had gone.[30]

De Lancre spends a whole chapter on the way in which witches attended the Sabbath, and then moves on to ointments. He has very little concrete to say about their composition but a great deal of highly imaginative information about their effects.[31] He cannot tell us much about poisons either. It always seems to be a question of some 'greenish and rather thick water' (*eau un peu épaisse et verdastre*), 'a little oil or grease' (*quelque huyle ou graisse*), solid and liquid poisons made out of toads for the purpose of ruining fruit crops, and even poison in powder form made out of grilled toads which, when mixed with clouds, harms fruit trees. The strongest poison was used for killing and even the old and skilled witches, those best able to changes themselves into beasts and perform other feats, were cautious with it.[32] Powder, cruses of ointment and bottles of liquid poison were assiduously sought. But the judge confesses that he could never find the slightest trace of them for examination purposes.[33] Ultimately, as so often, real experience is lacking, in spite of the professional air which the investigations tend to have. De Lancre, like Avellaneda, even believed himself to have been a victim of the machinations of the Devil.

In September 1609 he was staying in Saint Pé in the castle of d'Amou, who was the hysterical individual responsible for petitioning the king to take action against witches, and had blood sucked from his thigh whilst in bed. During the night of September 24th, the Devil came to the place where the judge was residing, to meet a witch called Sansinena. Then he unsuccessfully tried to enter the judge's room, but despite the assistance of three skilful witches (Sansinena was one of them) he was unable to do him harm. They said two Black Masses, one in the castle kitchen, and then went to the house in which one of the prosecuting fiscals was carrying on his work. From there they went back to d'Amou's castle where Sansinena and the old widows Arosteguy and Lurensena put a rope round the neck of the master of the house and did other unpleasant things to him. '*Or de tout cela,*' de Lancre says in conclusion, '*le sieur d'Amou ne moy n'en sentimes jamais rien.*' ('Apart from all this, neither d'Amou nor I felt anything at all.') Fortunately, there was always the invaluable evidence of two girls who had been involved in the whole business.[34] And so the details continue to pile up.

The witches' meeting-place was, then, an imaginary place from one point of view, and a spot where country people met, from another. What is most in doubt when we pose the whole problem of the 'reality' of the 'Sabbath' is what actually took place at these meetings. In the depositions of Catherine de Barrendeguy, or Cathalin de Bardos, a woman aged sixty from the parish of Hatso, it was stated that Catherine had seen Marie Pipy d'Olgaray acting as cup-bearer, and Joannes d'Olgaray as chief butler, to the Devil, at the 'Sabbath'. It was also revealed that Hirigoien, the vicar of the parish, was often to be seen dancing with two women, Marie de Haussy and another woman called Salbouharia, as were other priests also. When the witches wished to implicate someone in their activities, it was said that he or she was present but stood still. It was in this way that Petry de Lysalde, Estebanot de Bourhary and Jeanne Biscarrena became involved.[35]

The Church as Model for the 'Sabbath'

The 'Sabbath' not only imitates a royal court with its king and queen, cup-bearers, butlers, and other high dignitaries, it also resembles a cathedral or a church in which there are other dignitaries and where different functions take place. If one is sceptical of everything that de Lancre says, one is naturally suspicious of his statements about satanic masses and Devil-worship based on the services of the Christian church.

According to him, the Devil causes churches and altars to appear with music, small bells—not large ones—and devils decked out as saints. The dignitaries reach the rank of bishop, and sub-deacons, deacons and priests serve Mass. Candles and incense are used for the service, and water is sprinkled from a thurifer. There is an offertory, a sermon, a blessing over the equivalents of bread and wine and even an *ite missa est*. So that nothing should be missing there are even false martyrs in the organisation.[36] The details may vary but in essence the rite is the same: Christian ritual is so slavishly imitated that even the cerements which are still put in the family vaults in some Basque churches today, have their counterpart in the rites of the Devil, as do tapers and other things.[37] As if this were not enough, there are also references to well-known people in the satanic cult.

In Saint Pé, young Lancinena had been seen wearing a kind of tiara and pretending to be a bishop, dancing with the Devil and receiving homage.[38] But sometimes renegade priests officiated. A young man from St Jean de Luz claimed to have seen Maistre Jean Souhardibels saying a Black Mass in Cohandia and holding a Black Host; others denounced Martin Detcheguaray and a man called Escola, both clergymen, and other priests, who were even better known as sorcerers.[39] It is hardly surprising that de Lancre's investigations led to the detention, trial and torture of several of them.

The second discourse of Book Two of the *Tableau* is largely concerned with clergy who were accused of witchcraft. According to de Lancre, the region had been (as it is today) one of the most religious parts of France. Men were separated from women in the churches; the former sitting in the side aisles at the edge of the nave, as in the boxes at a theatre, and the latter praying over their families' vaults. But outward acts are no good if the spirit behind them is evil. De Lancre was scandalised by the familiarity of priests with their female sacristans and the ladies of their congregation, their fondness for dancing, playing *pelota*, and wearing military dress with sword and lance when going to local festivals.[40] At first he dared not lay hands on members of such a highly respected class. But finally he was given grounds for taking action by an old priest from Azcaín, called Arguibel, who was probably slightly mad.[41]

Arguibel confessed that he had given up worshipping the Devil some fifteen or sixteen years previously. But subsequently he had been so tormented by the Devil that he had been almost driven out of his wits, and his family hoped that they would be able to save him by alleging he was mad or not responsible for his actions. In this state, Arguibel confessed to having gone to the 'Sabbath', and to doing all the evil things that were said to be done on these occasions. He signed three declarations and reaffirmed them, when interrogated in the presence of the Vicar-General of the Diocese of Bayonne. He was unfrocked by the Bishop of Acqs (Dax) in the church of the Saint Esprit de Bayonne in the absence of the Bishop of his own diocese, and condemned and put to death in his own town as an example to others (*pour servir d'exemple*). The case had repercussions. Many priests used any pretext to escape.[42] But de Lancre, on the basis of evidence given by children, was still able to catch seven of the most notable priests from the best parishes in Labourd.

Amongst these an old man called 'Migalena', who was over sixty, and a young man called 'Maistre Pierre Bocal', both from Ciboure, were accused of still more serious crimes: of having said Mass in their parishes with feigned devotion after saying it at the 'Sabbath'. Bocal, three nights after singing his first real Mass, said a Black Mass, which was not so surprising since all his family were notorious witches and sorcerers. He suffered a similar fate to that of Arguibel. It seems that the old vicar of Ciboure was quite mad when he died, but de Lancre did not notice this.[43]

Credulity and lack of Critical Approach

When the period of time allotted to the commission came to an end—it was always fixed in advance—there were five priests under trial and awaiting sentence. An appeal was made and three were able to escape, so that the death sentence which the judge intended to pass was not carried out.[44]

Pierre de Lancre, like many of his predecessors in the same position, relied above all on the depositions of children, old people and individuals he had tortured. He probably could not understand Basque, for sometimes he transcribes names incorrectly. At other times he copies down Basque words which he takes at their face value, without interpreting them in the wider context of the declaration in which they appear.

Thus he asserts that the sorcerers were mocking Christian practices, when they crossed themselves with the following words:

> *In nomine Patrica, Aragueaco*
> *Petrica, Agora, Agora Valentia*
> *Iouanda goure gaitz goustia.*

And he translates the rhyme as follows:

> *Au nom de Patrique, Petrique d'Arragon,*
> *a cette heure, a cette heure Valence,*
> *tout nostre mal ' est passé.*

The translation and the rhyme may seem mere doggerel but

167

Pierre de Lancre could find a sinister explanation for anything. Three languages are used in the rhyme: Latin in the first line, Spanish in the second, and Basque in the third . . . and according to de Lancre the purpose of this was to mock the Trinity, like making the sign of the Cross with the left hand.

A similar jingle is:

> *In nomine Patrica, Aragueaco, Petrica,*
> *Castellaco Ianicot, equidac ipordian pot.*
> *(Au nom de Patrique, Petrique d'Aragon, Iannicot*
> *de Castille faietes moy un baiser au derrière)*[45]

Both rhymes probably allude to the wars between King Pedro of Aragon and Juan of Castile in the fifteenth century, when the people of Labourd supported the former. It is difficult to understand how such snatches of satirical poetry with historical allusions came to have such esoteric interpretations when they reached the judge's files.

Anyone as uncritical as de Lancre was obviously bound to be deceived time and again. But the excesses of officious individuals made even him suspicious sometimes, although he never seems to have had any qualms about the extraordinary nature of the depositions or evidence in his cases.

De Lancre tells us that at the beginning of September 1610 a quack called Don Pedro, a native of Pamplona with a knowledge of Basque, arrived in the town of Itchasou from Spain. This quack, apart from having the usual gifts of his kind, knew a lot about witches. The local parish priest thought that he might be capable of denouncing witches as well as curing people. However, he abused his powers to such an extent that an official complaint was lodged against him with the Bayonne authorities and he fled the town.[46]

Others enjoyed even greater prestige. According to de Lancre a foreign surgeon, living in Bayonne, became quite an expert at detecting the marks which sorcerers were supposed to have and in which the judge believed implicitly. This surgeon attended many trials in the company of a girl of seventeen, called Morguy, who had been taken to several 'Sabbaths'. The surgeon examined the witches, and Morguy the girls and young men who were witnesses. The former bandaged the eyes of the witches he was to examine and stuck a needle into them. If he managed to find an insensitive spot, guilt was established. Morguy did much the same with the girls, putting the needle into the place where the mark was supposed to be. De Lancre relates how some of these trials were carried out in the presence of the Governor of Labourd, Gramont, and the French Ambassador to Spain, Vausselas and his wife. The most insensitive person they found was twenty-four-year-old Jeanette de Belloc,[47] nicknamed 'Atsoua' (that is 'the old woman'), who had first been the protégée of another witch called 'Oylarchahar' and then of Marie Martin de Adamcehorena. Her statements followed the usual pattern.[48]

With the assistance of people such as these, and the evidence of children as the basis of his investigations, de Lancre managed to establish that there were more than three thousand people with the witches' mark in Labourd. The mark could not be attributed to any illness and was, therefore, considered to be invaluable as evidence in a witch-trial.[49] Yet when specific cases arose, de Lancre was as usual quite unable to establish the proof for himself. He was, for example, unable to see the toad's foot, which was said to be marked in the left eye of witches in Biarritz, nor other marks which witnesses, like 'Atsoua' herself, claimed to see.[50]

It is not possible to examine all the details of the points made by de Lancre in his treatises. It should not be forgotten, however, that there were some complaints about the judge who so plagued the Labourd region. The judge and his assistants had a number of very worrying moments.[51] It has sometimes been argued that this witch-hunt was really a political drive to establish the power of the central authorities. But however you look at him, de Lancre emerges as one of the most absurd figures of the movement to repress witchcraft, not so much for the astonishing things he says as for the way in which he says them; mixing a kind of Gascon 'bonhomie' with the most blatant superstition. The only difference between his superstitious beliefs and those of his unfortunate victims was that his were hidden under a layer of learning which seemed relatively extensive and profound.

De Lancre was able to establish the fact that witchcraft is the same wherever it is found: in Italy, Germany, France or even Spain (judging from the investigations of the inquisitors at Logroño) . . .[52] And this we can accept. However, de Lancre went on to expand his theories in a way that is interesting but more debatable. Drawing on his knowledge of Jewish and pagan writers, and particularly of books on the peoples of the New World, de Lancre reached the conclusion that the Devil always tries to imitate Christ, his church and its ceremonies in his own way.[53] Clearly a man who starts out with this belief will be rather un-critical in matters of religious morphology. And in this instance the morphological problem is exceptionally important. In subse-quent chapters we shall see how Spanish authors treated it in a subtler, more penetrating manner.

CHAPTER 13

THE WITCHES OF ZUGARRAMURDI

The structure of the supposed witches' 'sect' – Acts committed by its members

The Structure of the Supposed Witches' 'Sect'

A good deal of published material is available on the sorceresses and witches who were tried by the inquisitors of Logroño while de Lancre was extirpating witchcraft in Labourd, on the other side of the frontier. These were the witches whose meetings were held in Zugarramurdi and who died in the auto-da-fé of 1610. In spite of the extent of the material, much of it lacks interest, because it only repeats or summarises what had already been stated in the account of the trials published in Logroño by Juan de Mongastón shortly after they actually took place. This account is quite well known since the annotated edition of it by the eighteenth-century Spanish dramatist, Leandro Fernández de Moratín, has been reprinted on a number of occasions.[1] In its time, Moratín's edition seemed incredibly daring and irreverent and Menéndez y Pelayo described his comments as, 'Voltairean to the core, the true spiritual descendants of the *Dictionnaire philosophique*.'[2] It must be admitted, however, that on matters of witchcraft Moratín, with his rudimentary anti-clericalism, was not nearly as shrewd as Voltaire, for he lacked the Frenchman's acute historical sense. Moratín's notes too often miss the mark because the subject did not lend itself to the kind of humour which most suited him. Furthermore, Moratín was not very well acquainted

171

with developments which had taken place during the trials themselves.

We know now that the Inquisition was compelled to take action, in this as in other cases, by the civil authorities. The latter had felt impelled to do something because of the wave of panic which had swept through the Basque country (as it did from time to time), affecting more particularly the extreme north-western area of Navarre which lies next to the Labourd region. The civil authorities had already arrested large numbers of people and executed one or two when the Supreme Inquisition instructed the tribunal at Logroño to carry out an investigation.

An inquisitor named Don Juan Valle Alvarado was put in charge. He spent several months in Zugarramurdi and collected numerous statements; nearly three hundred people were under suspicion of crimes of witchcraft as a result of these accusations, not counting children. Out of these, forty, who seemed more obviously guilty, were arrested and taken to Logroño. About June 8th, 1610, a meeting was held in Logroño attended by Licentiate Juan de Valle Alvarado and his colleagues Don Alonso Becerra Holguín of the Order of Alcántara, who was the senior member, and Licentiate Alonso de Salazar y Frías. The ordinary of the diocese and four advisers were also present. It appears that as early as this meeting, there was a difference of opinion with Salazar who wanted more evidence.[3]

Salazar's colleagues did not share his scruples. They accepted the testimony and accusations of witnesses at their face value and went ahead with the trial. Subsequently, an extraordinary account of the sorcerers' and witches' activities was published, and it was on this that Moratín later poured ridicule, criticising the three judges and everything about the affair. Salazar's disagreement with the verdict, and his sharp critical sense, were not revealed until documents were discovered some time after he had been made an object of ridicule in company with the other judges.

Dr Vergara de Porres and Fray Gaspar de Palencia, whose licence to print and official approbation of the book appear in the best known, early edition of the *Account* of the trials,[4] are unanimous in praising the views put forward. But we must examine the work itself.

It is set out in a much simpler and more direct manner than Pierre de Lancre's Labourd account, which is long-winded, full of asides and irrelevancies, and weighed down with biblical and non-biblical references. The statements of those on trial and the evidence of the witnesses are set out with admirable clarity, and the book is so coherent that it gives a sharper picture than any other document of the sectarian nature of those who practise witchcraft, as a summary will show. It also points out the remarkable similarity between their activities and the mystery-religions of classical antiquity (*mysteria*, or, in the singular *mysterium*, Greek μυστήριον).

The main conclusions reached can be listed as follows:

a. Witchcraft had, in the first place, its propaganda organisation. This consisted of the older and more senior sorcerers, who were considered past masters of the Black Arts. These handed on the dogmas of the sect to others, for the ideology of the group was already fully formulated and far from being in process of evolution. Propaganda was carried out among people of a ripe enough age and intellect to promise to renounce God, but until they actually made their vows those under instruction were not taken to the 'Field of the He-Goat' (the *Aquelarre* or Sabbath): 'for the Devil whom they recognise as their Lord and God, usually appears at the Sabbath in the form of a He-goat.'[5]

b. Once the vow had been made, the ceremonial presentation of the novice took place. Two or three hours before midnight the Master of the Novices went to fetch him. He anointed him and they flew together to the 'field appointed for their meetings'. In the case of Zugarramurdi, a Navarre town on the borders of the Labourd region whence many of the witches tried at Logroño came, the 'field' actually existed. It lay outside a large cave or subterranean tunnel—a veritable cathedral for pagan rites and the cult of Satan. A river called the stream of Hell (*Infernukoerreka*) ran through it and there was a higher part on which, tradition has it, the Devil's throne used to stand.[6] The Devil's actual appearance was described in great detail. He would be 'sitting on a seat which sometimes seems to be made of gold, sometimes of black wood, looking very regal, imperious and severe . . . and with a sad, ugly or irate expression on his countenance'.[7] It is difficult to see how this kind of Gothic gargoyle, described in the *Account*, could have attracted anybody. But at all events the witch or sorcerer in charge of the instruction of the novice presented the latter to him and the formal act of renunciation was made: first of God, then of the Blessed Virgin, the saints, baptism and confirmation, parents and god-parents, the Christian faith and those who profess it. After the renunciation the neophyte worshipped the Devil and gave him an obscene kiss.

When the ceremony of adoration was over, the Devil marked the

173

novice with his finger nail, drawing blood which was caught in a vessel. The novice was also marked in the pupil of his eye with the form of a toad.

The master or mistress of the initiate was paid the price of the new slave in silver pieces, which tended to vanish if not spent within twenty-four hours. Then the initiate was given a toad, which had been kept in the charge of his instructress for some time, as a kind of guardian angel. 'When the renunciation has been made, the Devil and the other senior sorcerers present warn the novice not to name Jesus Christ or the Blessed Virgin Mary, nor cross himself nor make the sign of the cross.'[8]

c. The method of recruitment amongst children was different. They were lured to the 'Sabbath' by all kinds of false promises (or by giving them apples, nuts or sweets) once they had reached the age of consent, that is from the age of five or six upwards.

They were sometimes brought against their will, since the youngest were snatched from their beds whenever their parents had omitted to make the sign of the cross over them or to protect them from attack with holy water or relics. Children, like the novices, were put in charge of instructors and given a great number of toads to look after. These were used for making poisons and had to be treated with all due respect and veneration.

d. When the novices had made good progress in doing evil they were allowed to make poisons, but, before they were ready for this work, the Devil's blessing—a highly complicated affair—had to be administered. After this they were given sole charge of the toads that had been supervised by their masters from the time of their renunciation. 'From that time forward they are no longer under the orders of their masters, they feed their toads on their own and anoint themselves and go to the "Sabbath" unaccompanied, no longer needing their sponsors to go with them: they are also initiated into greater secrets and evils which are withheld from uninitiated sorcerers.'[10]

So far, then, we have information about the following grades of sorcerers within the sect:

1. Children who were taken by force to attend meetings (up to five years old).
2. Children who consented to be taken (from five or six onwards).
3. Older novices prepared to make their renunciation.
4. Neophytes who have made their renunciation.

All these categories were under supervision. Unsupervised we have:

5. Initiates in the first grade: makers of spells and poisons.
6. Initiates in the second grade: tutors, those in charge of novices and propagandists.
7. Senior sorcerers and witches.

At the auto-da-fé at Logroño a number of these masters and persons with 'high offices' at the Devil's court received various sentences. According to the published account, a woman called Graciana de Barrenechea was 'Queen of the Sabbath' at Zugarramurdi. She was probably getting on in years and was the wife of Miguel de Goyburu (who had the post of 'king'), and the mother of two girls who were also accused of being involved: Estevanía and María de Yriart. In charge of the children was Martín de Vizcar, and Joanes de Echalar was the executioner responsible for carrying out the Devil's sentences. The principal senior witches were María de Zozoya, who was burnt to death, and María Chipia, the aunt on her mother's side of a witch called María de Iureteguia. The latter played an important part in the trials, as we shall see.

In addition to these high offices there were also rather more peaceful occupations available. Joanes de Goyburu or Miguel himself played the *txistu* (a flute with three holes) to accompany the dancing and Juan de Sansin, for instance, banged the drum.[11] This latter was a cousin of the Goyburus who did not actually live in Zugarramurdi itself, but at a place two miles outside. At cockcrow they all had to fly off home.

Acts Committed by Sect Members

This is all the published account tells us about the peculiar hierarchy of the sect of witches in Zugarramurdi and neighbouring towns. As far as the activities of the witches are concerned, the account speaks of two classes of 'mysteries': one more important than the other.

Every Friday throughout the year there were ordinary meetings. But on the nights before certain festivals—Christmas, Easter and Whitsun, Epiphany, the Assumption, Corpus Christi, All Saints, the Purification, the Assumption and Nativity of the Virgin Mary, and St John's Day—more solemn feasts for the worship of the Devil took place. At these high feasts the Devil officiated and celebrated Mass himself, aided by lesser devils. He preached a sermon to the faithful on the usual lines, but in the Basque language, as a local priest of those or more recent times would have done. The details of the Mass, and the ceremonial adoration which followed it, are disgusting and seem to be the product of a perverted mind. The same is true of the physical union of the Devil with his flock; with men and women, old men and children.[12] In addition to the major and minor feasts, there were 'Sabbaths' of first, second and third class category, just as in village society there are masses, funeral services and so forth.

But apart from true acts of sacrilege, the sorcerers and witches of Zugarramurdi performed other acts which are more universal in the history of magic and witchcraft. These included:

1. Metamorphosis.

'Apart from dancing when they are attending the "Sabbath", they enjoy changing into different shapes so as not to be recognised and going out to frighten and hurt travellers. For the Devil, it seems, changes them into swine, goats and sheep, mares and other animals, whatever best suits his purpose.'

A typical case of transformation was that of María Presona who went out with other witches to frighten Martín de Amayur, a miller. The latter defended himself with a stick and struck and hurt a witch quite seriously. Equally typical is the case of the witches who set out to frighten three men from Zugarramurdi itself.[13]

2. Storms.

As Zugarramurdi is not very far, as the crow flies, from the Cantabrian sea, the witches who made it their centre frequently caused storms to wreck the ships entering or leaving the harbour at St Jean de Luz. On one occasion, according to certain depositions, some witches saw how the Devil himself produced storms:

'The Devil suddenly jumped backwards and swinging round to his left, raised that hand into the air and gave his blessing, calling out with a loud and hoarse voice: "Air, air, air." And immediately a storm arose with winds rushing from every direction, and carrying the ships before them on collision courses. . . .'[14]

Other storms were produced to ruin wheat and fruit, but it was only necessary to pronounce the name of Jesus to disperse them. Calling on His name put an end to situations which were far more horrible, such as the one described in the following passage:

'And María de Echalecu relates that after she had eaten, Queen Graciana de Barrenechea carried her through the air to a field where there was a cave and left her alone. She went towards the cave and after a little while the afore-mentioned Graciana and Estevania de Tellechea came out of the cave carrying the Devil between them in their arms. And his face was very terrifying, and all three of them came towards the place where she was. And being very afraid, she called out the name of Jesus and at once they all disappeared. And finding herself alone she realised that she was in the field called Berroscoberro, where the sorcerers and witches held their meetings. . . .'[15]

3. *Spells against crops and animals.*

'Many times in the course of the year, whenever the fruit or crops are beginning to flourish, they make powders and poisons. And to this end, the Devil chooses out those to whom he has given the power and the appropriate rank for making poisons, and he tells them the day on which they must make them. He divides the fields up amongst them, so that they can go forth in groups looking for reptiles and other things used for making poisons. And the next day, in the morning, they go forth with spades and sacks, and the Devil and his servants appear before them and go with them into the fields and the darkest and most cavernous places. And they seek out large numbers of snakes and toads, lizards and newts, slugs, snails and puff-balls. And having collected them in their sacks, they take them to their houses and sometimes there (in company with the Devil) and sometimes at the "Sabbath" they devise and make their poisons.'

The description which follows of the way in which they mass-manufactured their powders and ointments is straight out of Goya:[16]

'Once their work is done they leave the "Sabbath" in the shape of various animals led by the Devil, with Miguel de Goyburu carrying the cauldron and the magic powders. These they scatter over the places they wish to damage while the Devil says, "Powder, powder, ruin everything" or "Let half be ruined", and the more important sorcerers and witches repeat after him, "Let all (or half) be lost with the exception of anything that belongs to me".'[17]

According to the published account these spells were particularly made when a wind called 'Egoya' was blowing. This is the southerly wind which blows early in the autumn ('Egoa'). It is also called *sorguin aizia* or *wind of the witches*.[18] They used the powder to ruin the chestnut and apple crops, and the wheat.

4. Spells cast on people.

The ability to cause people to fall ill and even die was also attributed to the sorcerers and witches. Graciana de Barrenechea, as Queen of the 'Sabbath', had many victims to her credit, one of them being a rival for the Devil's love, Marijuan de Odia. Death was caused by giving a powder, wrapped in a toad's skin, to the person it was desired to kill, or by anointing them with ointment, pronouncing at the same time the following words: 'May the Lord make you sicken and die (or give you such and such an illness for so long)'.[19]

Not even members of the same family as the witch were always safe from the spells. If we are to believe the accounts of the trials, Miguel de Goyburu, Graciana de Barrenechea, her daughters Estevania de Tellechea and others, all killed close relatives. María Presona and María Ioanto, who were sisters, were accused of killing their son and daughter respectively.[20]

5. Vampirism and eating the flesh of the dead.

The account of the trials relates several horrible cases of vampirism, mainly involving children. The fear of witches experienced by children and their families must have produced states of collective terror in the region at that period. Those who were not threatened with loss of life or health were carried off to the meetings where they were made to suffer terribly.

To prevent children being stolen from their houses, the Vicar of Vera de Bidasoa is said to have taken them to his own house, letting as many as forty children sleep in one of the larger rooms. Before they went to bed, the vicar himself blessed them and they slept peacefully, despite the fact that the Devil ordered the meetings to be held near the vicar's house.

'And they went to the house every night to see if they could steal them away, going in through the front door (although it was locked)

178

and through the window, and making a great noise and terrifying all who were in the house. They laughed with glee to see the great pains taken by the Vicar who, clad in a cope and stole and with a book in one hand and a thurifer in the other, sprinkled holy water and adjured all the young children to remain in their beds. More than thirty of the sorcerers went up to the top of the roof and made a great din, breaking many tiles, because they were unable to steal away the children.'[21]

On one occasion, however, the Vicar was careless and the children were carried off to the 'Sabbath' and punished, according to the evidence of María Juanto, a witch who lived in Vera.

Other details of the declarations were no less realistic superficially. The trials, consequently, were very lengthy affairs and it took a whole day merely to read the sentences with all the charges. The auto-da-fé in Logroño lasted two whole days and it was on November 8th, 1610, that the witches and sorcerers finally heard their sentences.

Eighteen of the accused were reconciled with the Church, after confessing their guilt and asking for mercy with tears in their eyes. As a sign of magnanimity, the inquisitors removed the *sanbenito* (the gown worn by guilty persons) from María de Iureteguia in the middle of the auto itself. On the other hand, María Zozaya, an elderly lady who also confessed her guilt, perished in the fire with six others, who had refused to confess. Effigies of five others, who died before the auto took place, were burnt in the course of it. In fact, by comparison with earlier trials and those of de Lancre, this was not an excessively harsh affair, despite the fuss there has been about it in modern times, and the outcry that was made when the account we have quoted was published. Any civil tribunal would certainly have punished severely the crimes which the sorcerers were accused of committing, had it found them guilty.

179

CHAPTER 14

PRACTICAL AND THEORETICAL CONSEQUENCES OF THE ZUGARRAMURDI TRIALS

The theories of Pedro de Valencia – The action taken by Inquisitor Alonso de Salazar y Frías

The Theories of Pedro de Valencia

Ever since the *Malleus Maleficarum* was first published, and every time a similar work has appeared in print, attack and counter attack have followed almost at once, giving rise to some lively polemics. Devout people in the Middle Ages and the beginning of the modern era accepted without question the same dogmas as Catholics today. Belief in witchcraft, however, has varied in different sections of society at different periods.

The masses were sometimes inclined to panic and give way to their irrational fears. The civil authorities, local, regional, and even national, allowed the feelings of the majority to govern their actions. The Spanish Inquisition was as cautious and moderate as it could be under the circumstances. But its caution meant that the views of several of its members, and those of other persons whose advice it asked, were not published when they were in conflict with generally accepted opinions. They were put away in archives which were not easily accessible and, in consequence, it has only been possible in modern times to assess the real extent of the Inquisition's moderation on questions of witchcraft—a moderation which is in strong contrast to its severity towards people of Jewish persuasions and the more intellectual heretics.

Among the various writings of an advisory nature based on the accounts of the trials of 1610 there are two works by the great Spanish humanist, Pedro de Valencia, which have been available in print for some time.[1] Even before they were published two scholars made good use of them.[2] The second of Pedro de Valencia's pieces is merely a summary of the account of the trial with brief comments.[3] And even there, the opinions he expresses are full of critical strictures, as we shall see. But his first work gives an analysis of the facts from various hypothetical points of view which is of even greater critical value and historical interest. It is worth examining here.

Pedro de Valencia begins by expressing regret that accounts of trials such as the one under review, should be circulating in print. Not only do they give a bad name to the mountainous provinces of the north, in which live so many persons of noble birth who are obedient to the Catholic Church, but they also bring bad examples to people's notice which may lead them astray. Furthermore, if parts of the accounts are of doubtful veracity or actually false, the Holy Office itself may be discredited. After these preliminary observations, which are put in the most tactful and diplomatic manner,[4] Pedro de Valencia comes to the very heart of the matter. Leaving the general questions on one side, he begins by considering the possibility that the Zugarramurdi meetings are merely real gatherings of vicious people who 'have invented those meetings and evil mysteries—in which one person, the boldest of them all, pretends to be Satan himself and puts on the horns and other foul and obscene attire which are referred to—because they desire to commit fornication, adultery or sodomy'.[5]

There would be nothing miraculous about their actions if this were the case; the journey to the 'Sabbath' would be made 'on foot' by all those attending, and deaths would be caused by poisons. For the sake of secrecy, the pattern of the pagan mysteries, which took place under cover of silence and darkness, would be followed.[6]

At this point, Pedro de Valencia makes use of his scholarly knowledge of Greek civilisation, and he compares the 'Sabbath' of the Basques with the bacchanals, especially those described by Euripides.[7]

The Spanish translation of the passage from *The Bacchi*, which Pedro de Valencia quotes for the sake of comparison, is a lively one.[8] A shepherd brings a message to Pentheus when the latter is having a discussion with Dionysus himself, who has lately escaped from prison. And the holy fury of the Bacchantes he describes is certainly on a par with the lust for evil attributed to the *sorguiñak* (or Basque witches) when, with the Devil at their head, they go through fields and woods and over mountains, spreading evil everywhere in their train. The bacchanals, like the witches' 'Sabbaths', originally took place at night, and women play an equally important role in both. Euripides makes Pentheus say: 'This is dangerous for women, and proper for vice.' Τοῦτ ἐς γυναῖκας δόλιον ἔστι καὶ σαδρόν.[9]

The accounts of these bacchanals celebrated in a mythical period—and without historical foundation according to some scholars[10]—are not the only examples quoted by Pedro de Valencia in his attempt to give a concrete explanation of the activities of witches. He also refers to the famous case of the bacchanals which took place in Rome in 180 BC.[11] Livy gives an account of these but their occurrence remains largely unexplained even today.[12] It appears that they were not unconnected with the political struggles of the time, and the repressive measures carried out (involving women of the highest Roman families) were provoked by a wave of terror, fear of witchcraft and poisonings which arose as a result of the civil dissensions.

The Dionysian mysteries, which Pedro de Valencia describes as 'works of man and natural inventions of seducers, consisting of crimes and evil deeds of men and women, without visible magic or supernatural agency being involved,'[13] provide the Spaniard with a parallel case to the ones with which he is concerned. He also considers the possibility that some of the actions which are attributed to sorcerers and witches may be the product of mental aberrations and illnesses, including the following which were already known in classical antiquity:

1. Visions caused by 'melancholia' or sickness of mind (*morbum imaginosum*).
2. The desire to eat revolting foods, as a result of an illness which the Greeks called κίσσα or κίττα from the name of the magpie which likes such things. Valencia does not consider this a probable explanation, although he brings it forward.[14]

After considering the acts of witches as something real, which can be explained in various ways, Valencia goes on to discuss a second possible view. According to this the pact with the Devil is truly made, but everything that is said to take place at the meetings—sexual intercourse, banquets, etc.—is only a vision that occurs in dreams brought on by the Devil with ointments, poisons and other substances. Pedro de Valencia knows of several cases of witches who were induced, by way of experiment, to fall into a deep sleep—amongst them the one mentioned by Dr Laguna. Valencia even reaches the conclusion that parts of the visions may simply be due to the natural powers of ointments 'without the Devil's intervention at all'. In order to illustrate his point, Valencia again has recourse to his classical learning, recalling a number of cases of people who were taking part in religious cults (always of mystery-religions), and claimed to have had terrifying dreams brought on, amongst other things, by noises and perfumes.[15]

Finally, he puts forward the generally accepted view, which had led to the condemnation of those on trial at Logroño, and many others. According to this, everything to do with witchcraft is real down to the last detail. Valencia considers this opinion to be particularly dangerous when combined with the dream-state theory. By sometimes taking one point of view and sometimes another, guilty parties would have been able to accuse those who were basically innocent, and all kinds of extremely confusing situations might have arisen.[16]

In his second discourse Pedro de Valencia favours the first of the theories he advances—that wild orgies may have been taking place at night—as most probably the right one. 'The evidence of all my senses leads me to feel that the meetings have been between men and women who have come together for the same reasons they have always come together; to commit sins of the flesh.' Everything that takes place at the Sabbath is human and natural, and the Devil plays no larger a part in the proceedings than he does in every evil action committed by man. Pedro de Valencia goes no further than this. Had he developed his theories beyond this point, he would almost inevitably have reached the same conclusions as some modern writers, who see witchcraft as a relic of paganism in both form and content.

However, the concrete investigations which were carried out shortly afterwards led in a different direction.

The Action taken by Inquisitor Alonso de Salazar y Frías

One of the three judges who had presided at the 1610 trials, the inquisitor Alonso de Salazar y Frías, was commissioned by the Supreme Tribunal of the Inquisition to make further investigations after he had disagreed with the other judges over the conduct of the proceedings and the final verdict. He spent some time visiting towns in the basin of the River Ezcurra (a tributary of the Bidasoa), others in the Baztán valley, and the five main towns in the north of Navarre as well as some smaller ones. He established a sort of office in Santesteban so as to be able to carry out in the most efficient way possible the instructions of the edict pronounced by the Inquisition on March 26th, 1611—perhaps as a result of the consultations which had taken place and the advice given by men like Pedro de Valencia.[17]

In the course of his examination of the cases, interrogation of the accused, and frank conversations with the general public, he gradually reached the conclusion that the majority of acts attributed to witches in that particular instance never really occurred. This is apparent in a number of documents in Salazar's handwriting which have been preserved, and certain of them have already been discussed by Lea in his *History of the Inquisition of Spain*.[18] From one of them, which must have been written at a relatively late date, we can see that he wrote his first report in the Spring of 1612, on March 14th. This was divided into four articles with seventy-seven sub-sections, and was followed by another report which was sent to the Supreme Tribunal on October 3rd, 1613.

This second report followed the same basic plan as the first but put forward even stronger arguments. From then until some time in the 1620's, Salazar's activities as an inquisitor of higher rank were largely instrumental in making people see witchcraft in a new and very different light. Perhaps Don Alonso, when fulfilling functions which needed special tact and diplomacy before becoming an inquisitor, had acquired more flexible ideas than his colleagues.[19]

Salazar started off with the view that the majority of the declarations and accusations were the result of pure imagination. Initially, he examined 1,384 boys and girls (the young men were between six and fourteen years old and the girls were twelve or under) and they were discharged with a caution. Salazar felt that their declarations were full of inadequacies. In addition to these minors, there were some 290 other persons of all ages (including feeble old men of over eighty) who were reconciled to the Church, as well as forty-one individuals, guilty of lesser offences, who were dismissed with a caution and required to recant since they were under suspicion of unorthodoxy. Of those who were absolved and reconciled to the Church, six relapsed, subsequently declaring they had gone back to the witches' 'Sabbaths'. But there were also another eighty-one people who withdrew their original confessions of guilt: sixty-two of which had been made earlier before the district commissioner, nine in Logroño, and the remainder during the visitation of the inquisitors.[20]

The hard core of his investigations were 420 individuals who had given evidence on different counts and who were interrogated on the following vital points:

1. How did witches go to their meetings and where were these held?
2. What did they do at the meetings?
3. What external proof was there of this?
4. What evidence was there of the guilt or innocence of individuals?[21]

Summarising longer and earlier reports, Salazar, in answer to the first point, said categorically that the attempts to establish the meeting places of the witches, made by a commissioner of the Inquisition who examined thirty-six witnesses in the towns of Santesteban, Iraizoz, Zubieta, Sumbilla, Dona María, Arrayoz, Ciga, Vera and Alzate (which was a separate entity at the time), had produced no clear evidence, except in eight cases which referred to *two places*.[22] The evidence about the method used by the witches to travel to and from the 'Sabbath' was also contradictory or, at least, indecisive. Most of the accused said that they slept before they went; that they flew in the shape of a fly or a crow, leaving their houses through the narrowest holes and crannies. But there were some who thought that they went, or did indeed go, in a much more ordinary way—although, on the whole, most of the depositions emphasised the mystery which surrounded their activities. On the other hand, when twenty-two cauldrons and a list of ointments, powders and other concoctions (Salazar disdainfully called these 'soups') were found, 'it was shown by experiments and by the evidence of· doctors, as well as by the statements of the witches themselves that the properties of each and every one of them was sheer invention and deceit, and that they had been made by ridiculous methods and with absurd ingredients.'[23] Animals, to whom the various terrifying substances were given to eat, provided abundant evidence of the innocuous and ineffectual nature of those potions.[24]

But Salazar did not stop there. He went on to prove first to the witnesses and then to the sorcerers and witches themselves, that what they said had happened had not really taken place at all. An old woman, María de Echevarría, for instance, affirmed in an audience with the inquisitor that she had seen a number of people at the 'Sabbath', yet others who were there had not seen them. A young man, Martín de Arraçum, maintained that he had been taken two miles to a 'Sabbath'. No one, however, had noticed his going, and the same was true of Catalina de Sastrearena. Catalina de Lizardi, who claimed that she had had sexual intercourse with the Devil and lost a great deal of blood in the process, was found to be still a virgin. Several matrons found the same to be true of other maids who had made similar claims.

But this was not all. In Santesteban, some boys spoke of a famous 'Sabbath' that was held on St John's day in a particular place. Two secretaries of the Holy Office proved that 'nothing happened at all at that time and place'. A witch had to admit that she still had three toes, which she had said the Devil had taken from her. It was proved that neither María de Aranzate nor María de Tamborin Xarra nor their mothers had left their beds when they had slept tied together, despite what they had said. Everything that the published account of the Logroño trials had held to be a fact, everything that de Lancre had accepted as true, was shown to be a figment of the imagination thanks to the methodical approach of Don Alonso.

An amazing number of cases were examined. All the classic witch-stories which can still be heard in rural areas were subjected to a rigorous investigation. 'No certain proof was found of the noise and uproar that a girl from San Sebastian claimed to have made on the way back from a 'Sabbath', nor of the story of another girl, Simona de Gabiria, who declared, at the same place, that she had seen and wounded a dog who had appeared to her one night, and that the same wound had been found on a woman of evil reputation whom she had named. . . .'[25]

Nor did Salazar take any notice of what he was told about the ambushes the witches had prepared for him, the powder they had thrown at him, setting fire to his room or flying over him on his way into San Sebastian. Doubt was cast on everything, or as he put it, 'nothing was proved at all'.[26] The malice and ignorance of the witnesses had surprised many people, and, according to Salazar, after de Lancre's investigations they no longer thought of taking the matter further even in France.[27]

In 1613 the inquisitor finished his enquiries by looking up the precedents for witchcraft cases in the archives of the Inquisition. He was able to prove that nine cases had been brought up between 1526 and 1596 and 'the ambiguity and confusion that reigned in the matter had always been recognised, so that no one had been condemned or sentenced for witchcraft.'[28] This is rather surprising in view of what we know of Avellaneda and his work. But at least it was plain that the conduct of the trial at Logroño in 1610 had been hasty and ill-considered. Salazar blamed himself for not answering the feeble arguments of his opponents when first registering his dissent. He thought that they had not acted justly and with due 'Christianity' for the following reasons:

1. Because they had compelled the accused to make positive declarations and confess their guilt, promising them that they could go free if they did—thus insinuating ideas into their minds in various ways.
2. Because they had omitted to take note of many recantations, including those of people who had sought to recant through their confessor when they were on the point of death.
3. Because they had failed to 'investigate the rumour they had heard that the two most important witnesses in the case had boasted of inventing the whole thing'.[29]

The harsh treatment of those who recanted was so scandalous in certain cases that an unfortunate woman called Margarita de Jauri, when she saw that her recantation would not be accepted, killed herself by jumping into the sea. Salazar, borne along by his scrupulous concern for detail, made a note of as many as 1,672 cases of perjury and false witness in evidence given against innocent people, taking as the basis for his calculations the eighty recantations with which he was most familiar.[30] He also denied the value of 'public opinion and reputation', which were based on completely specious principles. He concluded:

'And so, having weighed up everything with the proper objectivity and rectitude, I have come to believe, and shall continue to do so, that none of the acts which have been attested in this case, really or physically occurred at all.'[31]

Such a radical conclusion as this could hardly be overlooked by Salazar's colleagues who during the trials at Logroño, and both before and afterwards, had shown that they were completely credulous. It seems that he had to write several new reports answering points raised by his colleagues, who were probably irritated that Salazar should have been responsible for the Edict of Grace with which they would both have liked to be associated: 'And being in agreement with the revision of view within the Tribunal, the Commissioners send news that the children sleep peacefully at last and have ceased going to the "Sabbath" now that these things are no longer talked or written about'.

Salazar finally concluded that all were aware of the great powers of the Devil, but that he saw little use in repeating theories about this. The question was whether or not the Devil really acted in the way and in the circumstances in which he was said to have acted. There was a great difference between what *may* be and what really *is*. If there had been mistakes in trials like those at Logroño, there was no point in continuing to make them or in covering them up, either for the sake of the honour of those involved or for political reasons. Such scruples should not be allowed to affect matters of justice and conscience. Furthermore, the purpose of the Edict of Grace was to put right what had been done wrong.[32]

Salazar had to struggle for all he was worth against colleagues and against the majority view, influenced by preachers who put forward the time-honoured theories of the classical books on the subject. In his reports, Salazar attached great importance to the influence of sermons on the masses. He said that one sermon on the subject from Fray Domingo of Sardo in Olagüe, near Pamplona, had been enough to make the people there ready to believe anything. Elsewhere, the Edict itself had caused children to start confessing and speaking of 'Sabbaths', flying through the air and so on.[33]

On August 31st, 1614, the Supreme Tribunal published a memorandum on witchcraft, which incorporated nearly all Salazar's ideas long before others began to spread similar views through Europe, after subsequent investigations. It is a pity that these later and less original opinions, came to be much better known than Salazar's, although the Spaniard was praised by certain liberal-minded writers at the beginning of this century.[34] He died some time after the events which made him famous, in 1635, a mere Canon of Jaen and a member of the Supreme Tribunal.[35]

CHAPTER 15

WITCHCRAFT IN THE BASQUE PROVINCES AFTER THE MAJOR TRIALS

A municipal trial: the Fuenterrabía witches – The views of Dr Lope Martínez de Isasti

A Municipal Trial: the Fuenterrabía Witches

From the first mention of witchcraft in the Basque country to the last incident of any significance, the actions of the civil authorities can be said to have provoked more general turmoil and concern in the region than the Inquisition's. Whether or not they really held 'Sabbaths', large-scale meetings or small family gatherings, Basque witches and sorcerers managed to keep people in a constant state of nervous tension, and families were frequently accusing one another of all kinds of witchery.

In 1621, Don Diego de Irarraga, lord of the manor at Iraeta, made yet another complaint at the provincial council meetings of Guipúzcoa, about the spells and witchcraft which were continually plaguing the country. He asked that an appeal should be made to the Inquisition to hunt out and punish the witches responsible. Two of them had, by a miracle, already been caught and tried, and were in prison at Azpeitia.[1] The deputies agreed with the proposal and passed the matter on to the Inquisition at Logroño. But the Tribunal there made an evasive reply, promising to see that justice was done but expressing, at the same time, its regret that municipal authorities were taking matters into their own hands, proceeding without due caution, and causing all kinds of harm by reason of their credulity.

This appeal to the Tribunal was the last of its kind, and the negative reaction to it is perfectly understandable, in view of what has been said in the last chapter.

In Vizcaya much the same thing happened. The inquisitors gave an evasive reply and even passed adverse comments on the commonly held views of witchcraft as well as on some of the appeals which had been made to them. However, this did not satisfy the civil authorities, and in 1617, as a result of a visit to the court by Padre Medrano and a deputy called Butrón, a special judge was appointed to look into the cases of witchcraft. The new Corregidor of Vizcaya, Licentiate Juan de la Puente Agüero, was given the job.[2]

At a meeting of the council in Astola, in the district of Durango, on October 8th, 1617, the decision was taken to prohibit Frenchmen from lodging in the area, since it was felt that the French were responsible for spreading witchcraft. The District Officer was to consult the Corregidor about the appropriate way of punishing the witches and sorcerers who were discovered. On June 5th following, two of the three witches, who had been in custody, were set free on the orders of the same District Officer.[3] This is as far as the local information goes.

There are plenty of documents, however, to show that local authorities, both civil and ecclesiastical, remained stubbornly opposed to the views of inquisitors like Salazar y Frías. There are also documents about municipal trials which throw new light on the approaches to the problem adopted at lower levels. One of these trials involving some women in Fuenterrabía is already well known. It took place in 1611 and has been discussed by at least two scholars.[4]

Two town councillors, Sancho de Ubilla and Domingo de Abadía, started the proceedings in the presence of a notary called Domingo de Aramburu by taking a statement from a thirteen-year-old girl, Isabel García, the daughter of Sergeant Diego García and Magdalena de Lizarraga. According to her statement, a certain María de Illarra, *alias* Mayora, had met her about a year previously when she was going to the spring at Laburheder to wash some clothes. María de Illarra had told Isabel that she would give her some money if she would go on an errand with her that afternoon, and the girl had agreed. But, in fact, María had not come to fetch her in the afternoon at all, but at night, when she had been in bed with her mother. Taking hold of the girl by her foot, María had dragged her to the window, and having got her there, had anointed her under the arms. Then she had seized her by the shoulders and had flown with her out of the house, over other houses and town walls, until they had come to the hill called Jaizquibel near the chapel of Santa Bárbara, where a 'Sabbath' was being held.

Isabel García described the meeting in the usual way. The Devil had sat on a golden throne, in the form of a man, but with burning eyes, three horns and a tail. María de Illarra had presented the girl to him, speaking in Basque; the Devil had then urged the girl, also in Basque, to renounce the Virgin Mary, Christ, the Holy Fathers of the Church, her friends and her god-parents. A dance to the accompaniment of flutes, rebecks and drums had followed. Many of those taking part had worn masks, but Isabel had recognised Inesa de Gaxen, who had played the drum, María de Echagaray and María de Garro—all three of them French. The Devil had spoken Gascon to those from San Sebastián and Pasajes, and Basque to those from Hendaye and Irún. He had had sexual intercourse with women, girls and young men, and had given an apple to Isabel which she had eaten. Two hours later María de Illarra had taken her back home the same way, and since she had put someone in the girl's place in bed to deceive her mother, the latter had not noticed anything amiss. During the next few days she had been taken to the 'Sabbath' again. It had been held near the Armoury and she had seen the Devil and Inesa de Gaxen say Mass there.

The description of the Mass and the form of words used to bless the pseudo-Host which was something like the sole of a shoe ('He-goat above, He-goat below') seems to have been inspired by the account of the trials at Logroño which had been published that year.[5] Other details, as, for instance, the fact that those who had not confessed could not see the Host when it was blessed during the Mass, also seem to have been inspired by the same work.

María de Alzueta, another girl of about thirteen, accused María de Echagaray, a Frenchwoman and the wife of a soldier, of having stolen her away in a similar manner to take her to a meeting held in a field near the chapels of San Felipe and Santiago. Her description of the 'Sabbath' was very nearly the same as Isabel García's. Yet it was on the basis of these accusations alone that the Fuenterrabía authorities gave orders for the women mentioned in them to be apprehended. There were María de Garro of Mendionde, who was sixty and married to a soldier called Joanes de Lizardi; Inesa de Gaxen, aged about forty-five, who was the wife of Pedro de Sanza, and came from Labastide Clairance; María de Illarra from Oyarzun who was sixty-nine, and forty-year-old María de Echagaray, from Hasparren. When they appeared before the judges all denied the charges.

Apparently Inesa had already been tried for witchcraft in France but, as she had had documents to prove her innocence, she had been discharged. She seems to have been an energetic woman. However, when they had all made statements denying the charge, María de Illarra asked to make a further statement, and this time confessed to being a witch. This was on May 6th, 1611. Under pressure from several people, she admitted that she had started being a witch while in the service of Joan de Tapia, in Marianto Street, forty-eight years previously. A tall, mysterious man, wearing long, wide trousers, with his hat pulled down over his eyes, had come into her room at about eleven o'clock one night and had adjured her to go with him. This man had taken her to the 'Sabbath' at Santa Bárbara, where she had met the Devil. When she had been presented to him and had made her renunciation, the Devil had given her some toads to pound up in water in order to make ointments, which the sorcerers and witches used to rub on their chests (down as far as the navel) and under their armpits before flying through the air to meetings or 'Sabbaths'. She also confessed that she had bewitched two sons of Joanes de Alchacoa and María de Salinas, a daughter of Juan Pérez de Espinal, the girl Isabel García and the grandchildren of Juanot de Hecheondo, but denied causing any damage on land or sea. Subsequently she said that she had had intercourse with the Devil more than twenty times, and when she was finally asked where she kept the pot in which she made ointments, she said that she had thrown it away a week before and that it had broken in pieces. An inventory was made of the belongings of the supposed witches. María Illarra had practically nothing.

After this more young children of both sexes came forward to give evidence and all of them made more concrete accusations and assertions. Isabel de Arano, aged fourteen, swore that Inesa de Gaxen had carried her to a 'Sabbath' in France, held amongst the reeds beside the river Bidasoa. There she had seen María Illarra supervising those who looked after the toads. Xacobe de Estacona, the daughter of a certain Captain Jacobo Estacona and Mariana de Isturizaga, who was eleven years old, spoke of a 'Sabbath' which was held near the chapel of San Telmo. She had also been taken there by Inesa de Gaxen, while María de Echagaray had taken her sister Mariana, who was four, and her cousin Francisca de Santesteban, aged two. Because Xacobe had not wanted to renounce God, they had thrown her down among some furze bushes and had beaten her bottom with a blackthorn stick. Then they had forced her to deny God, and the Devil had made a hot mark on her neck. This had not hurt her at the time, but it had become very painful after her return home. She also accused Inesa of wrecking ships in the harbour at Pasajes. The same or similar charges were made by a boy of twelve, called Joanes de Bidarray, a girl of seventeen, Mari López de Ezcorza, and three small children.

The women were in a very awkward position. María Illarra asked to be confronted with Inesa de Gaxen and María de Echagaray, after agreeing that she had been a witch for sixty, not forty-eight, years.

In her second hearing, María de Echagaray also confessed to being a witch, having become one at the instigation of Inesa, and she, too, asked to be confronted with the latter. This was arranged; but Inesa persistently and energetically swore that she was innocent. The appeals of the Archpriest of Fuenterrabía, Don Gabriel de Abendaño, the ecclesiastical judge, the imprecations of the older women who accused her, and various attempts to exorcise her, had no effect.

Since the confrontation had proved useless, the town councillors shut Inesa up in prison and decided to send all the details to Salazar de Frías, the inquisitor who was carrying out investigations in the mountainous regions of Navarre at the time. They must have been rather surprised by his lack of interest in the matter. In a letter which appears at the end of the copy of the proceedings, Salazar gave permission for the witches' belongings to be returned to them and that was all. Most of the women were, nevertheless, compelled to leave their homes, and were, with some difficulty, also forced to leave their husbands. María de Garro caused quite a disturbance over this. But these are details of minor interest, although they take up a good deal of space in the accounts of the trial.

The trial at Fuenterrabía, in spite of its relative lack of importance, throws into relief certain vital aspects of belief in witchcraft. It shows how one or two girls were able to have a number of foreign women thrown into prison, simply by accusing them of all the crimes witches were usually accused of in those days. Family feuds and pressures, and the juvenile desire to have witnessed mysterious and horrifying scenes (particularly sexual ones) must have played a considerable part in the whole matter. The children's tendency to harp on the sexual side of what they had seen will be discussed later, in the light of specific medical and legal investigations. But the mysteries of child psychology were unknown at the period, and most people continued to have the same view of witchcraft as the later Middle Ages.

The Views of Dr Lope Martínez de Isasti

A work by an historian of Guipúzcoa, Dr Lope Martínez de Isasti, provides adequate support for these points. Isasti was a fairly learned individual and a priest in Rentería, not very far from Fuenterrabía. In 1615 he met the Bishop of Pamplona, Fray Prudencio de Sandoval (who was a better-known historian than Isasti), when the latter was visiting his diocese. Both bishop and priest believed implicitly in the acts of witches. Fray Prudencio complained of the trouble they caused him in his diocese, particularly in Basse Navarre, and he told Isasti that he knew how numerous witches were in the district, and that he had been shown where they held their 'Sabbaths'. He urged Isasti to fight against the menace in the confessional, in classes of religious instruction, and also in the pulpit by preaching sermons in Basque. But Isasti liked writing—so he wrote an account of his own experiences and point of view: an account which proves his guilelessness but shows at the same time his general lack of critical acumen.[6]

Isasti began by soaking himself in the *Malleus Maleficarum*, Martín del Río, Torquemada (the author of the *Garden of Flowers* or *Jardín de Flores*[7]) and other texts and earlier authors whose credulity was not in doubt. He also found in his house a bundle of papers belonging to an inquisitor called Don Germán de

Ugarte, who was said to have been poisoned by witches in 1531 or 1532;[8] and he examined the instructions of Don Alonso Manrique. Yet in 1618, the date at which his book seems to have been written, he knew nothing of the actions and opinions of Salazar y Frías, although he was acquainted with the account of the auto-da-fé at Logroño and all its information about María Zozaya. Isasti tells us that the latter had lived in Rentería at one time. She had been taken prisoner and brought before the Inquisition by the local notary, Francisco Arano Michelena, who had 'discovered her by means of children'.[9]

Isasti's chief sources of information were texts like the *Malleus*, public rumours and evidence given by young children. It seems likely that methods of investigation were not his strong point. He also claimed that he had discovered the existence of rumours about 'an old Frenchwoman called Marichuloco', as if that had been very difficult.

'She had a bad reputation, lived in the town of Pasaje, and had been thrown into prison at San Sebastián by the Corregidor. When she was released, the Town Council of Pasaje threw her out of the town and the children followed, throwing stones at her because she had taken many like them to the "Sabbath". She went to France and died three years ago at St Jean de Luz.'[10]

His chief informants were two young boys and a girl of ten or eleven, who said they had been Marichuloco's disciples. One of the boys—the illegitimate son of a wealthy nobleman, who lived with a family from Navarre—was *rather sharp* to Isasti's way of thinking. He told the priest a series of details about the 'Sabbath', which reveal the boy's inordinate pride (doubtless due to his circumstances) at finding himself the object of a learned and highly-respected priest's attention. When speaking about the collection of toads which the children looked after, according to popular belief, 'he declared that one night when he was there, he had seen a beautiful and well-dressed woman coming slowly towards the place where the children were. When the witches saw her, they began to shout at her saying "a curse on the stranger" (*pechilinguesa*)[11] and when the boy asked who she was they said "Our Lady". But she went up to the children and said: "How did they bring you to this deceitful place? Come with me and I will take you back to your homes". And she carried them on her shoulders'.[12]

The boy, his imagination getting into its stride, also said that the men and women wore masks at the 'Sabbaths', but that the witches went dressed as gipsies, with mantles under their arms; and danced to the sound of a tuneless tambourine. He thought the Devil listened to everything he said, and only after Marichuloco had left the town did he really feel free from worry. Before that his father's beatings, relics and other remedies were of no avail against evil spirits.[13]

The stories of the other boy and the girl are less original—or less pretentious. The second boy said that when he had been to a meeting of witches, the Devil had appeared in the form of a large dog, sitting down; the meeting had taken place at Cocolot.[14]

Unlike the above cases, the others quoted by Isasti do not seem to have reached him at first hand; they were merely events or details about which information happened to be circulating. Isasti appears to have believed that all those being taken to 'Sabbaths' for the first time were given apples, or something to eat, so as to be prepared; and he also thought that there were quacks and other people who could recognise witches. He believed that the poison extracted from toads was a very powerful one, although he also thought that relics, the 'Agnus Dei' and other holy things could be used as antidotes.[15]

As a man from a coastal region, he felt that maritime life helped considerably in the spread of witchcraft.

'Witches, because of the pact they have made with the Devil, can give news of what is happening at sea or at the ends of the earth; sometimes they are right and sometimes wrong in what they say, but there have been people who have known about events which occurred a hundred or five hundred leagues away the day after they happened, and to be right, although it was impossible to find out who had told them. And this is their chief motive for becoming witches, to get news of their husbands and sons who are on their way to the Indies, to Newfoundland or Norway; although they do it out of evil lusts, and because the Devil pays them, and for the food, even though it be bad and ill-seasoned.'[16]

On the whole the first reasons seem more convincing than the last.

Witches who were mothers, wives and daughters of sailors could also cause storms. This was proved at the battle of Algiers and by the fact that the fleet of Don Antonio de Oquendo foundered on the bar at Bidart, according to María Zozaya's confession.[17] When Philip III went to Pasajes because of the double wedding of his son and Isabel of Bourbon, Anne of Austria and Louis XIII in 1615, Isasti says that 'all the witches in the district met and raised a storm to prevent the King from seeing the entrance to the harbour and the position of the mole which was being constructed to protect the port.'[18]

Storms, sickness, or bad harvests, could all be the results of spells made out of a desire for revenge. This was the common view. Isasti claimed that the Christ of Lezo helped those who were victims of spells or other troubles and misfortunes. He said:

'Many people complain that they are pinched at night while they are asleep, and find themselves in the morning covered with bruises and with black marks on their bodies and are greatly frightened. Great cats, rabbits, hares and rats appear by night to others and make much noise, and although they light a candle because they are afraid, it remains dark, and they are prevented from speaking, and are tormented in their beds.'[19]

Sometimes not even exorcism was any use, and preachers and other devout persons were violently attacked.

In spite of this, those who had already been brought before the Holy Office persisted in denying the accusations, or retracted earlier statements in which they had pleaded guilty. Like other writers of the period, Isasti believed that the power of the Devil could 'in no way be better advanced than by denying the existence of witches and claiming that it was all an illusion and deceit'. The Devil himself had admitted this,[20] and Isasti, far from believing that the evil could be eradicated by gentleness and kind behaviour, urged, in the name of all god-fearing people, that an investigation be carried out in Guipúzcoa. He demanded that inquisitors should punish the heretics 'and purge the region, where the suspicion falls on foreigners from France and Navarre'.[21]

There were people with the same convictions as Isasti in the Basque country long afterwards. But the authorities always restrained them.

PART FOUR

THE DECLINE OF WITCHCRAFT

CHAPTER 16

THE GREAT CRISIS

Major critical works – The witch-hunters discredited – Gassendi and Malebranche – Later trials

Major Critical Works

It was during the Baroque period that what might be called the great crisis in witchcraft took place. There were two clear signs of this crisis. Firstly, more people expressed the view that the acts of sorcerers and witches did not really take place and were more insistent about it. Secondly, witchcraft itself became confused with possession by the Devil and its classic manifestations were less common. We have already spoken of this tendency in Chapter 10 and outlined some of the factors which led to increasing doubts about the accepted views of witchcraft. We must now examine some of the individual contributions which helped to bring about this change of view.

Some histories of witchcraft and magic mention the German Jesuit, Friedrich von Spe or Spee (1591–1635), as one of the most important figures in the struggle against the ideas which led to so many people being condemned to death for witchcraft—ideas which were still widely held in the seventeenth century. Spe wrote an important book in Latin of which there was also a French translation by a French doctor from Besançon, F. Bouvot. Both Spe in Germany and Bouvot in Franche Comté attended many trials and saw many people put to death. They came to much the same conclusions about the unreality of witchcraft as some earlier writers; Spe's arguments, for instance, are very like those of Salazar.[1] But because he put his views into book-form in Latin they became public controversy and not merely private opinions. Consequently, while Salazar has been an object of ridicule because his name figures in the account of the auto-da-fé at Logroño in 1610 and his subsequent activities have remained virtually unknown, Father Spe has been held in high regard from the seventeenth century right down to the present day. Furthermore, the French translation of his book was used extensively by J. Tissot (who translated Kant) in a highly original book on imagination which is still worth reading.[2]

Spe did not deny the possibility of acts of magic nor the intervention of the Devil in human existence. But when he quoted, at the beginning of his book, the verse from Ecclesiastes which runs: 'And moreover I saw under the sun the place of judgment, that wickedness was there; and the place of righteousness, that iniquity was there',[3] it is plain that he considered that witchcraft trials had involved miscarriages of justice. He felt that there were serious abuses latent in the system of denunciations, accusations and the depositions of witnesses. The least indication was enough to incriminate a person; even too much outward show of piety might be suspect. The evidence of imbeciles and slanderers was not disputed, and the unfortunates who were implicated could not avoid scandal, regardless of whether they stood up to the accusations, or resigned themselves to accepting their fate.[4]

The use of preventive detention and interrogations to find marks or spots and signs of the Devil—and executioners and totally ignorant people carried out the search for these—meant that the accused were treated as if they were really guilty from the start. Torture and other methods used to extract information led to large numbers of false accusations: and often ideas were put into the minds of people by those administering (and inventing) the tortures. Subsequent retractions were disregarded. Those responsible for administering torture could only justify their existence by discovering guilt. 'Witchcraft proved by silence of the accused' was the verdict on any person who could stand torture without giving in. . . . But Spe believed that the majority of those whose torture he and others had witnessed, were innocent. As if torture itself were not enough, trial by fire and water was used in Germany. As late as the second half of the seventeenth century, magistrates, like a man called Rickius, could still argue in favour of its use although most countries had condemned it a long time before that.[5]

It should be remembered that trial by ordeal had been used in Germanic countries to prove the innocence or guilt of a sorcerer or a witch from the darker period of the Middle Ages onwards. The commonest ordeals are the following:

1. The duel or classic 'Divine justice'.
2. Ordeal by hot or cold water.
3. Trial by the Cross.
4. Ordeal by hot irons.
5. Ordeal by food.[6]

In Spain there were also many varieties, commonly called *salvas*, which had been condemned by writers of the later Middle Ages and Renaissance.[7] But the judges appointed to put down witchcraft used other ordeals, which were still more pointless, until a relatively late date. Worse still, such ordeals were supposed to be scientific!

In order to find out whether a witch was really a witch in an objective way, ducking was sometimes used. If the woman stayed afloat on the surface of the water she was guilty, if not, she was declared innocent. A similar test used in parts of Germany was the weighing of those accused of casting spells: if they did not weigh much, or their weight was not relative to their bulk, it was taken as a sign that they were sorcerers or witches.[8] Yet the very people who condemned the use of this kind of test, did not hesitate to introduce others which were far worse. In some cases a needle was stuck into the accused, and those who could not feel the pain were convicted.[9] Experts were engaged to look for the mark or sign that the Devil was supposed to make.[10] In some countries there were counterparts to the 'witch-finders' in England.

The Witch-Hunters Discredited

When Father Spe attacked current theories on witchcraft, he also attacked everything connected with the subject. Torture could be applied to extract the names of accomplices, and sentence could be passed without the counsel for the defence being able to do very much about it; the trials centred around the accusers and the judges rather than the defendants, and Spe would have liked the former to be lenient and merciful as well as learned and cautious.

This brings us to an essential point about witchcraft and sorcery in general. An individual's psychology determines the nature of his reaction to such things. And just as there is reason to believe that, for primitive peoples, witchcraft and sorcerers are the product of a pessimistic view of life (since belief in them increases when there are plagues, epidemics and catastrophes which affect society as well as the individual), so also pessimistic people both in the Middle Ages and since have tended to be more liable to believe in the existence of witches than optimists. The psychological theory of projection also throws light on witchcraft when it involves persecution mania, as it does on anti-semitism. Those appointed to judge witches, and more still those who specialised in hunting them down—like the famous Matthew Hopkins 'Witch Finder Generall'—were sometimes akin to the people they were trying to destroy: at heart they were inverted sorcerers, not unlike the female character in *King Solomon's Mines*, who hunted out false sorcerers partly to please an African tyrant, and partly to ensure she continued to be held in awe herself.

But it is not only the psychological make-up of the judge which is important. Admittedly, when there is serious doubt as to whether justice has been done, it is always tempting to assume that the judge is to blame. But this simplification (or over-simplification) means that we fail to take into account the actions of all the other people involved in the case. The complex problems of witchcraft have in the past been simplified in precisely this way. Only one aspect of the question was seriously discussed: did witches really fly to the 'Sabbath' and could they really change their shape? Once it was proved that they did not fly or change themselves into something else, it was assumed that everything else about witchcraft was unreal too. The scientific approach was thought to have solved the whole age-old problem. Yet in reality it had only disposed of the first unknown quantity.

Gassendi and Malebranche

Scientists have found a good deal of evidence to support the case for the existence of an objective world outside the human mind, which realist philosophical systems try to prove (as opposed to idealist systems which deny the reality of anything apart from the mental image). And those who, in the sixteenth and seventeenth centuries, made the experiments which seemed to prove that witches fell into dream-states (in which they saw themselves carrying out the acts which they later claimed had actually ocurred), helped considerably to fix the frontiers of reality. Apart from inquisitors and theologians like Salazar y Frías and Spe, who were interested more particularly in the legal and religious aspects of the subject (they were men with a humanist education let it not be forgotten), there were other philosophers who used frankly experimental methods to demonstrate that witchcraft did not really exist.

These experiments were carried out when the study of mathematical philosophy and the natural sciences was on the increase; and the most famous scientists involved were Gassendi and Malebranche. Gassendi gave a narcotic to several villagers living in the Basses Alpes and told them that they were going to a 'Sabbath'. This potion had been made up from a recipe given to Gassendi by a sorcerer. The villagers fell into a deep sleep and when they fully regained consciousness, they related a series of things they had seen. The defender of epicureanism was thus able to prove that the usually accepted view of witchcraft was wrong. His proof had a much greater influence than earlier experiments, like that of Dr Laguna. Possibly the intellectuals of his time were better equipped to appreciate such theories than were their predecessors.[11]

Malebranche, for his part, had a very clear idea of the role of the imagination in witchcraft. In his famous treatise *De la recherche de la vérité* (Book II, Part III, Chap. VI), for instance, he writes as follows:

'I know that some people will find something to criticise in my theory that the larger part of witchcraft is the result of imagination. For I know that men like to be frightened, and are annoyed with those who try to make them see the error of their ways. They are like those who imagine they are ill and who listen with respect to their doctors' dire warnings, following out their instructions to the last letter. Superstitions are not easily destroyed, and one cannot attack them without running up against numerous defenders; and this tendency to believe blindly in the dreams of demonographs is caused by the very same thing that makes superstitious people obstinate, as can easily be proved. Nevertheless, this should not stop me from describing briefly the way in which I believe such opinions arise.

'A shepherd in his cottage one evening after supper tells his wife and children what happens at a "Sabbath". Since his imagination has been fired by the wine he has drunk, and he believes he has attended this imaginary meeting on several occasions, he speaks about it in vivid and striking terms. His natural eloquence, given the willingness of his family to hear him talk about such a new and terrible subject, will doubtless make a very strong impression on their feeble minds, and it is perfectly possible that the mother and her children will be terrified, struck and wholly convinced of the truth of what they hear. There is the husband and father telling them about what he has seen and done; they love and respect him. How should they not believe him? The shepherd repeats the story on a number of occasions. It makes a deeper impression on the imagination of the mother and her children. They become used to it and are no longer frightened, but are utterly convinced; finally, they are so inquisitive that they want to go to the "Sabbath" themselves. They rub themselves with an ointment with this end in view, and go to bed. Their willingness to go fires their imagination, and the impression that the shepherd's story had made on their minds is strong enough to make them believe, while they are asleep, that they can see all the stages of the ceremony, which had been described to them, going on before their very eyes. They get up and exchange ideas about what they have seen. In this way they strengthen the impression of their dream. The person with the most vivid imagination can persuade the others all the better, and in a few nights the whole imaginary story of the "Sabbath" is worked out. The shepherd has made full-blown sorcerers out of his family. And in time they, too, will do the same to others, unless their imagination is not vivid enough and fear prevents them from telling such stories. Bona fide witches have on several occasions told people that they went to the "Sabbath", and they were so convinced of this that, although a number of persons watched over them and could assure them they had never left their beds, they refused to accept their assurances.'[12]

Here we have a very radical point of view put forward by a philosopher who, if one is to believe reports about him, was not entirely free from imaginary fears of his own. Malebranche, however, does not deny that genuine sorcerers exist, although he thinks they are very rare. The 'Sabbath' itself, on the other hand, he believes to be no more than a dream, and he feels that the fairest way for the Law to deal with accusations of witchcraft is to reject them. Enchantments, spells and so forth may be the work of the

Devil, who is only on occasion (*quelque fois*), when given special permission, allowed to work in this way by a Higher Power. The Devil was always thought to have been more deceitful before the coming of Christ than afterwards.[13]

Later Trials

Such ideas as these had relatively little effect on the majority of judges and other individuals responsible for the execution of justice. During the eighteenth as well as the seventeenth century, witches and sorcerers continued to be burnt, on the grounds advanced by Sprenger and others—more so in Protestant countries than in Catholic ones, as has often been observed. The cases were hardly ever as sensational as they had been in the old days, but there are one or two interesting examples of relatively late trials.

In 1670, for instance, there was a memorable trial in Sweden. The children of a town called Mohra, in the Elfdale (or Elfdalen) district of the province of Dalecarlia, declared that they had been carried by witches to a place where they had never been before, called Blockula. There a 'Sabbath' had been held, and Satan himself had been present. When they were ready to depart, the witches had called on the Devil three times with the following words: 'Antesser, come and take us to Blockula!' Sometimes they had called the Devil, Locyta. The Devil had usually appeared in a grey overcoat, red trousers and blue stockings, wearing a high-peaked hat and having a red beard. Every witch who had gone to the 'Sabbath' had had to take a child with her. When the child was there, he had been obliged to renounce God and make a pact with the Devil; then he had been baptised and even confirmed by a priest of Hell. After this, there had been a banquet at which all the sorcerers, witches and devils sat down to eat. The food had varied, being sometimes very tasty but sometimes quite flavourless. After the feast, dancing had taken place. The sorcerers and witches had gone round and round together, riding on halberds, while the Devil roared with laughter and played the harp with his sharp, claw-like fingers. Girls and boys had been born as a result of the Devil's intercourse with witches, but only toads and snakes had been conceived by the sorcerers and witches amongst themselves. The only original detail in the evidence is a reference to the death of the Devil on one occasion and his resurrection shortly afterwards. All the rest seems to have been taken from one or other of the many books on demonolatry published at an earlier date.

The explanation for this is that the evidence was taken down by theologians who were familiar with the earlier outbreaks in Germany. But as a result of the children's statements (and there were three hundred of them), seventy women were burnt and fifty-six scourged. Fifteen of the older boys, over sixteen years old, who made the accusations, were also burnt. Forty were whipped. The incoherence and inconsistency of the details do not seem to have disturbed the judges any more than they had on similar occasions previously.[14] But just as certain ill-conducted trials in modern times have led to violent campaigns for reforms, because of the shocking sentences that have been passed, so also this and other trials provoked into action those who were no longer prepared to accept that law should depend on custom.

CHAPTER 17

THE ENLIGHTENMENT

Critical currents in the early eighteenth century – Voltaire and Feijoo's views on witchcraft – Criticism in the late eighteenth century

Critical Currents in the Early Eighteenth Century

Those who start a movement never get much praise for it when it succeeds. Applause is reserved for those who have the good fortune or the ability to represent the movement in a way which the general public appreciates. The result of this is that we sometimes lose sight of the true facts of history and accept doubtful generalisation. It is often said that the crime of witchcraft ceased to exist thanks to efforts made by men during the enlightenment. Yet in many countries witches and sorcerers continued to be condemned and severely punished throughout the eighteenth century; and in others, the supposed crime of witchcraft came to be reckoned no more serious than fraud or deceit[1] thanks to magistrates who had as little to do with the enlightenment as the Spanish inquisitors of the seventeenth century.

The most interesting consequences of the critical movement of the eighteenth century were the tentative scientific investigations of witchcraft and related topics. Sometimes these were conclusive rather than tentative. As always, the most radical attacks on the old opinions came from Holland.

It was there that Bayle (the source of many of the futur~ ~as of the Encyclopaedia), wrote about magic at the end of the seventeenth century. Yet in spite of the audacity of his views,[2] we still find hints from time to time of his theological background, first as a Protestant, then as a Catholic and finally as a sceptic. Bayle, in fact, did not dare to deny absolutely the reality of stories about witchcraft current at the time, nor reject all the material contained in the enormous quantity of books which he read on the subject. The true sceptic doubts rather than denies, and Bayle doubted everything. Nevertheless, in Holland itself, and in Bayle's time, a large number of short works were published which approached the same subject in a highly unprejudiced and critical way, sometimes reaching extremely radical conclusions. Of all these critical works of a largely negative nature the one which caused most outcry was *Betoorverde Weereld* (*The Enchanted World*) written by a Dutch theologian called Balthasar Bekker (1634–1698). It was published in Leuwarden in 1691 and was quickly translated into a number of European languages. The French edition came out in 1694.[3]

The nature of the book and the ugliness of its author (whose portrait appears at the front of the French translation) must have been equally striking. The poet La Monnoye wrote the following epigram on him:

> *Oui, par toi de Satan la puissance est brisée:*
> *Mais tu n'as cependant pas encore assez fait;*
> *Pour nous ôter du diable entièrement l'idée*
> *Bekker, supprime ton portrait.*[4]

> Yes. Thanks to you the Devil's power is broken
> But there is not yet time for breathing space.
> If you would root out the last Devilish token
> Bekker, get rid of your face.

To prove that the Devil played no part in the life of man was a dangerous task even in Holland in the middle of the eighteenth century. Bekker's work was condemned by a synod and his employment was taken away from him. Till the end of his days, he lived an unsettled and precarious existence. As far as sorcery and witchcraft were concerned, it is perfectly understandable that anyone who was as radically rationalistic in his approach as Bekker should have considered the facts accepted both at that period and earlier[5] to be ridiculous—mere old wives' tales which led to shocking miscarriages of justice. But other writers attacked the subject with rather more wit and humour.

In 1710 an anonymous book in French entitled *L'histoire des imaginations extravagantes de Monsieur Oufle* was published in Amsterdam.[6] In this satirical work, the author adopts much the same attitude to books on magic, as Cervantes did to novels of Chivalry in the *Quixote*. But there is none of the wit and subtlety of the Spanish original in the turgid and discursive arguments, tiresome adventures and feeble jokes of the imitation. It was, in fact, written by Bordelon (1653–1730), and must have had some influence in a basically rationalistic Europe, since it was reprinted on several occasions.

Better written than the adventures of Monsieur Oufle were some letters of a doctor, St André, which appeared in 1725. These again emphasised the importance of books on witchcraft and their influence on the statements and confessions made by those who admitted going to the 'Sabbath'.[7] St André was not without his opponents, however. Given the scholarly character of the age, and its fondness for pamphlets and polemics, one is not surprised to find numerous similar disputes in other countries,[8] and also fictional satires, as boring, usually, as they were superficial, on subjects which had been the terror and nightmare of Europe a hundred years previously.

In Italy, it was Maffei who attacked witchcraft most radically. A writer called Girolamo Tartarotti had published a work in 1749 entitled *Del Congresso notturno delle Lammie*, which strongly criticised Del Río and other authors like him. The work was very erudite and followed the old theory that witches only attended covens in their imagination. The evil activities of which they were accused, existed only in their minds. Tartarotti did, however, believe that the Devil was able to control the conscious actions of corrupt individuals, and he nowhere denied the existence or the power of magic outside the circle of ignorant witches.[9]

Maffei was asked to express his opinion on Tartarotti's book. And he wrote a short piece about it, praising its author's learning, but confessing that he could not accept the theories Tartarotti advanced. The latter answered Maffei in an *Apology*, following his opponent's arguments paragraph by paragraph and rebutting them, in the manner of Origen answering Celsus. But most influential people were on Maffei's side.[10] Montesquieu in his *De l'esprit des lois* (Book XII, Chapter V), summarised the various points of view expressed in the following terms:

'An important maxim: one must be very cautious in persecuting magic and witchcraft. A charge laid for these two crimes may endanger liberty and be the source of numerous tyrannies, if the legislator is not careful. Since it is less a question of the actions of a citizen than of his reputation, the charges become most dangerous where the mass of the people are most ignorant. Consequently, a citizen is always in danger, since the best conduct in the world, the purest morals, and the fulfilling of all social duties are no guarantee that an individual will not be suspected of committing these crimes.'[11]

In this instance, Montesquieu was obviously thinking of persons of some standing in society. But in practice his advice was valid for all classes of people.

Voltaire and Feijoo's Views on Witchcraft

The battle between those who believed in magic and those who attacked it wholeheartedly was nearly at an end by the middle of the eighteenth century. The attackers were winning, at least as far as the ruling classes were concerned. Voltaire, in his article on persons possessed by the Devil in the *Dictionnaire philosophique*, could write as follows:

'It is a great pity that there are no longer any persons possessed by the Devil, or magicians, or astrologers, or genii. One cannot conceive how useful all these mysteries were a hundred years ago. In those days the nobility lived in castles. The winter evenings were long and everyone would have died of boredom if these noble entertainments had not been available. There was hardly a castle which was not visited by some spirit from time to time, as the spirit Merlusine visited the Château de Lusignan. The great hunter, a wasted black figure, hunted with a pack of black dogs in the woods at Fontainebleau. The Devil twisted Marshal Fabert's neck. Every village had its own sorcerer and witch; every prince his astrologer; all the ladies had their fortunes told; those possessed by the Devil wandered all over the place; everyone wanted to know who had seen the Devil or who was going to see him; and all this provided an endless topic of conversation which kept everyone in suspense. Nowadays we play insipid card-games and have lost a lot by losing our illusions.'[12]

Elsewhere, in less flippant style, he could roundly affirm on the subject of the 'Sabbath': 'Philosophy alone has rid mankind of this abominable chimera, and has taught judges not to burn imbeciles'.[13]

Religious people may well be disposed to feel hostile to Voltaire's pronouncements. But it is easy to show that what he and the *philosophes* were saying (which is sometimes considered the height of heterodox rationalism) was also being said, in slightly more moderate language, by persons of very different beliefs and backgrounds. Speaking of witches' 'Sabbaths' in a commentary on a book by Dom Calmet (to which we have already had occasion to refer) the Spaniard Padre Feijoo, a Benedictine monk like Calmet himself, wrote as follows:

'In countries and periods plagued by witchcraft, those who took down the evidence showed how stupid they were, and the defendants did the same. Accusers and witnesses alike were generally rustics, who are always inclined to explain things in terms of witchcraft, which, in reality, fall well within the bounds of possibility in Nature or in Art. The unworthy zeal with which the legal proceedings were conducted, and the frequent application of torture, drove many unfortunate people out of their minds. No sooner were they accused than they began to believe quite sincerely that they really were witches and sorcerers. They confessed to the acts of which they were suspect, in spite of the fact that they had not committed them. Excessive fear naturally upsets the balance of timid people's minds, and this is the inevitable result. Some judges were scarcely less credulous than the accusers and accused. And were judges not rather better these days, there would be as many sorcerers as ever.'[14]

These observations of Feijoo's are, in fact, more perceptive than Voltaire's. They are similar in tone to many of the opinions expressed at the same period by religious persons who felt obliged (as they had at an earlier date) to disagree with the conclusions reached by others of the same persuasion. They had no hesitation in doing so. It should be remembered that the views of Father Spe were repeated, in other theological works, a long time after the publication of his book. Abbé Bergier's article on witchcraft in the *Encyclopédie méthodique* is a case in point.[15] Thanks to these later mentions, Spe's ideas reached a much wider public at a time when it was possible to get the witch-trials into perspective. This new public was, however, rationalistic to an almost incredible degree and was, to some extent, influenced by the views of dogmatic materialists such as no longer exist today.

Criticism in the Late Eighteenth Century

The second half of the eighteenth century saw the publication of many books attacking belief in witches and all kinds of superstitions from a rationalistic viewpoint. Opinions that men of previous generations had expressed with a certain diffidence could now be advanced without any such restraint, often in a jocular manner. It was rare for a witch or a sorcerer to be condemned to death at this time, and not to believe in witchcraft was the done thing.

Jovellanos, an author and statesman who admirably reflects the views of moderate but progressive Spaniards at the end of the eighteenth century, read a number of books on witchcraft in August 1798 (as his *Ninth Diary* tells us), shortly after he had been deprived of his post as Minister of Justice. One of them was by Cándido María Trigueros (1736–1800) called *Las brujas* (*The witches*) and Jovellanos did not find it very interesting. Another entitled *Memorias de la gitana Pepilla la Ezcurripa* (*Memoirs of the Gipsy Pepilla*) provoked the following comments:

'Excellent ideas for banishing *pointless belief in witches*, *spells*, *spirits*, *diviners*, *etc.*; a good dedication to Cervantes; but the plot on the whole, is ridiculous, the characterisation poor, the episodes improbable or fantastic and it is written without style, wit or brilliance . . .'[16]

This is the general failing of the satirical works of the period, both in Spain and elsewhere. Authors, concerned to rationalise their existence, were better at sentimental, humourless and melancholy types of work than at witty or brilliant ones.

Finally, during the political struggles of the early nineteenth century, belief in witchcraft came to be identified with ultra-conservatism. Those who supported absolutism and despotic forms of government could legitimately be accused of it. In one of his *Diálogos Satíricos* (*Satirical Dialogues*), Francisco Sánchez Barbero does just this. A character called Floralbo, who stands for conservative ideals, comes on and says:

> *En presencia del orbe, que me escucha,*
> *Provoco, desafío, cito, aplazo*
> *A su reverendísima Feijona*
> *Con toda la caterva de sectarios,*
> *Pretéritos, presentes y futuros,*
> *Que con lengua procaz, y sin recato,*

La existencia real y verdadera
De brujas niegan, nieguen y negaron.
Existen, yo lo digo; si no basta
Mi dicho, pronto estoy para probarlo,
Con razones, con armas, como quieran,
En calles, plazas, cátedras y campos.[17]

In the presence of all those who hear me now
I challenge to a duel, when and how
They will, Father Feijóo and all his crew,
Present, past and future, old or new,
Who shamelessly and evilly dismissed,
And still do so, the fact witches exist.
And that they do, I give my solemn word,
And if my word is not enough, my sword,
My arguments or anything they please,
I'll take them on and with the utmost ease
In street or lecture hall or open air
I'll prove my case to any, anywhere.

The expression 'to believe in witches' has ultimately come to be used only about people of the most credulous kind, with very limited mental resources. But did this general change of opinion come about purely as a result of the discussions of lawyers, theologians and philosophers? It is easy to show that this is not the case. In fact, intentionally or unintentionally, it is artists and writers treating witchcraft from their own individual points of view, who have led men of taste and intelligence to take up these new positions, as we shall now show.

215

CHAPTER 18

WITCHCRAFT IN ART AND LITERATURE

Hieronymus Bosch, or objective criticism - Realism in literature - Goya and the modern mentality - Romanticism and folklore

Hieronymus Bosch, or Objective Criticism

Writers on problems connected with magic are, as a rule, primarily concerned with psychology, sociology, history or theology. They tend to neglect aesthetics and are not often interested in art. Yet I believe that an aesthetic approach could sometimes throw a good deal of light on aspects of anthropology and the history of religion which have so far been discussed almost wholly in relation to ethics and the moral sciences. Witchcraft is a subject which particularly lends itself to investigation by scholars with an interest in art (and an interest in humour too, for that matter). Frequently humorous or satirical treatment of witchcraft has deterred people from embarking on wild witch-hunts and from falling victim to the panic which belief in witches causes. Horace, Ovid, Petronius and other Latin authors, who approached witchcraft from a burlesque point of view, probably succeeded in fighting the fear of witches in their own times to good effect. A clever satire may make a greater impact on people than any number of learned books by philosophers, moralists or theologians seeking to prove that witches do, or do not, fly. This was true in the past and it is still true today. But to recognise the importance of humour and art in acquiring a proper perspective is not enough. There is a very real connexion between critical humour (which is ultimately sceptical) and credulity or terror.

Nietzsche finished writing his *Origins of Tragedy, or, Hellenism and Pessimism* at the end of 1871. It deals with ethics and aesthetics as is well known. The most significant part of the book is the famous distinction between the Apollonian and the Dionysiac in the first chapter, which has been used by a number of subsequent writers in many different countries. In it, Nietzsche begins by emphasising the extraordinary antagonism which existed in the Greek world between the plastic arts on the one hand (belonging to Apollo) and the less formal art of music on the other (the art of Dionysus). Plastic conceptions of things occur in moments of great vision and they give rise to an art of appearances, and images which are serene and full of majesty. Dionysiac art, however, is produced in states of intoxication and frenzy, brought on by alcohol and other stimulants. It is violent and irresistible. The states which we can call Dionysiacal are induced by drunkenness, have a musicala ccompaniment, and lead to conflicting emotional states: first of all, uncontrollable joy and merriment, then profound sadness. The Apollonian spirit is dominated by notions of space, while the Dionysiac is ruled by notions of time. The Apollonian likes what is static, orderly, organised according to rules. The Dionysiac prefers what is dynamic, irregular and constantly changing.

It is clear that these two forms of artistic expression are not restricted to Greek society, and when Pedro de Valencia compared the witches in the north of Spain with the Greek Bacchantes, as described by the Greek tragedians, he evidently felt that the Dionysian type of frenzy could occur in Spain as well as in Greece, and for much the same reason. He was, in fact, making a not invalid generalisation about human psychology.

The witch is, indeed, a Dionysiac type, and for a number of reasons: amongst others, because of her link with rhythm, music and violent and ecstatic dancing. The witch, like Dionysus and the Devil of the Middle Ages himself, sometimes causes laughter, and is the butt of satirical humour; but at other times, she strikes terror and fear into people. The step from joking and satire (and even from ecstasy) to anger and terror is a natural one for people who are drunk. The true witch, a turbulent and slightly unbalanced person, must often have been drunk,[1] and so caused laughter or terror, or both at once, in simple people whose instincts and emotions are less straightforward than books on psychology tend to suggest. But it should be noticed that the movement from fear to laughter or mockery in the great mass of society was precisely what led to the decline of witchcraft as a collective problem. In pointing out the way from one to the other, and in helping people to lose their faith in witchcraft, artists, poets, novelists, and, above all, painters, have made a considerable contribution, whether deliberately or not.

The intention of many artists in the Middle Ages in reproducing grotesque scenes in places dedicated to religion and worship, seems, in general, to have been an extraordinarily pious one. But the result was not always consonant with the intention, and so it is not surprising that some people of the seventeenth century felt that Bosch was an atheistic painter.[2] In reality, he must have been something of a mystic, who abominated sensuality above everything else. Of all the pleasing sensations which encourage sin, music seems to have preoccupied Bosch in particular. Sound is always represented in his satirical work, and with it rhythm and movement. The drawings of witches by Bosch in the Louvre show very clearly the way in which the painter associated jerky movements, strange balancing acts, and uncontrolled muscular exertions with the Devil.[3]

Several of Bosch's paintings allude to common beliefs about witchcraft, the most striking references being to unusual methods of transportation from one place to another, and extraordinary movements. In one of the Temptations of St Antony in the Prado (No 2051) he deals with the typical case of a pair of witches riding through the air to the 'Sabbath' on a flying fish. The man in front carries a rod on his shoulder from which hangs the cauldron used for making magic potions; the woman riding behind has a skirt with a long pretentious train.[4]

Bosch aimed to criticise human behaviour in his paintings. Philip II bought them because he was impressed by the moralising and religious spirit behind them. But more recently the fantasies of this brilliant artist have tended to cause laughter and irreverence rather than anything else. Nowadays, few people visiting the Prado—which contains the largest collection of his best work— sense the religious symbolism of Bosch when looking at his paintings. The more common reaction probably is to feel coldly satirical or titillated.

Realism in Literature

Other Flemish painters chose similar subjects to those of Bosch, and their work was immensely popular in Spain. In some, the technique of caricature was taken to extraordinary lengths, as in the picture in the gallery at Bilbao representing the banquet at a 'Sabbath'.[5] Gradually and insensibly, as the number of these works increased, the original moralising intention gave way to a more aesthetic and humorous purpose.

Who can feel edified by a Temptation of St Antony in the style of Teniers, or scenes in Hell like those of Brueghel, to the same extent as he can by a picture of Fra Angelico? Religious painting in the sixteenth and seventeenth centuries became either realistic and dramatic (as in Spain), decorative (as in Italy) or fantastic. The religious theme itself took second place to the landscapes and local colour in the background (as in the Low Countries). What began by being an end became a means, a pretext for producing beautiful scenery with figures dotted about, or large-scale compositions after the manner of Rubens.

In literature a similar change took place. As far as our particular subject is concerned, the approach of some medieval authors, who treated witches and sorceresses with pious realism, lashing out at their vices and perversions, was superseded by a realism which was an end in itself (that is, aesthetically satisfying). In this latter case the witches became a theme for literary variations in which any condemnation of their actions played a very secondary part.

The remarkable evolution of the novel in Spain in the sixteenth and seventeenth centuries is well known, and as control over language developed, the delineation of the witches improved, and they became yet one more type of character in the varied world of the novel.

Already Cervantes was filling in the outlines of a witch with humorous touches in his short story *El coloquio de los perros*, part of one of his *Exemplary Novels*. Quevedo, too, in the first chapter of his picaresque novel *El Buscón* (*Pablos of Segovia*) referred to the protagonist's mother as a witch and a sorceress (as well as a procuress) in an equally comic and satirical tone.[6] Yet in the lifetime of these two great authors the 'Sabbaths' of the Basque Provinces were a byword throughout Spain. Although a large number of witches were found guilty in Castile and Andalusia at that period, these two writers and others who lived in those parts preferred to speak of the 'Sabbaths' of the north, even though they also referred to witches of other parts, when discussing spells and incantations.

Cervantes himself, in *El coloquio de los perros*, which is an admirable piece of observation, when he makes one of the speakers describe an Andalusian witch, who had been his mistress, claims that she had been 'in a valley in the Pyrenees, on a great tour'. Details of what actually happened there Cervantes forbears to mention:

> '(We go) far from here to a great field, where great numbers of people, both sorcerers and witches, gather together, and (the Devil) gives us tasteless food to eat, and other things happen, which, to tell the truth, before God and on my soul, I dare not relate, they are so disgusting and repellent, having no desire to offend your virginal ears.'[7]

Others might have put these reflections into the mouths of solemn magistrates, but Cervantes makes a dog say them, and this makes all the difference.

A little later in the seventeenth century the fame of Basque witches was on the increase. Vélez de Guevara, in his book *El diablo cojuelo*, published in 1641, makes Don Cleofas pronounce the following words from the top of the tower of San Salvador in Madrid:

> 'Look, there is some new-fangled hypocrite anointing herself to go to an important meeting of witches which is held between San Sebastián and Fuenterrabía. By my faith we would go there too if I did not fear that the Devil (who plays the part of a He-goat) might recognise me, for I struck him in the mouth with my open hand when we had words in Lucifer's ante-chamber . . .'[8]

The intention is moralising. But what about the tone of the passage? With its half-joking, half-serious comments, it was inevitable that those who read the work would acquire a fairly sceptical view of the subject.

Even as late as the reign of Charles II the *costumbrista* author, Francisco Santos, could still write about the trials at Logroño (which took place years before), and about witches in a work attacking commonly-held superstitions.[9] But again, his book took the form of a literary satire. The moral purpose of all these writers did not prevent the tone in which they wrote, and their style of writing, from making an impact on the reader. They were bound to be taken in joke, partly at least. And by using humour in small but effective doses, other equally able writers at a later period made well-read people believe that witchcraft was an absurdity. Finally artists used the subject not to condemn the sorcerers and witches themselves, but those who believed they existed, and those who had persecuted and put them to death.

Goya and the Modern Mentality

An objective view of the world, such as existed in antiquity and in the greater part of the Middle Ages, fostered belief in acts of magic and witchcraft. The subjective view adopted in modern times, from the seventeenth century onwards, was to a considerable degree responsible for the disintegration of that belief and the break-up of the coherent and orderly systems founded on it. As the old view disintegrated, satirical ends became inverted. Already in Spain in the last days of the old régime the object of satire was— as I have previously suggested—anybody who still clung to ideas which would have been considered normal a century earlier. Here is an example which proves it:

Antonio Ponz, a Spanish critic and art historian of neo-classical leanings, tells how, while on one of his journeys through different parts of Spain during the reign of Charles III, he arrived at a village in the Cuenca district one rainy day, and was welcomed into a nobleman's house. After he had dried himself by the fire and was sitting down to dinner, various local worthies arrived, anxious to meet the traveller—as such people always were in those days, because of the infrequent contact they had with the world outside. Quite soon one of the gentlemen began to monopolise the conversation. He had a high opinion of his own learning and began a fierce attack on Padre Feijoo, denying that his works would rid the country of ignorance. 'Everything he says about witches', the good gentleman explained, 'is utterly false, apart from anything else; I am not just repeating stories I have heard from others, but I am quoting from my own experiences.'[10] And he began to tell the most tremendous tales, which Ponz refrained from copying. What really interested Ponz was the man himself. He was not unintelligent, yet he clung to *out-of-date* ideas and *still* believed in witchcraft. Ponz's sketch is quite witty at the gentleman's expense.

There was no lack of writers at the same period who tried to fight against that 'preoccupation'—as it was called in those days—which was particularly widespread amongst the lower classes. They chiefly employed the satirical novel and allied forms as we have already seen in the previous chapter. But the eighteenth century in Spain was not a good period for novels and their works were totally devoid of interest.

Those who wrote them thought they were following in the footsteps of Cervantes. But their discursive and clumsy style cannot seriously be compared with the trenchant and lucid prose of the author of the *Quixote*. By a strange paradox, that orderly and restrained period ultimately gave birth to an irrepressible genius, who tried to satirise in pictures the same views that Ponz and his friends satirised in words. This was Goya, of course. But his treatment of witchcraft is so forceful that it is more likely to produce terror and panic than laughter in the spectator. Many an inquisitor of an earlier period would probably rather have had an artist like Goya at his service than Bosch—with his medieval vision of things—to convey the horror and repulsiveness of witches' covens and all their other activities.

Goya treated witchcraft at two different periods and with very different techniques. First in the *Caprichos* and in four paintings for the Dukes of Osuna; then, much later, in the *Pinturas negras* or Black Paintings. He was working on the *Caprichos* between 1793 and 1796 or 1797, and the Osuna paintings (one of which is now in the National Gallery, *El hechizado por fuerza*) date from much the same period. He produced a large number of preliminary drawings for the eighty etchings which finally made up the *Caprichos*, as well as a number of proofs for most of the plates. There are also some related drawings and some etchings which were not included in the work when it was finally put on sale in 1799. This first edition had to be withdrawn almost at once, since it was reported to the Inquisition.[11] This is hardly surprising since there is evident hostility towards the Holy Office in the work. The last plate, No 80, which is called *Ya es hora* ('It is time'), seems to look forward to the time when inquisitors and friars would cease functioning in Spain.[12] Other etchings are no less obviously hostile towards theologians and friars of the minor orders.[13]

But when we look through the etchings in which witches appear 'hunting for teeth', sucking children, flying or attending their covens in a variety of ways,[14] it is difficult not to feel profoundly disturbed in a way we do not when we contemplate works by Bosch. The latter's works are certainly disturbing too, but they are much more burlesque in manner and therefore less deeply so. The fact is that Goya, while working on these plates, had become deaf, and consequently embittered. His affliction may well have caused him to treat these subjects with a deeper emotion than is usual in purely intellectual or cultured satire.

The Black Paintings which decorated the walls of Goya's country house just outside Madrid (the 'Quinta del Sordo', the 'Deaf man's estate', as it is called) are, if anything, even more tragic in their treatment. These paintings, thanks to Baron d'Erlanger who bought them, now hang in the Prado in Madrid. The ones which are supposed to refer to belief in witches are No 755 (a 'coven'), in the Prado Catalogue, No 756 (two witches flying), No 757 (four witches flying through the air), No 761 ('Sabbath') and 762 (a witch eating with her family). These paintings, which also date from a period of deep depression in Goya's life, are perhaps the deepest expression of pessimism in art. The world is black and what happens in it is blacker still. The 'Sabbath', in fact, with all the details recorded in early accounts of witchcraft, is a perfect symbol of an ugly and bestial society, dominated by all kinds of crime and violence. Personally, I believe that Goya may well have been inspired by reading the account of the auto-da-fé at Logroño in 1610, which his great friend Moratín had edited. Certainly the emphasis on the vital part played by movement which we find in the *Account* recurs in Goya's paintings.

In the *Caprichos*, too, Goya may well have been influenced by the dramatist's orderly mind, in spite of his own more violent nature. But he took Moratín's ideas one step further. He was a true precursor of more modern times and somehow managed to feel intuitively what we can now see quite plainly: that the problem of witchcraft cannot be solved by purely rationalistic analysis (as those who mocked and criticised the lawyers responsible for the repressive measures against witches tried to do); but that it requires the examination of the dark states of mind of both witches and bewitched. There are, of course, in these and other works of

Goya clear allusions to friars, pretentious and muddled writers, and fanatical authorities whose sole aim seems to have been to strangle truth.[15] But apart from the misery for which miscarriages of justice are responsible, apart from the horrors of war and material deprivations, there are other more mysterious forms of mental suffering. Goya said that human life consisted—like his three great series of etchings—of caprices, disasters and follies ('Caprichos', 'Desastres' and 'Disparates'). Once this was recognised, there would be no more to fear.

No one who looks at the works of Goya today can believe that they were the product of the cold analysis of human affairs we find in his contemporaries, Jovellanos and Moratín, concerned to root out bad legal practices, corrupt political institutions and out-of-date beliefs. Goya is a remarkable forerunner of modern man; an anthropologist, a psychiatrist, a psychologist and a sociologist all rolled into one. Above all, he is a tremendous humorist, not an ironist like his friends, who were nearly always sure that it was the others who were wrong. Goya both mocks and is sorry for everything at the same time. And his sorrow perhaps stems from his awareness of his own weakness and infirmity.

Romanticism and Folklore

Art, in fact, thanks to the brilliant intuition of some of its practitioners, opens up new paths and suggests new directions that slow reflection may well fail to discover. But romanticism brought a set-back in this, as in other fields. For the romantics, witchcraft was simply a picturesque subject full of 'local colour', as in Mérimée's pieces on Spanish witches,[16] or full of 'historical colour', as in novels and books written under the influence of Scott. Something of the original power of the subject was inevitably lost in the process.

Artists began to see the witch-trials from a distance and described them with an eye to theatrical effect. The idea was to use them in a way which would prove striking to those interested in the literary contests, exhibitions of paintings, books and periodicals of the moment—and a more essentially bourgeois and completely self-satisfied public there never was. Forgetting Goethe's 'Sabbath', which was still eighteenth-century in character—a pretext for innumerable satirical, political and philosophical allusions—it is to Victor Hugo that we must turn for a good example of romantic treatment of the subject. I refer to the ballad which gave rise to a lithograph by Louis Boulanger which was in its time as famous, if not more so, than Hugo's poem itself. The poem stresses the visual element.[17] Hugo shows off his immense powers of invention and rhetoric. On the same lines is Gautier's later description of a 'Sabbath' in *Albertus ou l'âme et le péché*.[18] There colour is all-important—colour which is brilliant and sombre by turns. But in the poetry of both Hugo and Gautier there is a virtuosity, a technical skill, which we also find in Gustave Doré and other painters and draughtsmen of the period—very different from the primitive directness of Bosch, and from the more profound directness of Goya.

The romantic movement did, however, give rise to numerous investigations and scholarly enterprises: the study of folklore may be said to have developed under its auspices. Artists, having looked to medieval history as a source of inspiration, and to the ancient unscholarly chronicles more particularly, now turned to the *people* to find exciting new elements for their inventions.

At this period and even earlier, scholars like J. Grimm were claiming to have found a rich source of German mythology in the oral tradition. They believed that the primitive beliefs of the Germanic peoples had been preserved almost intact by country folk. Other writers carried on the same work in the Celtic field. But the quality of these investigations gradually declined until they produced little more than 'miscellanies', rag-bags of supposedly amusing facts, which are nearly always the same, and very rarely have any originality or wit to recommend them.

The witch herself became more and more banal, with parts in musical comedies and operettas, melodramas and novelettes. Regional literature made considerable use of her, and *fin de siècle* poets, decadents and the like, also exploited her. Hundreds of Italian works used the *stregha* as a major or minor character. And it is not so long ago that critics thought D'Annunzio's *La figlia de Iorio* on a par with Sophocles, while in Spain, Valle-Inclán filled his works with witches, sorceresses and ghosts.

So we come to the moment when a painter like Zuloaga, who had an international reputation in his time, and was a great admirer and collector of Goya's work, could paint a picture like 'Las brujas de San Millán' (The Witches of San Millán). The painter's intention is obvious. He would have liked some poet and artist of a later age to be able to describe him, in the same way that Gautier described Valdés Leal, as:

> *Un vrai peintre espagnol, catholique et féroce,*
> *Par la laideur terrible et la souffrance atroce,*
> *Redoublant dans le coeur de l'homme épouvanté,*
> *L'angoisse de l'enfer et de l'éternité.*

But styles do not last. The folklore movement of the neo-romantics at the beginning of this century, the history-cult of the romantics themselves, and other more recent and conflicting trends, all seem to us now to be a little lacking in sincerity, and in consequence less profound than they might have been. The historian comes to realise that if he is to say anything useful on the subject, he must rid himself of the romantic vision of witchcraft and the folklore version of it, which is hard at a time when romanticism and folklore continue to exercise an influence in education and the ordinary life of society; at a time when folk-dancing and country-dancing, which are properly rural pursuits, are cultivated by the sons and daughters of middle-class families trained by well-paid 'professionals', while the real country-folk no longer dream of having fairies and witches at their command, but of owning refrigerators and television sets.

In spite of this, it is still possible to explore the minds of some who are less materialist in their ideals, and it is of these I shall speak in the next chapter, avoiding out-of-date romantic approaches and folklore anecdotes.

CHAPTER 19

MODERN VIEWS OF WITCHCRAFT

Devil-worship in the Basque Provinces today – A first-hand account of a typical witchcraft case – More data on witchcraft in the Basque country – Witchcraft amongst people in other areas

Devil-worship in the Basque Provinces Today

It happened in 1826, in the old frontier town of Fuenterrabía. On April 18th, the leading citizen of the town issued a proclamation stating that Francisca Ignacia of Sorondo, a neighbouring town, was not a witch, still less a sorceress, but a practising Roman Catholic. He reminded Francisca Ignacia that she was henceforth forbidden to practise medicine, for she was so incompetent at it that she had acquired a bad reputation.[1] The proclamation was a bureaucratic attempt to vindicate Francisca, but the authorities realised that there was not much hope of shaking the majority of people out of their beliefs, since it is apparent that Francisca Ignacia was an unfortunate quack, who had been accused of witchcraft as a result of her ineptitude.

It is very probable that a considerable number of women prosecuted as witches in earlier times were, in the same way, unsuccessful quacks, exposed to the fury of unsatisfied clients. Furthermore the Basque language of today seems to make a distinction between:

1. Witch (m or f): *sorguin, sorguiñ, zorguin.*

227

2. Enchanter or enchantress: *azti*, *azta*, someone who generally limits himself to the practice of fortune-telling and divination.[2]

The quacks and medicine-men were in a separate category with special dispensations.

It is relatively easy to obtain objective information about diviners, quacks, and bone-setters; about soothsayers, it is less easy, and about witches, it is much more difficult, although some modern experts on folklore have blazed a trail. In the light of their investigations, and other researches of which I shall speak later, we can distinguish fairly sharply between the traditions dating from the time when witchcraft was connected with the devil, and those much more fruitful traditions stemming from a different source, in which Satanism and Devil-worship are hardly involved at all—traditions that are pagan in character. It is the latter which I have been able to study most directly. But to clear the ground a little, I will speak first of certain typical manifestations of Satanism, which have been related to me by friends who knew I was interested in this subject.

A First-hand account of a Typical Witchcraft Case

In the Basque provinces it is still possible to find traditional views of the *sorguiñak* or witches as worshippers of the Devil, who appears to them in the form of a goat: *akerra*. In one of the verses of a song, known as *Iru damatxo*, which has little obvious connexion with the rest (apart from its burlesque character) we read:

'The people of San Sebastián have brought a he-goat from Guetaria. They have put it in the bell-tower and they call it the Holy Father.'

This must be an allusion to a story handed down from the time of the witchcraft persecutions.

The lovely French-Basque song *Iragan besta bigaramunian* also has an allusion in the last verse to four witches going to a coven—three spinsters and a widow, companions in games and amusements and in less innocent pursuits. Among the papers of my grandfather, Serafín Baroja y Zornoza (born in San Sebastían in 1840 and died in Vera de Bidasoa in 1912) there was a poem called *Larunbata akelarren* which contained a classic description of the coven. And on the feast of the patron saint of Vera, the inhabitants of Vera itself and the neighbouring families and their guests still sing the song of the witches which begins *Ama zazpi serore, eta bost emaguiñ* . . . in which there are clear allusions to the witches' 'Sabbath'.

It might, of course, be said that in all these burlesque or humorous compositions the subject is treated much as it was by Goya, by Moratín, and by other artists; that is, with an obviously satirical intention: the black goat *akerra* is an object for laughter and mockery, as are his admirers. However, although the subject is difficult to investigate, there are indications that even in our own time people have held mysterious meetings, with the same intention of worshipping the Devil so often satirised in the past. My information comes from a variety of sources; here are some examples.

In 1932, the following story was told to me by Doctor R. . . ., a surgeon, working in Madrid, but a native of Deva in Guipúzcoa, who knew I was interested in witchcraft:

'One summer night three or four years ago (about 1929), I was going by car from Deva to Bilbao along the coast road. Somewhere between Lequeitio and Ispaster, when approaching the latter, I saw a dark shape in the middle of the road. It remained motionless even though I tried to attract its attention by blowing my horn. When only a couple of metres away, I realised that it was a woman. Somewhat put out by her lack of attention, I stopped the car and asked her in Basque: "Why don't you take any notice when I blow my horn?" The woman hesitated for a moment, and then she burst out laughing and said: "Can't you see that I am at the witches coven?" As soon as she had spoken, I heard the voices of others in a neighbouring field, and the woman ran off to join them. I went on my way without thinking any more of the matter.'

At about the same time I heard from reliable people, who must remain anonymous, that there were similar meetings in a certain town of Guipúzcoa. But it was after the Spanish Civil War that I received the most sensational information from a friend, a well-known doctor and linguist who lives in San Sebastián and is a native of Navarre. He, too, must remain nameless. It concerned certain happenings in August 1942, in the G . . . . district of the town of L. or V., very near the frontier in the direction of Roncesvalles.

'At eleven o'clock at night on an unspecified day of the week various

229

people were together on a farm, eating and drinking copiously. After dinner they went on drinking wine and vermouth. The party was held in a barn (*ikulla*), which had a wooden upper floor and loft (*sabai*). It consisted of the lady of the house and six men and two more women. In spite of the heat, logs were burning in the central space. What with the warmth from this fire and the inner warmth caused by their libations, the main characters in this drama must have been feeling pretty hot. Anyway, at the command of the master of ceremonies, a middle-aged man and father-in-law of another participant, they all undressed completely and hung their clothes from nails on the wall. In this state they went out from time to time into the road, where dusk was beginning to fall, in order to have a little fresh air. After a period of increasing merriment, the mistress of the house took a cauldron of soup into the barn and placed it on the embers. Then the leader, climbing up into the loft of the barn, threw down a live cat into the cauldron, which was immediately covered with a lid by someone else.

'This cat soup was communally eaten with much ritual. Between spoonfuls, some sort of spell, litany or incantation was recited in the Basque tongue.

'Afterwards, another of the guests—not the ringleader—rigged up a kind of altar out of planks and began to parody a celebration of the Mass. At one point in this travesty he seized a sausage, cut it into slices on the planks, and parodied the Communion, with various irreverent and blasphemous observations. Each person present took a piece of sausage, uttering the Communion formula in Latin, although throughout the "Mass" they intoned their litany in Basque. At another point, two or three of those present played with their private parts to the rhythm of the incantations. Afterwards, they went out naked into the fields on a hunt for toads, which was not surprisingly unsuccessful. Throughout the whole session there was much play with the women.

'The man, who conducted this typical coven, had always been regarded in the town as a practising Catholic. But he died soon afterwards, mocking Christian beliefs and enquiring if there was good liquor in heaven.'

This is as far as my information goes. It was furnished by doctors. What should one make of it?

I have no doubts that in the Basque provinces, where strange sects of an unorthodox nature are apt to spring up within the community (because of the intensity of religious feeling), there have been recent outbursts of demonolatry. But it remains exceedingly difficult to obtain the final proof. From a historical point of view, it is perfectly possible for attitudes and beliefs to remain dormant for a time and then reappear. Not so very long ago, in Durango, there was an outburst of a heresy with roots in communism, strangely reminiscent of the *fraticelli* groups which were very strong there in the middle of the fifteenth century.[3] One must remember, however, that in Ochandiano, another Vizcayan town, the men perform a dance on the feast of their patron saint which is called the *sorguiñ dantz*. This commemorates the repression of witchcraft by the faithful in remote times and so helps to keep the old traditions alive.

More Data on Witchcraft in the Basque Country

There are very few conscious adepts of Satanism nowadays, and those who still believe in witchcraft in the Basque country tend to fear the activities of witches although they have very little to do with Satanism. The current theory of witchcraft as far as I have been able to deduce it from information collected in Vera de Bidasoa between 1935 and 1950 from various persons—mainly women, some of whom are now dead—is as follows:[4]

1. There are some districts which produce more witches and sorcerers than others. Apart from Zugarramurdi, they are said to abound in Areso, Zubieta, and other towns of the Ezcurra basin. The people of Aranaz on the other hand are thought to be specially subject to the fear of witches.[5]

2. Strangers and people speaking an unfamiliar Basque dialect are suspected of witchcraft. Elsewhere I have related how, many years ago, my mother had a friend to stay who was from Vizcaya. One day they went for a walk. They approached a local farmstead called 'Itzekoborda'. My mother fell into conversation with the farmer's wife, who was quite amicable until my mother's friend joined in, speaking the Basque of Biscay. The woman became confused and angry and broke off the conversation. Afterwards, to make things right with my family, she explained that she had heard that people who spoke in a strange way were witches.[6]

3. Apart from geographical locality and fashion of speech, it is said that certain acts or possessions can make a person a witch. For example, walking round a church three times is enough to make someone a witch. In any case, it causes great misfortune.[7]

The most usual way of becoming a witch is, nevertheless, by

receiving certain objects from another witch. Also, if a witch on her death-bed touches another person, she may transmit her witchcraft and be free of it herself. The cases cited to illustrate this are all very similar. The object most often given by a dying witch seems to be her pin-cushion or needle case: *Kuthun*. It should be noted that this word, which has been the subject of some detailed studies,[8] can have all the following meanings: scapular, amulet, pin-cushion, letter, book. All these objects are associated in the Basque language for the same reason that all paper with writing on it is held to have magic power, which makes it difficult to distinguish the Christian emblem from the pagan amulet.

It must be stressed that only very rarely does one hear it said that one becomes a witch by means of pacts like those described so often in the early treatises, between the Devil and a man or woman with certain desires.

4. Witches have special times for exercising their power—always during the hours of darkness. There are stories which explain that it is better not to perform certain actions by night, such as the one frequently told about the daughter of the house at Argata de Yanci:

'There was a very pretty girl known as "Joxepa ederra" (Josephine the beautiful), who was as sceptical as she was lovely. She maintained that there were no such things as witches. One night she was in the house with a friend, and on being reproached for her disbelief, she said: "I am going this very moment for water to the well where you say there are witches, and you shall see that I will be home again quickly without anything happening at all." She went, but she did not return. Instead, a voice was heard singing:

> *Suguilla zuretzat*
> *eta Joxepa ederra neretzat*

(The pail for you and 'Joxepa ederra' for me) and the pail was hurled into the kitchen. According to a fuller version, this is what was heard:

> *Gabazkuak, gabazkuentzat,*
> *eta Argatako alaba neretzat*
> *eta suguilla zuretzat.*

(The night-walkers for the night-walkers, the girl from Argata for me and the pail for you.)

This idea of the 'night-walkers' has been illustrated by Barandiarán with examples from various parts of the Basque country.[9] The phenomenon is similar to that of the classical sorceresses, described at the beginning of this book. The night (*gau*) is complemented by its geographical counterpart: the cross-roads (*bidekurtze*). But in this, our Basque witch differs from those of antiquity, who met together in *compita*.

An old lady who lived near us told me the following story a long time ago, about events of her youth:

'At the time of year when the fern was cut, my brothers went into the hills and when they had cut it, they left it spread out over the fields and went home. One night after their coming home, a terrible gale blew up, which grew fiercer as the night advanced. When they had already gone to bed, my father told them to get up again and go to the fern fields to see how things were, for he was afraid the fern might be blown away. They obeyed him, and on approaching a cross-roads, they saw bright lights and heard the most marvellous music, singing and dancing, which so terrified them that they came straight home without seeing their fern.'

5. The activities of witches are almost always nocturnal; at least the most outstanding. At night, they leave their houses and indulge in many pastimes other than doing evil. For instance, the following story refers to night-rides on horseback:

'In Sumbilla there lived a pretty, young, fair-haired girl who had a horse. Every morning the girl's relatives found the horse tired and covered with sweat. One night they decided to keep a watch and saw the girl leave the house through the key-hole of the door, mounted on her horse. She galloped off across the fields. The following nights, to prevent this from happening, they put a heap of corn together with a taper that had been blessed in front of the door to block the key-hole. Thanks to this neither horse nor girl could leave the place. Later, when the young witch was dying, she stretched out her hand to touch the hand of some other person in order to pass on her witchcraft to another. But no one would take her hand.'

Another version of the same story gives Sare as the place where it all happened. There, when a bushel-and-a-half of corn was placed before the door, both girl and horse came out. According to this version, books were used to cure the girl of her witchcraft.

Other accounts which are often told, set out to prove that witches

233

really can change their shape. One of these, which has been mentioned earlier in this book, goes as follows: A man in a certain village noticed that when he put fresh milk out on the window-sill to keep cool every night, some of it disappeared in a suspicious way. So he decided to keep a watch on it. The next time he put the milk out, he hid by the window. Shortly afterwards, a black cat appeared who jumped up on to the sill and began quietly drinking the milk. The man was furious and, since the window was already half open, he threw it wide and caught the cat a blow on the front leg with a stick, while it was getting away. The cat cried out like a human being when it was struck, and disappeared. The next day it was discovered that an old lady in a neighbouring village had one arm in a bandage. She claimed to have fallen downstairs, but the man knew well enough that she was really the cat which stole his milk.

Other stories also refer to the good appetite of witches, often in a slightly comical fashion. One of the more curious ones runs as follows:

'In the old days, all girls used to learn how to spin. A girl who could not spin well was badly thought of. Now there was a girl in a certain village who was very good at spinning. Every night she would sit all alone in the kitchen, after the others had gone to bed, and spin. One night, a witch appeared and said to her—*Ekarran gantx* (Give me some lard). The girl heated a frying pan on the fire and threw a large piece of lard into it. Then the witch quietly ate it all up. She came again several nights running and made the same request. The girl gave her what she wanted because she was frightened until, finally, she grew tired and told her father what had happened. The next day, her father dressed up like his daughter and sat down to spin at the usual hour. The witch came and, noticing the clumsiness of his spinning, remarked: *Leiñ pirri, pirri, orañ mordó, mordó*—(meaning that the thread which had been spun before, *lein*, had been thin and fine, *pirri-pirri*, whereas now, *orañ*, it was thick and coarse, *mordó-mordó*.) However, she made the same request as usual. The man put candle-grease in the pan instead of pig's lard; the witch tried it, and never came back to the house again.'

But these are the least harmful acts done by the witches.

6. As elsewhere, witches are also believed to have the power of the evil eye in the Basque country. It is called *beguizko*. There are stories about a large number of cases, most of which occurred

in the past, and these throw some light on the belief. In Aranaz, for instance, many years ago, a number of children in one particular street are said to have been repeatedly under the influence of the evil eye. A man maintained that the first old woman to walk down the street each morning must be responsible. The mothers, sisters and aunts of the children then prepared an oven to burn the old lady, and she was only saved from death by some men who intervened after she had been caught.

The idea that the first person to pass by, or ask about a child's health, is the person responsible for the latter's sickness, is found in a number of different stories. These also show that diviners (*aztiyak*), quacks, and others skilled in such matters, are sometimes consulted by people who want to find out about illnesses caused by witches (*sorguiñak*). The diviners provide them with remedies to cure the illness or reveal its source. The way to make witches lose their powers of invisibility, for instance, is to light a taper that has been blessed, and pour out half a bushel of grain. This was how the person who bewitched a cow in a village near Alcayaga was discovered.

Another way of getting rid of spells is to scrutinise the mattresses and palliasses in houses where things attributable to witchcraft are occurring. The theory is that the spells are carried in little shapes made out of twists of wool from the stuffing of mattresses and supposed to look like animals—cocks, dogs, cats and so forth. *Sorguinkeri* is the generic name for these in Basque. If the power of the spell is not great, scissors, put in the shape of a cross on top of the mattress, will get rid of it. But when spells are really powerful, the whole mattress and other furnishings have to be burnt.

7. Sometimes witches take on the form of rats, cats and asses, or even of herbs and dry leaves, when they are trying to deposit a spell in the right place. Many animals, plants and actions are, in fact, related to witchcraft in the Basque language. Wild garlic is called *sorguin baratsuri* for example; a type of fern, *sorguin-ira*; a reed is *sorguin-khilo* (witches' distaff); a butterfly, *sorguin-man-datari* (witches' messenger); *sorguin-oilo* is another name for butterfly; *sorguin-orratz* is a dragonfly; *sorguin-piko* a wild fig; *sorguin-tsori*, a mason-bird (or witches' bird . . .). A gust of wind and the wind which blows from the south in the autumn both have the same name, *sorguin-aize*, also connected with witches.[10]

There are also certain signs which indicate that witches are at hand. A cock crowing at an unusual hour, for instance. When this happens, the best thing is to throw a handful of salt on to the fire. Crossing the fingers on both hands (*hacer la higa* in Spanish, or *puyes* in Basque) is also supposed to be a protection against witches. And when some illness arises without any obvious reason, it is a good idea to put a stew-pot upside-down at a cross-roads, with a comb and some stones inside, so that the witches do something about it.

Sometimes, however, witches cannot be stopped from tormenting a person and no amount of protection helps. When I was a boy, for example, we had a cook called Tomaxa. She always kept her bedroom windows completely shut at night because the witches followed her about, laughing and upsetting her with their suggestions. Other people also claim to have been maltreated by witches—seized by the feet and dragged through rooms and noisily pulled downstairs, or lifted up into the air.

8. According to popular traditions, the witch can be both terrifying and ludicrous. A good illustration of both these sides of her is the story of the hunchback. This is an extremely popular tale, and I have recently found a version of it in some letters written by Jesuits in the seventeenth century and published by Gayangos.[11] But I have found very few references to any connexion between witches and the Devil himself (with his usual attributes) in the course of my researches.

Around 1934, I talked to an elderly man about witches in the town where I carried out most of my investigations. He must have been born about 1860 and was seventy-odd years old when I met him. He used to tell the most extraordinary stories about men flying through the air, changing themselves into animals, talking to animals, and so forth, as if this were the most natural thing in the world. He was thought to be slightly mad. But when the Spanish inquisitor, Salazar, had visited the same town hundreds of years previously, it had clearly been from people just like him—of the same age, and just as cut off from the world outside —that he had got most of his evidence. This old man never mentioned witchcraft, still less pacts with the Devil. But he told stories like the following one, for instance, without turning a hair:

236

'Once when my father was engaged in smuggling near Tolosa he got into a tight spot. God gave him the power (*birtutia* in Basque was the word he used, virtue) to change himself into a dog, and so he could get back home without any trouble. He also flew and sometimes walked through the air, cutting the topmost branches of the trees with an axe as he went. You cannot do such things without special powers (*indarr*) of course. . . .'

This is very different from the classical kind of Satanism. In Basque folklore, witches and those spirits closely connected with them, have nothing to do with the horned figure of Evil. On the other hand, they can be linked up with the goddesses of classical antiquity, who presided over sorceresses, and also with the spirits to which medieval theologians referred in commenting on the 'Canon Episcopi': 'Holda' or 'Frau Holle', 'Bensozia', 'Abundia' and the 'Good Wives'. These were satirised with their elderly female companions by Vincent de Beauvais, as we saw in Chapter 4. Various facts support this conclusion.

In the first instance, there are a number of areas in the Basque country, particularly in the western regions, where the witches' meeting-place is called *eperrlanda*, the place of the partridge[12]— on the assumption that this bird is propitious to witches—and is never referred to as *akelarre*.

Secondly, the classical meeting-places for witches are caves, like those at Azcondo (Mañaria) and Zugarramurdi (Navarre). A tale is told about a young girl from the village of Izunza, who used to walk by the first of these every night on her way to another village to spin, until the witches warned her against it. She paid no attention apparently, and was carried off the very next night and was never heard of again.[13] Other meeting-places are the dolmens (at Arrizala in Alava for instance), springs (like that at Narbaja and also in Alava), steep places (like those at Osquia in the Iza valley in Navarre) and other unusual natural sites. Precautions used to be taken, and sometimes still are, when passing these. When going near the cliffs at Ozquia or Arkaitz, for instance, it was customary to collect some pebbles and make the sign of the cross with them to ward off the witches.[14]

Much more significant, however, than these connexions with old pagan places of worship (caves, springs and dolmens) is the strong belief which exists in parts of Guipúzcoa and Vizcaya, that Mari, a mountain spirit believed to inhabit the highest peaks of mountains like Amboto, Aizkorri, and Muru, presided over the witches. This spirit is also called 'Lady' (*Dama*) and 'Mistress' (*Señora*), and can make storms. She is depicted as a remarkably beautiful woman who flies through the air in a ball of fire. Her dwellings in the caves are full of gold and precious stones, although the presents she gives by light of day turn into coal. The legends which exist about her make us think of cthonic deities like Proserpina and others.[15] This is not very surprising, considering that the language and folklore of the Basques presents a world-picture similar to that given in the Introduction. The figure of Mari has often been described. But not enough research has been carried out to determine exactly how much belief in witchcraft there is in any given society, or rather, in any society at one-given period.

Nevertheless, as far as I can see, there were certainly towns like Aranaz which were so obsessed with witchcraft during the Spanish Civil War of 1936–1939 that they ascribed many of the evils which inevitably occur in a civil war to witchery. According to reliable people who were in a position to know what happened in that town, there was a notable increase in the number of mattresses burnt and other classic measures to counteract spells. Again, as far as I can tell, witchcraft in that area is ultimately limited by the restricted range of emotions and ideas of those who believe in it; their emotions are closely connected with their day-to-day preoccupations, and consequently fairly rudimentary.

Witchcraft amongst People in Other Areas

It would be possible to make a deeper study of Basque witchcraft, and to choose other areas for similar investigations. All country people in Europe believe that witches exist, or have done so in the past. Without going outside Spain, we can still find the same strong fears of the 'hosts' of witches and evil spirits among countryfolk in Galicia today, as existed a hundred years ago.[16] According to popular belief, the witches in Galicia met in the sandy area at Coiro near Cangas, by a spring called Arenas Gordas on the feasts of St John, St Peter and the Virgin Mary. A he-goat— a Devil with three horns—usually presided over the meeting, although he was sometimes replaced by the mysterious St Comba, probably a kindred spirit of the German St Walburga. The

Galician witches also treat, or treated, Saturdays as holy, had secret prayers and were great blood-suckers (*meigas chuchonas*).[17]

If one were to explore Galicia, one would almost certainly find a variety of conceptions of witchcraft, as one does in the Basque country. There is also some material on witchcraft in Asturias in books on folklore,[18] but there has been no serious study of its deeper aspects, and the same applies to the Montaña region of Santander. Cernégula, in the province of Burgos, is supposed to be the meeting-place of witches in that region. They gather round a thorn-bush, and the Devil presides in the usual manner; broomsticks are used for getting to and from the meeting-place in the classical way. The witches anoint themselves before leaving their houses with an ointment that is as black as pitch, kept under the flag-stones on the hearth. When leaving they shout:

> *Sin Dios y sin Santa María,*
> *¡ Por la chimenea arriba!*

> (*Without God and without the Virgin Mary,*
> *Up we go, up the chimney!*)

At the meetings at Cernégula there is supposed to be a lot of dancing and a good deal of time is spent talking of the deeds which have been done, and asking for advice about future activities.[19]

The witches of the Montaña region follow the same archetypal pattern. For witches further south the equivalent of Cernégula is the Barahona district of the province of Soria. Still confining ourselves to Old Castile, and simply looking at place names, we find a glen 'of the Witches'[20] in Sos del Rey Católico in the Aragonese area of the Pyrenees, a Witches' spring in Almendral, in the province of Badajoz,[21] and in the Somontano de Trasmoz region of Saragossa, another place famous for its covens[22]—witches' fields, in fact, and witches' castles, springs, bridges and roads leap to the eye everywhere.[23] Everywhere, too, the same classic stories are told; the tale of the hunchbacks, for instance, or others, which seem to justify the reputation some places have for mystery. It is difficult to find out what really lies behind these commonplaces. But if we are to believe the nineteenth-century Spanish poet, Bécquer,[24] there were still young men about in 1861 or 62 who could get excited enough to kill a poor old woman called Tía Casca, because they thought she was a witch and responsible for spells, whose secrets she had inherited from others. The poet described

239

the whole vile scene in moving language: a scene which has occurred time and again, where the strong young man flies at the poor, weak, old, helpless woman. It is a scene that psychologists ought to study, to explain why such streaks of cruelty and moral weakness can occur at moments of physical euphoria.[25] The legal authorities of the time sent the perpetrators of the crime to prison, much to the annoyance of the local inhabitants.

Even long after that, the witch continued to be both feared and consulted in Aragon. But the witch whose advice is sought, as it is there and elsewhere, is a different kind of witch. Something is being asked of her and she is looked upon as a useful citizen. Juan Blas y Ubide, an Aragonese novelist of the beginning of the present century, has described her well, I think, in his *Sarica la borda*.[26]

One must not, however, go too far into the field of literature. Southern European authors of novels and plays with rural themes have used and abused belief in witchcraft,[27] the Italians above all. Less is known, on the other hand, of the city witch who has lived, and still lives, on the shores of the Mediterranean. In Rome at the turn of the century, A. Nicéfore and S. Sighele found her still at work.[28] A Spanish journalist, at the beginning of the present century, tracked her down in Barcelona, and claimed that witches were still making a living by selling philtres and spells to bewitch, cure and kill, and by practising the arts of conjuration and divination. 'Some add to these professions procuring, corrupting youth, protecting thieves and acting as a fence for stolen goods.'[29] The recipes of witches in Barcelona at the beginning of the century, and of some in Andalusia that I have come across, are remarkably feeble, like those used in other parts of Europe. They are more ingenuous than those that appear in French booklets like *Le dragon rouge*,[30] *Solomon's clavicles*,[31] and others which enjoyed a certain popularity from the sixteenth century right down to the nineteenth. Such books as these are sequels to the novels of chivalry; they seem to be the last products of the medieval mind, and went on being printed cheaply until very recently.

Faced with such facts as these, what are we to think of the complicated theories which judges at witch-trials put forward in the past, what of the isolated cases of Satanism we have been able to find, and what of all the speculations about the prehistoric cult of the horned gods and the secret rites which have achieved some publicity in our own times? If I had to choose between the meandering discussion of certain aspects of religious beliefs in antiquity by Schelling or Bachofen and those of some modern scholars (supposedly more scientific and objective), I would choose the former as being more helpful in the search for the truth. Not invariably, but frequently at least, the witch prefers left to right, night to day, moon to sun, death to life, and the dead to the living. . . . These preferences were also characteristic of the 'nocturnal' religions of the pre-hellenistic period, as described by Bachofen, starting out from a hypothesis of Schelling's.[32] Apart from their historical hypotheses and reconstructions, the most valuable contributions of these two scholars were the broad relationships they established between European religious systems. These help us to orientate ourselves in a field which, however much we try, still contains irrational and obscure elements: τὸ ἄρρητον as the Greeks would say. For this reason, modern interpretations of witchcraft, which adopt a specialist viewpoint —be it theological or psychological—will always be slightly arbitrary and inadequate, as we shall show in the last chapter.

CHAPTER 20

SOME MODERN INTERPRETATIONS OF WITCHCRAFT

Anthropological interpretations – Theological interpretations – Modern demonologists – The views of psychiatrists – The witnesses – Witchcraft and politics – The personality of the witch

Anthropological Interpretations

The facts about witchcraft which can be ascertained from the books written by the judges and inquisitors of the fifteenth, sixteenth and seventeenth centuries, have interested many people in recent years. They have been studied by legal historians; doctors specialising in psychiatry; anthropologists; and a horde of Satanists and anti-Satanists, who believe in witchcraft (or say they do) in the same way as Pierre de Lancre and other earlier authors.

Historians of religion have also had their say. And consequently there is a continual danger of getting lost in the maze of contradictory opinions to which all these investigations have given rise. Perhaps, in the long run, it will be possible to make a close analysis of the various theories, although it is clear that many of them have been worked out very superficially, and put forward more with a view to causing a sensation than anything else, to satisfy the appetite for violence of the general public.

Any serious discussion of the subject must ignore the conclusions of at least two-thirds of what has been written, perhaps even three-quarters. And one has to be particularly wary of the methods of reconstruction used by archaeologists and anthropologists of the old school, who are prepared to find some common ground or transcendental significance behind documents of widely different periods and totally different historical and ideological contexts.

From my presentation of the historical facts about witchcraft it can be seen that the subject involves a unique complex of emotions and beliefs. Unfortunately, we know less about what the sorcerers and witches themselves believed than what was believed about them. Possibly witches and sorcerers had more complicated emotions and systems of beliefs than those who believed in them. And this makes them more difficult to study. Furthermore, it must be admitted that it is easier to find out what *is said* to have occurred than what *really happened*. The real witch may be very different from the witch who appears in accounts of the trials. Some modern writers on the subject have attached a great deal of importance to the evidence given at the trials and yet have neglected to see this in its proper historical context.

It is common knowledge, for instance, that Margaret Murray accepts most of the material about 'Sabbaths' given in the witch-trials and, at the same time, holds that witches worshipped a mysterious Horned-God of extreme antiquity, dating from pre-historic times. As I have already suggested, I cannot accept this view. Such interpretations are, in any case, nothing new. Pierre le Loyer, a lawyer who was a contemporary of de Lancre himself and as credulous as he, and whose natural talent was perhaps obscured by an excess of sacred, profane, oriental and classical learning,[1] maintained that the he-goat worshipped by the witches was Attis himself, and that the worshippers of Bacchus, the Great Mother and Cotyto[2] were the precursors of the witches of his own times.

Nowadays we go even further: pre-history is fashionable. The disciples of Margaret Murray are even capable of writing things like this:

'It was shown earlier that the Horned-God of the primitive palaeolithic peoples, known in a number of different forms everywhere, took on a special significance in Mesopotamia and Egypt, where he became associated with the whole ancient magical system.'[3]

There is no need to follow the trail of this Horned-God right down the centuries, and, in any case, there have almost certainly

been numerous other gods with the same attributes from Palaeolithic times to the modern age. To look, in the witch-trials, for
such a god disguised as Satan or the Devil (the form in which he
constantly appears from the time of the miracle of Theophilus
onwards) is an abuse of method: one that was easily committed at
a time when anthropology was based on a comparison of isolated
details and on theories of association and survival.

It is perhaps more reasonable to look for specific historical
antecedents for witchcraft in the pagan cult of certain female
deities in Europe on the one hand, and in medieval Devil-worship
on the other.

Basically there seem to be two sides to the subject, which can
be represented as follows:

Active Belief	*Passive Belief*
(What witches believe)	(What is believed about witches)
That they can perform acts of magic and witchery producing good or bad effects, with the aid of spirits like Diana, Hecate, Holda, Bensozia, etc.	That they can perform evil acts under instructions from the Devil whom they worship.

The problem of belief in witchcraft is, in fact, much more complex than most problems of belief. It is not simply a question of
the truth or falsehood of the belief itself, but also the reality or
unreality of many of the persons and actions involved. It is also
necessary to find out why it has been so difficult to prove that
certain acts do not take place. Having made the initial distinction
between active and passive belief, further clarifications may be
possible.

Theological Interpretations

After our preliminary encounter with a somewhat specialised type
of anthropologist, we must turn to that still less familiar body of
scholars, the theologians. The reality of witchcraft is obviously not
in question so far as they are concerned. But they are willing to
argue about the nature of the cases involved; and there is a much
wider divergence of opinion between modern theologians than
between those of the past, as to the possible effects of witchcraft,
however remote. But there is no room for doubt on the basic

issue. As a theologian wrote at the beginning of this century in a booklet on witchcraft (one of a series of Catholic publications):[4]

'We can fight the scepticism of those who persist in believing that witchcraft is a product of the imagination and not an objective reality, by quoting any number of facts which any unbeliever would have to accept.'

The facts he adduced to support his case, which were taken from a variety of sources, tended to suggest that the Devil was actually present at innumerable rites and services. Certain cases of *envoûtement* were taken as proved. But the evidence of the Devil's presence accepted by this theologian would hardly satisfy the objective standards of the historian.

Another apologian of the same period tried to prove that pagan antiquity was not so wrong in its views as was generally thought. Pagan cults either centred around Jupiter or Zeus or Dionysus, so that some pagans really worshipped one god, while others worshipped the Spirit of Evil.[5] Devil-worship, according to this scholar, was, in effect, a constant, unchanging factor in European communities, and in those of other continents as well: one that was not subject to normal processes of evolution in the course of history. This theory, which may be tenable from the theological point of view, will again not satisfy the historian. The mystery religions were by no means the hodge-podge of evil they appeared to be on a superficial or prejudiced examination. Other modern theologians, more objective and penetrating in their approach have, in fact, found the mystery religions of great interest from a theological point of view in their search for traces of primitive revelations, etc.

What of the theologian's view of medieval and modern witchcraft, with its infinitely more concrete context in time? One of the best-known theologians who has attacked witchcraft and, apparently, firmly believes in its existence, is an English clergyman, Montague Summers. He has published several original works on the subject and edited translations of early texts, with introductions and commentaries.[6] He speaks of men like Institor, Sprenger, Bodin, Daneau, etc., with unhesitating respect, as if they were responsible for uncovering real facts. He spares no adjectives in his criticism of those accused of witchcraft: they were or *are* impious, damnable and abominable people. The teaching of the magic arts in Toledo is as real for him as the 'Sabbath' or as clubs of Devil-worshippers in English universities. The ancient laws and most questionable edicts are full of significance for Summers. His English prose style even seems to have an archaic flavour about it, if I am not mistaken, and the ideas of rationalist historians of the early years of this century (like Hansen, Lea and others) are anathema to him. There is, of course, no fear that this kind of person will wield a decisive influence on modern society. But there is something symptomatic about the way in which large sectors of society enjoy old-style approaches to the subject (whether orthodox or heterodox), and fail to see how unhistorical they are.

Modern Demonologists

In the field of theological investigation, the methods and criteria normally used by the historian are disregarded and others (of which the historian has little to say) are put in their place. Writers who adopt a theological approach are all too ready to base their conclusions on unorthodox and even un-Christian works of no real scholarly value. Equally unscholarly in approach are the large numbers of books which have recently been published on black magic, sorcery and witchcraft by practitioners of these ancient arts.

As far as I can see, these writers are usually mystifiers and charlatans or clever and slightly unbalanced exhibitionists; that is, those of them who are not simply writing for money and cashing in on the public taste. The pseudonyms they favour presumably hide hard, unprofitable and insignificant lives, whose ends are very different from those of the true Devil-worshippers. Yet their books are widely read. Even authors like the defrocked priest Alphonse Louis Constant (1816–1875), better known by his *nom-de-plume* Eliphas Lévi, who are half-visionaries and half-cheats, still enjoy quite a large public. The books they wrote nearly a century ago (and which never had any reputation at all amongst intelligent people), are still reprinted and translated by Rosicrucians and other followers of esoteric mystery cults. And this in spite of the fact that Eliphas Lévi himself had to become a fruiterer in his old age in order to earn a living, and was ultimately reconciled with the Church.

These theoreticians of magic are in agreement with those who are otherwise their opponents, on the basic reality of crimes of witchcraft and sorcery. They also reprove these crimes before losing themselves in a maze of cabbalistic speculations. One has only to read what Stanislas de Guaita, for instance, has to say about witches in one of his famous books.[7] Yet even men like Maurice Barrès took such nonsense seriously. For the fact is that magic, and demonolatry to an even greater extent, tends to be practised or appreciated by individuals with a highly developed artistic sense. More than one Protestant has been converted to Catholicism for aesthetic reasons, and in the same way there have been people who chose to live a turbulent and scandalous existence out of sheer dandyism, or attended black masses, copied 'Sabbaths' and were perverts for some other not particularly religious motive.

J. K. Huysmans was the great mentor of such people with his novel *Là-bas*, a work that has been taken very seriously by those who write books on 'Practical Witchcraft',[8] as if they were recipes for cooking or hints on carpentry.

As far as I can judge—and my information about such people derives from written references rather than personal contact— I would say that they predominantly belong to a very limited number of social groups in cities and towns, and are chiefly 'decadent' writers, ageing ladies with an appetite for sensuality and, sometimes, maladjusted young people. The study of these social groups, full of frustrated, disillusioned, perverted and emotionally-disturbed people, would be a useful contribution to the theory of demonolatry. Some of them even claim that they belong to a very ancient sect which still practises witchcraft in western Europe.[9] But it would be difficult to produce such a study, since the books these people write about their circles contain either badly organised historical material or sheer pastiche.

The Views of Psychiatrists

Some societies are certainly more prone to belief in witchcraft than others. Dr Fortune, in his book *The Sorcerers of Dobu* (New York, 1932) has shown, for instance, that groups of human beings in Dobu live in a world where spells play a vital part in every aspect of their existence.[10] And when the civil authorities in Guipúzcoa, Vizcaya and other old parts of Europe complained of the number of spells which were upsetting the inhabitants, and

asked for legal action to be taken, they were admitting the full significance of magic in those places and at that time. The misfortunes and illnesses of individuals, and of society as a whole, were
ascribed to spells. But judging from historical examples, it was
the *victims* of spells, not witches and sorcerers, who usually
caused official steps to be taken about witchcraft—although this
is contrary to what is found in primitive societies. In fact, the
passive belief of those who are bewitched does more to create a
social climate like that of Guipúzcoa in the fifteenth or sixteenth
century, than the *active belief* of the sorcerers. The same is true
of the more important individual cases at a later date.

In Spain, for instance, Charles II was convinced that he
was bewitched, and nearly the whole of society, from the highest
aristocrats to the lowest plebs in Madrid, accepted the idea and
spread it about. The nature of the spells and the personality of
the sorcerer remained obscure and anonymous. And those who
tried to relieve the unfortunate king by exorcisms and other processes were later tried and condemned by the Inquisition.[11]

Such societies are fair game for those who are interested in
mental sickness and psychical disturbances, particularly if magic
—as Malinowski thought—is primarily based on feelings of frustration and impotence. The magician may well be driven to act
by such feelings; and the victims may suffer from persecution
mania. In societies which believe in magic such phenomena
would be particularly important factors. Non-religious communities are prone to a variety of complexes.

The distinction between active and passive beliefs is also useful
as an aid to understanding the psychiatrist's point of view. In the
first half of the nineteenth century, psychiatrists were already
putting forward the theory that witchcraft, at least in the major
witch-trials, was a kind of mass hysteria. Calmeil, in his important
book entitled *De la folie*, collected together quite a number of
examples of what he called 'Demoniomania' to support this
view.[12] More recent psychiatrists have been able to draw on his
large fund of material.[13] However, a clear distinction has never
really been made between the demoniacal neurosis of those who
are bewitched, possessed or liable to fits on the one hand, and
witches and sorcerers on the other. The psychopathology of the
witch herself remains blurred, while that of the other people
involved has been clarified. Richet, for instance, did not hesitate

to compare the chronic cases of hysteria which Charcot studied in La Salpetrière with the 'demoniacally possessed of the past'. These cases of hysteria were also found to produce symptoms remarkably like those of witches. They lost the sense of feeling in parts of their bodies for instance. This was the starting-point for Richet's study of witchcraft as a 'contagious disease', in which he also discussed cases of possession in some detail.[14]

Subsequently, A. Marie drew attention to the link between the incidence of witchcraft cases and long periods of moral and physical suffering.[15] But Marie, inevitably, concentrated on later cases where possession by the Devil is all-important rather than on cases of witchcraft proper. The same is true of other students or 'demonpaths', as they came to be called. The views of psychiatrists of the late nineteenth and early twentieth centuries are, in fact, diametrically opposed to those of the theologians. But it should be pointed out that they, too, used early texts in a rather cavalier manner and were not always very scholarly in their approach to documentary sources. The practical work they carried out on living persons was, in reality, much more useful than their researches into cases of the past. The examples they gave of modern women from urban backgrounds who had feelings of anxiety, accompanied by the sensation that there was somebody with them, are particularly interesting. On occasion, such feelings are followed by voluptuous sensations, so that there is medical evidence for 'succubi', although I do not know whether such cases are at all common.[16]

There are also one or two other isolated cases which can be linked with witches, or with the physical characteristics ascribed to them, such as the lack of feeling in certain parts of the body. But, unfortunately, there is no fully elaborated analysis with hospital and clinical evidence. For this reason I must insist that the theory of *contagion* amongst the victims of repressive measures against witches and sorcerers can only be accepted with strong reservations. In reality, the most obvious cases of contagion that can be studied in the light of modern psychiatric research are those of the judges and witnesses at witch-trials. In the first place the latter are responsible for such information as we have and, what is more, they also provide first-hand documentation about themselves. I hope that earlier chapters of this book will already have demonstrated this adequately. But it is not only in dealing with the psychiatric problems involved in the study of witchcraft that the mentality of judges and witnesses is of the first importance. The same approach is valid when legal problems are under examination.

On this particular point (in connexion with the judges) it is worth recalling an essay of Jules Valles. In the view of this forceful writer and member of the Commune, *books* were the motivating force behind the vast majority of human actions. And he wanted to replace the rule 'cherchez la femme', dear to historians and psychologists, by 'cherchez le livre'.[17] The extent to which books influence or have influenced both individual and collective action, is indeed remarkable. A clear example of this in the history of witchcraft is the case of the *Malleus Maleficarum*. The views it advanced spread rapidly through Italy, Spain, France and countries in the north of Europe. Both Catholics and Protestants were influenced by it. And the more learned was the judge in charge of a trial, the more notice he took of it. Pierre de Lancre was undoubtedly more erudite than Alonso de Salazar y Frías. And King James I of England was no bad scholar. But pedants with power in their hands, supported by a whole arsenal of authorities and the opinions of other pedants like themselves, can be dangerous; more especially if there is a mass of people only too willing to give in to their ideas and pay tribute to their pedantry, because they are too frightened to do anything else. And this is how the pedant in authority comes to judge real or supposed witches, and is ready to condemn any spell which is said to have been cast.

Now let us turn to others who are hostile to the accused, namely the witnesses. Here the practical experiences of psychiatrists are of far greater value than in the case of witches themselves.

The Witnesses

It was E. Dupré, a doctor working in Paris at the beginning of this century and a specialist in forensic medicine with many scholarly books to his credit, who first used the word 'Mythomania'. He used it to describe the pathological tendency to lie and invent imaginary stories which he had observed in a large number of cases in the course of his professional work.[18]

A person who is 'mythomanic', even though he may lie deliberately, finally comes to believe what he has said. The majority of those who do this are either children or mentally retarded.[19] In children, continual lying does not necessarily indicate a pathological state, whereas in adults it does.[20] In children or abnormal adolescents mythomania is most frequently associated with vanity, maliciousness and precocious sexual appetites.[21] In cases where the mythomane tends to be vain or malicious, a suggestion from outside may well set him off on a particular course of action.[22] This form of mythomanic activity prompted from outside was what particularly interested Dupré and most concerns us here. As a result of auto-suggestion, Dupré tells us, a number of children have given utterly false testimony in courts of law, with a good deal of imaginary detail, more particularly about supposed attempts to outrage their innocence.

Dupré also tells us (after describing several cases of mythomania involving auto-suggestion) that it is frequently the conversation of people around the child who is supposed to have been attacked, or the questions of members of his family, which ultimately forms the substance of his accusations.

'In spite of their surprise and indignation which restrains them somewhat, friends, and above all, the family, anxious to know all the details of the attack, the time, the place, the motives and so on of the criminal act, bewilder the perturbed and embarrassed child with their questions; they ascribe his confusion to shame or repentance, and without knowing it put into his mouth the very answers they are so anxious to hear. In this way, the whole tale is prepared and arranged, learnt by heart by the child so that nothing can shake him from it. The child wishes not to forget anything when telling it, and so sticks rigidly to the version now imprinted in his mind. If he does add anything it is only new material suggested to him in the course of further interrogations.'[23]

Other aspects of evidence and its relative value in criminal enquiries have been studied by doctors helping with police investigations. These could be mentioned at this point, since they would show how certain of the witch-trials have been used as the basis for a scientific study of the use of evidence to prove guilt in criminal cases. According to a number of experts, witnesses who are genuinely concerned to speak the truth (let alone those who are not) have a tendency to exaggerate or even lie when giving evidence.[24]

In Paris or other capital cities today, judges and lawyers can be shocked by crude or obscene stories from young perverts or psychologically disturbed adolescents. But in older societies with a deeper respect for the mysterious, crudeness and obscenity could be seen quite simply as an aspect of magic, or as being inextricably linked with the power and activities of the Devil. In the evidence given by young boys and girls in the witch-trials there are always, or nearly always, numerous mentions of the most obscene occurrences. It is often difficult to see exactly how much of this was put into the minds of the children by their relatives or the judges, although, at times, the influence of the family or the judges is clear, as in the case of the witches at Fuenterrabía.

Margaret Murray, and other authors who take a similar line (not to mention modern Devil-worshippers who celebrate Black Masses in large hotels or in luxurious, air-conditioned houses complete with central heating), seem to be harking back to those who accepted the reality of everything connected with witchcraft in earliest times. When they speak of the survival of the cult of the Horned-God and that sort of thing, they are, in fact, rejecting all serious, factual investigation of the subject, without religious bias (and the sixteenth century is far enough away from us for this), in favour of more or less arbitrary archaeological fabrications. They also fail to take into account writers who treat the witch-trials as an essentially legal problem and discuss them in a lively and interesting manner from that point of view.

There have been a number of instances of this legal approach recently, and the witch-trials have often been compared with the methods used to repress certain present-day political activities. Arthur Miller, for example, has written a successful play about the trials of the witches of Salem, which is a covert attack on the political tribunals operating in the United States at the time when it was written. Miller, in reality, does little more than give artistic shape to the conclusions of scholars who, for a variety of reasons, see the problem of witchcraft in terms of a vast miscarriage of justice resulting from an abuse of power.

It is, however, important to distinguish between two kinds of persons who have approached the witch-trials from this standpoint. On the one hand, those like Alonso de Salazar, Father Spe and other Catholic lawyers and ecclesiastical authorities, who were trying to find a solution to a serious problem. On the other, those who, many years later, used the mistakes of the Catholic Church and the Pope, to question their authority. Protestant historians, like Lea, used them in this way, and so did Catholic theologians who disagreed with the official views of the Church, like Canon Döllinger. Finally, at the end of the nineteenth century and beginning of the twentieth, rationalists went still further: Jules Baissac, for instance, and the writer whose pseudonym was 'Jean Français'. On very little foundation—these writers declare—a vast legal structure was erected by the Catholic Church, which was really to blame for the injustice done—although Protestants did not hesitate to use the same methods.[25] This kind of view may seem rather puerile today. In any case what we really want to know are the basic facts which gave rise to the legal mistakes. There is nothing new in inventing a crime and finding people guilty of it in retrospect, nor in making laws which are unrelated to real facts, and refer only to imaginary crimes dreamed up by those who make the laws or by unreliable witnesses. These are legal abuses into which man or rather society has fallen on many occasions both before and since the Middle Ages. But since we are living in a period when the same abuses are again rearing their ugly heads, we may well understand our subject the better for considering the political trials of today. For life tells us more about history than history about life. Whenever there is an abuse there are real circumstances which give rise to it.

Witchcraft and Politics

Present-day politicians will forgive me when I say that their position is very similar to that of the witches. This is no paradox. Both are thought to be much more powerful than they really are; both are looked to for help in times of trouble; they both disappoint; and ultimately they get the blame for all that is wrong with society. Furthermore, politicians are held to form secret societies with their own private pass-words; are believed to seek to do evil, and to have their own mysterious meetings and even banquets. When they fall from power, the same sensational trials take place, in which austere magistrates and innocent witnesses reveal all their sins. If people could be burnt alive these days, the politicians would be the first to go to the stake. Luckily for them there is no such form of capital punishment in the more civilised countries, and when they are found guilty, they are found guilty of false pretences and misrepresentation—as witches were by the Spanish Inquisition in the eighteenth century.

But let us not pursue the parallel any further. We should like to think that the politician might one day become as insignificant as the witch is today.

The Personality of the Witch

At last we come to the witch herself, or the person who thinks she is a witch. What are the characteristics of these followers of Simeta and Canidia? Sometimes they are, like Celestina, procuresses and go-betweens. Sometimes, an altogether stranger type of person emerges, slightly mad, weird, but not wholly improbable, and perhaps nothing like so fantastic as she is made out to be. The witch of country areas is usually an old woman, an outsider, who is both feared and despised, and who has some knowledge of quackery. She foretells the future from time to time, and maybe finds consolation in the dream world which certain European herbs can give her. Without accepting the tall stories about maleficent powders, ointments made from toads and so on, which have so often been uncritically repeated, it must be admitted that the witch could often have used drugs to induce dream-states in others and in herself.

It was from plants of the nightshade family, like belladonna, henbane and the common thorn-apple, that most of the sleep-inducing drugs used in Europe were made. Further east scopelia was used, and mandragora in the Mediterranean. There were a number of ways of inducing sleep with these plants. Sometimes their leaves were boiled, sometimes they were smoked. Drinks were concocted and an oinment was made from them, which was probably the basis of the unguents so often referred to in the witch-trials. Sleep induced in these ways brought with it fantastic dreams. In Europe today, and in central Europe more particularly, poor people still use plants of the nightshade family as an opiate. They take them for pleasure since wines and liqueurs are usually beyond their means, and they are sometimes used to strengthen weak beer, although laws have been passed to prevent this. Specialists maintain, in fact, that nightshade is a far more harmful opiate even than hashish. And another great disadvantage of it is the depressing nature of the dreams it usually produces.[26] We have already found references to the use of this sort of opiate in connection with witchcraft in sixteenth century writers.[27] But knowledge of it was by no means confined to men with medical knowledge at that period. Authors of works of literature also seem to have been aware of its effects, and some of them realised, as early as that, that it could be the explanation of the belief that witches could fly. In a play called *Lo que quería el Marqués de Villena* (*What the Marquis of Villena wanted*) by Rojas Zorrilla, for instance, we find the following piece of dialogue:

Marquis	..	Others believe that witches can fly.
Zambapalo	..	And can't they?
Marquis	..	Certainly not, you ignorant fellow.
Zambapalo	..	Since I'm no specialist in these matters, I must ask you what happens.
Marquis	..	They all rub themselves with ointment.
Zambapalo	..	And then what?
Marquis	..	The ointment, which is an opiate made from henbane given them by the Devil, sends them to sleep, and they dream such a dream that they think they are not dreaming at all. And since the Devil has great power to deceive, he makes them all dream the same dream. And that is why they think they are flying through the air, when they are really fast asleep. And although they never fly at all they think, as soon as they wake, that they have all been to see the calf, and all visited the fields at Baraona. When, by God, in reality, more than two of them have been seen sleeping in their rooms with the ointment on them.[28]

If one has only a very remote and academic idea of what the Devil is like, and finds it difficult to imagine his omnipresence, I suppose one really ought to experiment and try one or two of these opiates, to see what kind of effect they have. But although I would be in a better position to discuss this point if I had tried them, I have never been able to bring myself to do it. I can only apologise for this failure on my part at such an important juncture in my book.

It is these opiates, then, and not flying brooms or animals, which carry the witch off into a world of fantasy and emotion. And it is a pity that modern psychologists have not had a chance to examine some of the women in question. They would almost certainly have found them to be rather insignificant people in their normal environment, who wanted to be far superior to, and very different from, what they really were. Ultimately they came to believe they had the status they desired. They were perhaps rather like Emma Bovary in their own particular way, but living in a rather different kind of society from the lower middle-class background of Flaubert's character.

The few reliable descriptions of witches which have come down to us are nearly all of people with an overdeveloped sense of their own importance, quite convinced that a woman with a humble town or country background could do the most remarkable things. They usually started their activities when they were middle-aged or old, although there have been some cases in which demoniacal powers developed early in life.

In any case, a woman usually becomes a witch after the initial failure of her life as a woman; after frustrated or illegitimate love affairs have left her with a sense of impotence or disgrace. This, in turn, drives her to use improper means to achieve her ends, although this does not always involve the work of the Devil in the Christian sense of the word. Her situation changes as she grows older, and no longer has any strong sensual desires. In old age, perhaps, her only satisfaction is to see younger women go the same way as she, living a life of false or inverted values. For them evil becomes good; the crooked, straight. What is public loses its importance, and what is private and carried out in the strictest secrecy becomes significant. The sorceresses of antiquity did, in fact, form a female secret society. But I believe that field work is needed to prove that this feminine witchcraft is quite different from Devil-worship, although the two are often inextricably linked. It also seems to me that the important thing to bear in mind when discussing the two is the distinction between passive and active beliefs. Many of the documents quoted in the past by historians and students of folklore need to be reinterpreted, and many questions re-examined, from a sociological and philosophical rather than from a religious viewpoint.

I do not doubt that Black Masses and similar activities still take place today, and that there are one or two cases of Devil-worship from time to time. But I believe that the people involved nowadays are usually fairly sophisticated in spite of their tendency to be self-important, and their morbid interest in anything psycho-pathic—sexually psychopathic particularly. They are, in fact, very different in every way from the witches of rural areas in medieval, sixteenth and seventeenth-century Europe. And they are not in the least like those unfortunate sick people who were put to death at that period because nobody knew what was wrong with them.

I make this last point with the so-called lycanthropes more particularly in mind. For lycanthropy is no more than an illness in reality. It has, for some time past, been studied by specialists in mental diseases, and has recently been discussed (like sadism and masochism) by Eisler, in a posthumous work, in relation to Jungian psychology.[29]

In conclusion, it seems to me, as a historian, that witchcraft makes one feel pity more than anything else. Pity for those who were persecuted, who wanted to do evil yet could not do it, and whose lives were generally frustrated and tragic. Pity, too, for the persecutors who were brutal because they believed that numberless dangers surrounded them. Perhaps we are in a better position nowadays to appreciate the feelings of the people involved, who discovered one day that they had a devilish power in them, or were subject to the devilish power of a close enemy who had lived near them for years, watching and hating. For ours is no period of calm, with an optimistic view of public morality and religious philosophy and beliefs. It is an age of existentialism and an existentialist way of life, which leads man to break down the barriers and conventions and face up to his own *angst*.

It is not, after all, so hard for us to understand those men and women. Their age, like ours, was an age of *angst*. Only their idea of reality radically separates them from us.

NOTES

CHAPTER 1: A PRIMARY CONCEPTION OF THE NATURE OF THE WORLD
AND OF EXISTENCE

1. H. Frankfort, 'Myths and Reality' in *Before Philosophy* (Harmondsworth, 1951), p. 13.
2. Leopold Von Scroeder, *Arische Religion*, I (Einleitung-Der Altarische Himmelsgott das Höchste Gute Wessen) (Leipzig, 1923), pp. 418, 454, etc.
3. *Ibid*, II, pp. 69–81.
4. *Ibid*, II, pp. 164–96, 241, etc.
5. *Ibid*, II, pp. 659–74. Significantly little attention is paid to the moon.
6. *Ibid*, I, p. 309. There is no adequate development of ideas relating to the earth. For essential information, cf. Albert Carnoy, *Les indo-européens*, pp. 214–16. A. Dieterich's *Mutter Erde* (Leipzig-Berlin, 1925), is also of great interest.
7. *Ibid*.
8. B. Malinowski, 'Myth in Primitive Psychology' in *Magic, Science and Religion and Other Essays* (New York, 1955), p. 97.
9. Scholars who won the sympathies of this school by attacking evolutionary theory turned their attentions to the school itself later. Cf., for example, A. Goldenweiser, 'Cultural Anthropology' in *History, Psychology and Culture* (London, 1936), p. 149.
10. Gordon Childe, *What happened in History* (Harmondsworth, 1950), pp. 64, 66, etc.

11. Strabo III, 4, 17–18. A commentary on this and other passages will be found in my book *Los pueblos del norte de la península ibérica* (Madrid, 1943). This book is now in need of revision but contains some original observations.

12. I quote from the selection of his works made by Carl Albrecht Bernouilli, *Urreligion und antike Symbole* (Leipzig, 1926), I, pp. 64, 109, 122, 264, 266, 278, 314; II, pp. 49, 52, 62–71, 298, 361, 419, 468, 509.

13. B. Malinowski, 'Myth in Primitive Psychology', *op. cit.*, pp. 93–148.

14. For Frazer's account of his theory of magic, cf. 'The Magic Art and the Evolution of Kings', in *The Golden Bough*, I, chapters III and IV.

15. Plotinus, *Enneads*, IV, 4, 40 and more especially 43. In the Bréhier edition (Paris, 1927), IV, pp. 147–8 and 150–1.

CHAPTER 2: THE NATURE OF THE WITCH IN GRAECO-ROMAN TIMES

1. For the following pages I have drawn on my essay 'Magia en Castilla durante los siglos XVI y XVII', in *Algunos mitos españoles y otros ensayos* (Madrid, 1944), pp. 185–213, particularly. But I have revised my views since writing this work.

2. A good deal of well-organised material can be found in the article on magic by H. Hubert, in the *Dictionnaire des antiquités grecques et romaines*, edited by Darember and Saglio (Paris, 1904) III, 2, pp. 1494–1521. Hopfner is less systematic in the *Real-Encyclopädie der Classischen Altertumswissenschaft*, ed. Pauly-Wissowa, N.B. (Stuttgart, 1930), XIV, cols. 301–93. L. F. Alfred Maury's book, *La Magie et l'Astrologie dans l'Antiquité et au Moyen Age ou étude sur les superstitions païennes qui se sont perpétuées jusqu'à nos jours* (Paris, 1877), can still be read profitably in spite of its poor organisation.

3. General histories of witchcraft contain a fair number of passages from works of the classical period. Cf., for example, Soldan, *Geschichte der Hexenprozesse* (Stuttgart, 1880), I, pp. 35–51, for references to the Greeks; pp. 52–85, for the Romans.

4. A significant passage is that of Seneca, *Nat-Quaest*, IV, 6–7.

5. The investigations of Frazer on this point have already been referred to in note 14, chapter 1.

6. Cf., for example, Cato's *De agr. cul.*, 160. Cf., also 5, 4, of the same work.

7. Cato in his *De agr. cul.*, 5, 4, writes 'Haruspicem, augurem, hariolum, Chaldaeum nequem consuluisse velit'.

8. Columela, *De re rustica*, I, 8.

9. Plato, *Leg.*, XI, 932 e, 933 d.

10. *Ibid*, X, 909 b.

11. Lucan, *Bell. civ.*, VI, lines 440–1.

12. *Ibid*, lines 492–496.

13. Rudolf Otto, *The Idea of the Holy* (Oxford, 1928), pp. 121–3.

14. *Ibid*, p. 4.

15. Bacchanals were persecuted in Rome at certain periods because of their anti-social nature.

16. Virgil, *Aen.*, II, line 255, '. . . tacita per amica silentia lunae'.

17. Ovid, *Metam.*, VII, lines 192–3.

18. Horace, *Epode*, 5, lines 49–54:

> 'O rebus meis
> non infideles arbitrae,
> Nox et Diana, quae silentium regis
> arcana cum fiunt sacra,
> nunc, nunc adeste, nunc in hostilis domos
> iram atque numen vertite.'

19. Theocritus, *Idyl.*, II ('Pharmac.'), line 10 *et passim*.

20. Cf. Heckenbach's article on 'Hekate' in Pauly-Wissowa's *Real Encyclopädie der Classischen Altertumswissenschaft*, N.B. (Stuttgart, 1912), VII, cols. 2769–82. Even more important is Erwin Rohde's invaluable book *Psyché. Le culte de l'âme chez les grecs et leur croyance à l'immortalité*, ed. Auguste Reymond (Paris, 1928), pp. 328–35, 607–11.

21. Certain of Hecate's banquets can be compared to those of the witches. The Εκατικὰ φάσματα have much in common with witches.

22. Cf. Erwin Rohde, *Psyché, ed. cit.* p. 325, note 1, for references to mental illnesses.

23. Diodorus Siculus, IV, 45.

24. She also controls animals, cf. *Odyssey*, X, 240. Circe has a pleasant singing voice (X, 220–1) and can make people forget (X, 236).

25. Homer, *Od.*, X, 240.

26. Euripides, *Medea*, more especially lines 401–9. There are frequent references to Medea as a sorceress in Latin poets. Cf., for example, Horace, *Epodes*, 17, lines 76–81.

27. Cp. Seneca's rhetorical invocation in his *Medea*, 1–55, and the more restrained speech in Euripides.

28. Horace, *Epodes*, 17; lines 16–81.

29. B. Malinowski, 'The Art of Magic and the Power of Faith', *op. cit.*, p. 74.

30. Apuleius, *Metam.*, I, 8. Malinowski has pointed out geographical areas where Black Magic is much more extensively practised than in parts of the world which are relatively close to ours, in his *Sex and Repression in Savage Society* (New York, 1955), pp. 85–7.

31. Apuleius, *Metam.*, II, 22.

32. Apuleius, *Metam.*, I, 10.

33. Apuleius, *Metam.*, II, 21–2.

34. Apuleius, *Metam.*, II, 5. Cf. Lucian, *Lucio*, 4.

35. Apuleius, *Metam.*, II, 12–14.

36. Apuleius, *Metam.*, I, 9.

37. Apuleius, *Metam.*, I, 14.

38. Cf. Aulus Gellius, XV, 11, i; Horace, *Epodes*, 5, lines 75–6 and 17, lines 28–9.

39. Apuleius, *Apol.*, 27–8.

> 'Philtra omnia undique eruunt:
> antiphates illud quaeritur,
> trochiscili, ungues, taeniae,
> radiculae, herbae, surculi
> saurae, inlices bidoculae
> hinnientium dulcedines.'

40. B. Malinowski, 'The Art of Magic and the Power of Faith', *op. cit.*, 79–84.

41. Cf., for example, A. L. Kroeber, *Anthropology* (New York 1948), pp. 308–9.

42. Theocritus, *Idyl.*, II ('Pharmac.'). Similar themes are to be found in other Greek poets.

43. *Ibid*, lines 17, 22, 27, 32, 37, 42, 47, 52, 57 and 63.

44. *Ibid*, the spell begins at line 18 and goes on to line 63.

45. *Ibid*, lines 69, 75, 81, 93, 99, 105, 111, 117, 123, 129 and 135.

46. *Ibid*, lines 165–6.

47. *Philosophumena*, IV, 35 (in Migne's *Patrologia Graeca*, XVI, 3) (Paris, 1863), cols. 3100–1. The Greek word βόμβος seems to be onomatopoeic. It is used to convey the dull sound involved (assuming that it is not connected with *rhombo*). Hecate must have made this noise when she appeared (cf. Lucian, *Philopseud.*, 22–4). Gorgo and Mormo are other names for Hecate. Cf. also Erwin Rohde, *Psyché*, *op. cit.* p. 607.

48. *Ovid, Ars amoris*, II, 1, lines 23–8.

49. Cf. Stéphane Mallarmé, *Divagations* (ed. Paris, 1922), p. 326 'Je dis qu'existe entre les vieux procédés et le sortilège, que restera la poésie, une parité secrète.' ('Magie'.)

50. The passage begins at line 413 of Bk. VI of the *Pharsalia* or *Belli civilis libri*, by Lucan.

51. Lucan, *Bell. civ.*, VI, line 431.

52. *Ibid*, VI, lines 499–506.

53. *Ibid*, VI, lines 507–69.

54. *Ibid*, VI, line 577.

55. *Ibid*, VI, line 699.

56. *Ibid*, VI, lines 719–20.

57. Euripides, *Medea*, lines 214–66.

58. Cf., p. 29–30 above.

59. Horace, *Epodes*, 5, lines 17–25.

60. *Ibid*, 5, lines 37–8.

61. *Ibid*, 5, lines 71–2:

> 'A, a, solutus ambulat veneficae
> scientioris carmine.'

62. *Ibid*, 5, lines 87–8:

> 'Venena magnum fas nefasque non valent
> convertere, humanam vicem.'

63. *Ibid*, 5, lines 87–102 (the curse); lines 97–8 describe the stoning of witches:

> 'Vos turba vicatim hinc saxis petens
> contundet obscenas anus.'

64. Porphyry refers to this. See Villeneuve's edition of the Odes and Epodes (Paris, 1927), p. 207, note 2.

65. Horace, *Serm.*, I, lines 8, 24, 48; II, 1, 48 and 8, 95.

66. Apuleius, *Metam.*, II, 5.

67. Apuleius, *Apol.*, 27–8.

68. B. Malinowski, *op. cit.*, p. 23.

69. Petronius, *Satiric*, 134, 8. Oenothea (οἶνος θεά) is very similar, even in her liking for wine.

70. Ovid, *Ars amoris*, I, line 8. Lines 1–18 describe her as a witch, and 19–34 speak of her activities as a procuress. Cf., lines 35–48 for a description of loose women.

71. Petronius, *Satiric.*, 132, 5.

72. Lucian, *Dial. mer.*, IV, I, 4–5.

73. Tibullus, I, 2, lines 43–64. Another protégée of Hecate (see line 52).

74. At times there is some confusion about the properties of certain substances, as 'hippomanes' for instance. Cf. Stadler's article in Pauly-Wissowa's *Real Encyclopädie*, N.B. (Stuttgart, 1913), VIII, cols. 1879–82.

75. Lucian, *Lucius or the Ass*, 12. Cf. the passages from Apuleius referred to above.

76. Horace, *Epode*, 5, lines 71–2.

77. The witch to whom Tibullus refers (I, 2, lines 59–60), boasted that she could destroy the poet's love by 'chants' and 'herbs'.

78. Petronius, *Satiric.*, 130, etc.

79. Ovid, *Ars amoris*, III, 7, lines 27–35. There is an allusion to Medea's activities as witch and poisoner ('Aenea venefica') in line 79.

80. Petronius's *Satiric.*, 63, includes a typical story of a lycanthrope ('versipellem').

81. Ovid, *Fasti*, VI, lines 131–50. See lines 141–2 for the hypotheses. Cf. *Ars amoris*, I, 8, lines 13–14.

82. Petronius, *Satiric.*, 63. The idea of the 'mala manus' in the story is interesting.

83. Cf. C.I.L., VI, 19–747.

84. Cf. Kuhnert's article on 'Fascinum' in Pauly-Wissowa's *Real Encyclopädie*, N.B. (Stuttgart, 1909), VI, cols. 2009–14.

85. Petronius, *Satiric.*, 134. Cf. the description of the moon with that of Euripides in *Medea* (lines 395–8), Aristophanes in *The Clouds* (lines 749–50), and Horace in *Epode*, 5, lines 45–6.

86. Apuleius, *Metam.*, I, 9, 14, etc.

87. Ovid, *Fasti*, II, lines 571–82. For Tacita, see II, lines 616–683.

88. Seneca, *Nat. Quaest.*, IV, 7: 'et apud nos in XII tabulis cavatur, nequis alienos fructus excantassit. . . .'

89. Tacitus, *Ann.*, II, 69; III, 13. Cf. Suetonius, *Caligula*, 3.

90. Ammianus, XIX, 12.

91. *Ibid*, XXVI, 3.

92. Gibbon, *The Decline and Fall of the Roman Empire* II, XXV, (ed. London, 1951), pp. 471–5.

CHAPTER 3: CHRISTIANITY, PAGANISM AND WITCHCRAFT

1. Tertullian, *Apol.*, 7, 9, 16, etc.

2. Early collections of *obscaena* have been known to include passages from Arnobius describing obscene rites and the scandalous behaviour of the gods.

3. Tertullian, *Apol.*, 43.

4. *Cod. Theod.*, IX, 16, 3 (Ed. Mommsen, I, 2, p. 460).

5. *Cod. Theod.*, IX, 16, 7 (Ed. Mommsen, I, 2, p. 462). Subtitle 16 contains twelve laws relating to maleficent mathematicians and other similar persons (pp. 459–63).

6. *Cod. Just.*, Ed. Krüger, pp. 379–80 (as many as nine).

7. Article on 'Magic' in *A Dictionary of Christian Antiquities*, by William Smith and Samuel Cheetham (London, 1880), II, pp. 1074–8. The whole of chapter 2 of Hansen's *Zauberwahn. . .* , pp. 36–121, is a typically thorough study of these laws from AD 400 to 1200.

8. St Augustine, *De civ. Dei*, XVIII, 18.

9. Joseph Hansen, 'Zauberwahn, Inquisition und Hexenprozess im Mittelalter und die Entstehung der grossen Hexenverfolgung' (München-Leipzig, 1900).

10. Zosimus, V, 28 (Ed. Reitemeier, pp. 459–60) proves that the first wife of the emperor died a virgin. In spite of this he married again, this time with Stilicho's daughter. When he died the girl was sent back to her mother. See V, 28 (Ed. (*op. cit.*, p. 477).

11. *Ibid*, pp. 61–2.

12. William of Malmesbury seems to have been the first to tell the story. Vincent de Beauvais took it from him, and Molitor and others got it from Beauvais.

13. I have used the two-volume edition of his homilies published in Basle in 1504. It is difficult to make concrete references to passages in this text.

14. *Op. cit.*, Homily XXI, i, fols. XLI r–XLIII r—especially the last page. In Homily II, fols. XXII r–LXIX v.

15. Gibbon described this event with his usual force in *The Decline and Fall of the Roman Empire*, III, ch. 32 (*ed. cit.* pp. 306–11).

16. Procopius, *Anec.*, I, 1.

17. *Ibid*, I, 7.

18. *Ibid*, XII, 10; XXII, 7 and 8.

19. *Ibid*, IX, 12; XXII, 6 and 7.

20. Nicetas Choniates, III, 4 ('De rebus gestis Alex. Commeni').

21. A. L. Kroeber, *Anthropology*, pp. 298–9.

22. John Magnus, *Gothorumque sueonumque historia, ex probatis antiquorum monumentis collecta* . . . (Basle, 1558), XVII, ch. 12, p. 640.

23. Mlle R. du Puget. *Les Eddas traduites de l'ancien idiome scandinave* (Paris, n.d.), p. 21 (page 5 of Gylf's voyage) and p. 249 (page 32 of Hyndla's poem).

24. H. Ch. Lea, *Histoire de l'Inquisition au Moyen Age*, III, pp. 486–90.

25. Fernand Mossé, *La Laxdoela Saga. Légende historique islandaise traduite du vieux norrois avec une introduction et des notes* (Paris, 1914), pp. 99, 103, 104, 105–7, 111–12.

26. Tacitus, *Germ.*, 8.

27. Tacitus, *Hist.*, IV, 61–6; VI, 22–4. Dio Casius, LXVII, 5.

28. Velleda's successor.

29. *Les Eddas*, *op. cit.*, p. 138 (pages 4–5 of Lodfafner's song).

30. *Ibid*, p. 27.

31. *Ibid*, p. 188 (page 24 of Aeger's feast). Cf. also p. 115 (page 34 of Wola the Wise's prediction).

32. *Ibid*, p. 190 (page 32 of Aeger's feast). A further accusation is on p. 195 (page 56 of Aeger's feast).

33. A. Krantz, *Regnorum Aquilonarium, Daniae, Sueciae, Noruagiae Chronica* (Frankfurt, 1583), fols. 20 v–21 r (Bk. I, 32).

34. See, for example, Pierre le Loyer, *Discours, et histoires des spectres, visions et apparitions des esprits* (Paris, 1605), Bk. II, ch. 7, p. 142.

35. A. Krantz, *op. cit.*, fol. 16 v (Bk. I, ch. 23).

36. Jordanes, *De rebus gothicis*, 24. Many years afterwards, John Magnus maintained that witches had intercourse with men and not with spirits (*Gothorumque sueonumque historia*, VI, 24, pp. 258–9). The number of witches varies considerably from one edition to the next.

37. 'Chronicon Bohemiae', Bk. II, ch. III-X, in *Reliquiae manuscriptorum omnis aevi diplomatum ac monumentorum ineditorum* (Halle, 1737), XI, pp. 131–45. Cf. P. J. Schafarik, *Slawische Alterthümer*, II, (Leipzig, 1844), p. 421.

38. H. Boethius, *Scotorum Historiae a prima gentis origine* (Paris, 1574), Bk. XI, fols. 220 v–221 v. Pierre le Loyer, *Discours*, *op. cit.*, Bk. IV, ch. 15, pp. 369–70.

39. *Fuero juzgo en latín y castellano, cotejado con los más antiguos y preciosos códices por la Real Academia Española* (Madrid, 1815), pp. 81–2 and 104–6 (Latin with Spanish translation).

40. Pomponius Mela, III, 7.

41. *Scriptores Historiae Augustae: Alex-Sev.* (Biography ascribed to Lampridius): *Numerianus* (biography ascribed to Flavius Vopiscus).

42. Gregory of Tours, *Hist. franc.*, VI, 35.

43. *Ibid*, V, 40.

44. *Ibid*, VII, 44.

45. Jules Garinet, *Histoire de la magie en France, dépuis le commencement de la Monarchie jusqu'à nos jours* (Paris, 1818), pp. 6–7, 39–40, etc., and appendices.

46. Baluze, *Capitularia regum francorum*, I, (Paris, 1677), cols. 150–2—chapter 4 of the Capitular, comprising an 'Indiculus superstitionum et paganiarum'.

47. Baluze, *op. cit.*, I, cols. 220 (Chapter 18, dated 789), 518 (chapter 40, of uncertain date), 707 (chapter 21 of Book I of Ansegisus' collection), 837 (chapter 69 of Book V of the same collection), 929 (chapter 26 of Book VI), 962 (chapter 215 of Book VI), 999 (chapter 397 of Book VI), 1104 chapters 369–70) of Book VII).

48. Baluze, *op. cit.*, II, cols. 230–1 (§ VII).

49. J. B. Thiers, *Traité des superstitions qui regardent les sacremens*, I (Paris, 1741), pp. 178, 198, and *passim*.

50. Title 3 of Canon 42. Cf. Hansen, *op. cit.*, pp. 66–7.

51. Agobard's work, 'Liber contra insulsam vulgi opinionem de grandinem' can be found in Migne's *Patrology*, CIV, cols. 147 ff. Nearly all writers on the subject quote it. See, *inter alia*, Hansen, *op. cit.*, p. 73.

52. Cf. J. B. Thiers, *op. cit.*, note 49.

53. Baluze, *op. cit.*, I, cols. 251–2: 'VI. Si quis a diabolo deceptus crediderit, secundum morem paganorum, virum aliquem

aut feminam strigam esse et homines comedere, et propter hoc ipsam incenderit, vel carnem ejus ad comedendum dederit, vel ipsam comederit, capitis sententia punietur'.

54. Hansen, *op. cit.*, pp. 76–7, also refers to the laws promulgated by Stephen of Hungary (AD 997–1038). General histories like Soldan's, or the more recent one by Baissac, contain plenty of material on this period.

1. Julio Caro Baroja, 'Ideas y personas en una población rural', in *Razas, pueblos y linajes*, pp. 293–323.
2. Cf. Chapter 3, section 2.
3. Cf. Du Cange, *Glossarium* (Paris, 1733), II, cols. 567–8.
4. *Pactus Legis Salicae Antiquior.*, LXVII, 1–3; id., *Reform.*, LXVII, 1–3 (P. Canciani, *Barbarorum Leges Antiquae* (ed. Venice, 1781–92), II, pp. 107–8 and 153 respectively). Cf. Garinet, *op. cit.*, pp. 6–7.
5. Shakespeare, *Macbeth*, I, scenes 1 and 3.
6. Hector Boethius, *Scotorum Historiae a prima gentis origine*, fols. 249 r – 249 v (Bk. XII). It should be noted that the women in his text have a supernatural nature, they are 'Parcas' or 'Nymphas aliquas fatidicas', not sorceresses (veneficas, etc.). The narration, therefore, begins as follows: 'Nam Maccabaeo Banquhonique Forres (ubi tum rex agebat) proficiscentibus ac in itinere lusus gratia per campos, sylvasque errantibus medio repente campo *tres apparuere mulieri specie*, insolita vestitus facie ad ipsos accedentes . . .'
7. 'Illud etiam non omittendum, quod quaedam sceleratae mulieres, retro post Satanam converseae, daemonum illusioni bus et phantasmatibus seductae, credunt se ac profitentur nocturnis horis cum Diana paganorum dea (vel cum Herodiade) et innumera multitudine mulierum equitare super quasdam bestias et multa terrarum spatia in tempestate noctis silentio pertransire, ejusque jussionibus velut dominae obedire, et certis noctibus ad ejus servitium evocari.' Cf. Pierre de Lancre, *La mescreance du sortilège* . . . (Paris, 1622), pp. 528–9, for an early example of its use by a writer on witchcraft.
8. Baluze, *op. cit.*, II, col. 365; Canciani, *op. cit.*, III, pp. 76, 112.
9. Reginus, *De disciplinis ecclesiasticis et religione christianae*,

ed. Baluze (Paris, 1671), II, 364. Cf. also Hansen, *op. cit.*, pp. 78–82.

10. See section IV of the present chapter.

11. Burchard of Worms, *Decretorum libri XX* (ed. Cologne, 1584), fols. 194 v – 195 r (XIX, 5). For information on Burchard, cf. Hansen, *op. cit.*, pp. 82–7.

12. Burchard, *op. cit.*, fol. 195 r: 'Si credidisti has vanitates, duos annos per legitimas ferias poeniteas.'

13. *Ibid*, fol. 195 r: 'Nam innumera multitudo hac falsa opinione decepta, haec vera esse credit, et credendo a recta fide deviat, et in errore paganorum volvitur, cum aliquid divinitatis aut numinis extra unum Deum esse arbitrantur.'

14. *Ibid*, fol. 194 r (XIX, 5): 'Credidisti, ut aliqua foemina sit, quae hoc facere possit, quod quaedam a diabolo deceptae, se affirmant necessario et ex praecepto facere debere, id est, cum daemonum turba in similitudinem mulierum transformatam, quam vulgaris stultitia Holdam vocat, certis noctibus equitare debere super quasdam bestias, et in eorum se consortio annumeratum esse? Si particeps fuisti illius credulitatis, annum unum per legitimas ferias poenitere debes.' (Cap. LX in other editions).

15. *Ibid*, fol. 199 v (XIX, 5). Hansen, *op. cit.*, especially p. 84. Other editions of Burchard make this Chapter CLVIII. Cf., for example, *Mélusine*, XI (1912), cols. 11–15.

16. Ivon of Chartres, *Decretum*, XI, 30; Hansen, *op. cit.*, pp. 89–90.

17. Gratian, *Decretum*, II, XXVI, v, 12; Hansen, *op. cit.*, pp. 94–6.

18. Other works on witchcraft to be consulted, apart from those we have mentioned, are, *inter alia*, Jules Baissac, *Le diable* ... , p. 277; Soldan, *Geschichte der Hexenprozesse*, I, pp. 107–10; J. Français, *L'Eglise et la Sorcellerie* (Paris, 1910), p. 216 (texts and documents). Cf. also H. Ch. Lea, *op. cit.*, III, pp. 591 (= 494), 592 (= 495), and the same author's *A History of the Inquisition in Spain* (New York, 1907), IV, pp. 208–9.

19. John of Salisbury, *Policraticus* (Leyden, 1639), p. 83 (II, 17): 'Qui in quosdam exigentibus culpis, Domino permittente, tanta malitiae suae licentia debacchatur, ut quod in spiritu patiuntur, miserrime et mendacissime credant in corporibus evenire. Quale est quod Nocticulam (Noctilucam) quandam

vel Herodiadem, vel praesidem noctis afferunt convocare, varia celebrari convivia, ministeriorum species diversis occupationibus exerceri, et nunc istos ad poenam trahi pro meritis, nunc illos ad gloriam sublimari. Praeterea infantes exponi lamiis, et nunc frustatim discerptos, edaci ingluvie in ventrem traiectos congeri, nunc praesidentis miseratione reiectos in cuna reponi. Quis vel caecus hoc ludificantium daemonum non videat esse nequitiam? Quod vel eo patet, quod mulierculis et viris simplicioribus et infirmioribus in fide, ista proveniunt.' Hansen, *op. cit.*, p. 134, reproduces the ideas of John of Salisbury and other passages.

20. The Venice 1591 edition of Vincent de Beauvais' *Speculi maioris* consists of four large volumes. The last volume is not his work, and the third contains the majority of cases used subsequently by moralists and others.

21. These occurrences are to be found in relatively late authors. See also Note 22 *infra*.

22. A. Calmet, *Dissertations sur les apparitions des Anges, des Démons et des Esprits* (Paris, 1746), pp. 161–2. These pages give the published sources of this story: Jacobus de Voragine (*La légende dorée* . . . I, Paris, 1843, p. 196), Pierre de Noels, St Antonin, and early breviaries of Auxerre. The story is also to be found in collections like that of Henningus Grosius *Magica de spectris et apparitionibus spirituum*, p. 20, which also includes the two stories from the *Speculum*.

23. Margaret Murray, *The Witch-Cult in Western Europe* (Oxford, 1921). Other more recent books and articles by the same author enlarge upon or modify her earlier views. Cf. for example, *The God of the Witches* (London, n.d.).

24. There is also a male spirit, 'Dianum', perhaps the Asturian 'dianu'.

25. St Martín Braga, 'De correctione rusticorum', 3, in *España Sagrada*, XV, p. 427: 'in fluminibus Laminas, in fontibus Ninfas, in silvis Dianas.'

26. Cf. C. Cabal, *La mitología asturiana. Los dioses de la vida* (Madrid, 1925), pp. 71–5, and Aurelio de Llano, *Del folklore asturiano; mitos, supersticiones y costumbres* (Madrid, 1922), pp. 28–47, for information about Santander. Cf. M. Llano, *Brañaflor* (Santander, 1931), pp. 25–9, 43–4, 60–2, etc., for the Santander region.

27. Information is summarised and bibliographical details given in Oswald, Erich and Richard Beitl's *Wörterbuch der Deutschen Volkskunde* (Stuttgart, 1955). p. 348 (Holle), 74–5 (Bercht), etc.

28. Du Cange, *Glossarium*, I, col. 1127. They date from AD 1280 according to col. 1467 in Vol. II.

29. Cf. the magnificent books of E. Mâle. English translations of these are now accessible, for instance, *The Gothic Image. Religious Art in France of the Thirteenth Century* (New York, n.d.).

30. For information about 'Abundia' and 'Satia', cf. Hansen, *op. cit.*, pp. 134–5.

CHAPTER 5: THE DEVIL'S PART

1. The Devil is not represented in this way in the earliest Christian pictures of him. See, for example, the Devil in the sixth-century church at Bauït in Egypt.

2. For contemporary views of women, cf. G. G. Coulton, *Medieval Panorama. The English Scene from Conquest to Reformation* (New York, 1957), pp. 614–28.

3. This kind of pictorial representation lasted until the time of Hieronymus Bosch, who was undoubtedly a master of medieval symbolism.

4. Obviously there were some defenders of the female sex with chivalrous ideals.

5. Cf. St Gregory, *Dialogues*, II, 2.

6. Cf. Fray Alonso del Pozo, *Vida de la Venerable Madre Doña Michaela de Aguirre* (Madrid, 1718), relevant extracts from which are included in Manuel Serrano y Sanz, *Apuntes para una biblioteca de escritoras españolas desde el año* 1401 *al* 1833, I (Madrid, 1903), pp. 14–15.

7. Cf. Fray Antonio Arbiol, *Exemplo de Religiosas en la penitente . . . vida de la Venerable Madre Sor Jacinta de Antondo* (Zaragoza, 1716), in Serrano y Sanz, *op. cit.*, pp. 49.

8. Gonzalo de Berceo, *Milagros de Nuestra Señora*, ed. Solalinde (Madrid, 1922), I, pp. 167–9 especially. Cf. E. Mâle, *The Gothic Image*, pp. 260–1, for details of the legend of Theophilus in Christian art; also, Hansen, *op. cit.*, pp. 168–9, for the general background.

9. The best known Spanish example is that of the Cid. Cf. R. Menéndez Pidal, *La España del Cid* (Buenos Aires, 1943), pp. 186–7.

10. Arturo Graf, *Il diavolo* (Milan, 1889), pp. 221–46.

11. It should be noted that popes, emperors and kings figure largely in the traditional 'Dance of Death' series. In more modern times, artists have continued to place these figures in purgatory, showing them being purified in the fire.

12. I have used the text given by Soldan, *op. cit.*, I, pp. 161–3. The relevant section begins on p. 159.

13. Hansen, *op. cit.*, pp. 307–98 (Chapter V).

14. *Ibid*, pp. 214–34, and more particularly pp. 229–32.

CHAPTER 6: THE 'SABBATH'

1. St Thomas Aquinas, *Quodlibet.*, XI, 10: 'Fides vero catholica vult, quod daemones sint aliquid et possint nocere suis operationibus et impedire carnalem copulam.' This is the basis of the most famous book on witchcraft, the *Malleus Maleficarum*, of which more will be said later. Aquinas puts forward similar ideas in his *Comment. in Job*, I. Cf. Soldan, *op. cit.*, I, p. 143, and Hansen, *op. cit.*, pp. 155–6, more particularly.

2. The Greek text has Φαρμαχοὺς οὐ περιποιήσετε. The Hebrew version, however, uses a word equivalent to witch or sorceress: 'Megasshepha'. Cf. H. Ch. Lea, *Histoire de l'Inquisition au Moyen Age*, III, pp. 477–8.

3. A. Cohen, *Everyman's Talmud* (London, 1949), pp. 161, 280, 295, 319.

4. J. Michelet, *La sorcière* (Paris, 1867), pp. ix–xii.

5. Ignaz Döllinger, *El Pontificado*, Spanish translation by Demetrio Zorrilla (Madrid, n.d.), pp. 171–80.

6. *Fuero de Cuenca*, ed. Rafael Ureña (Madrid, 1935), p. 329.

7. Witches were condemned to be burned as early as AD 943 in Spain (the reign of Ramiro I). Cf. H. Ch. Lea, *A History of the Inquisition of Spain*, IV, p. 179.

8. *Siete partidas*, partida VII, title XXIII, law III.

9. Pierre Clément, *Enguerrand de Marigny, Beaune de Semblançay, le chevalier de Rohan, épisodes de l'histoire de France . . .* (Paris, 1859), p. 103.

10. Emile Gebhardt summarised and commented on the work cited in Note 11 *infra* in his 'Un évêque satanique au XIV siècle', in *Les jardins de l'Histoire* (Paris, 1911), pp. 107–21.

11. Abel Rigault, *Le procès de Guichard évêque de Troyes* (1308–13) (Paris, 1896), pp. 66–8 and 271–2—legal measures proposed by the Bailiff of Sens to the ecclesiastical commissioners in August and October 1308 against certain types of spell.

12. Abel Rigault, *op. cit.*, p. II, note 6.

13. It should be remembered that the Graeco-Roman tradition remained in force until only a short time before this. Authors like John of Salisbury accepted the validity of Varro's classification of types of magic. Cf. *Policraticus*, Lib. I, Caps. xi and xii, *op. cit.*, pp. 36–9.

14. Hansen, *op. cit.*, pp. 153–67, has studied the influence of scholasticism on the development of new ideas. Subtle minds like Bacon's were unable to prevent this influence from having its effect. Bacon wrote a work titled *De nullitate Magiae* (cf. Hansen, *op. cit.*, pp. 150–1).

15. H. Ch. Lea, *Histoire de l'Inquisition au Moyen Age*, III, pp. 589–660; also the same author's *A History of the Inquisition of Spain*, IV, p. 207, note 1, and Hansen, *op. cit.*, p. 315.

16. This text, which is taken from the archives of the Inquisition in Toulouse, has been quoted by Lamothe Langon in his *Histoire de l'Inquisition en France*, III (Paris, 1829), p. 235 and ff. (which I have been unable to consult), and Th. de Cauzons in *La Magie et la Sorcellerie en France*, II, pp. 349–54. Cf. also Hansen, *Quellen und Untersuchungen zur Geschichte des Hexenwahns und den Hexenverfolgung im Mittelalter* (Bonn, 1901).

17. H. Ch. Lea, *Histoire de l'Inquisition au Moyen Age*, I, Chapters IX–XI, pp. 399–457.

18. Hansen, *Zauberwahn*, p. 411; Th. de Cauzons, *op. cit.*, II, pp. 389–93, 413–26.

19. Pennethorne Hughes in his *Witchcraft* (London, 1952) and other disciples of Margaret Murray have continued to discuss this point in an equally useless way in my opinion.

20. Cf. Chapter 5, Dualism.

21. The goat is also a symbol of sensuality.

22. Thomas Wright has dealt in a very scholarly way with the pictorial representation of the Devil in the Middle Ages in his

Historie de la Caricature et du Grotesque dans la Littérature et dans l'Art (Paris, 1875), pp. 58–69.

23. This is what we may call Margaret Murray's 'second theory' on the origin of the witch cult. Cf. Pennethorne Hughes, *op. cit.*, pp. 38, 40–3, etc.

24. E. Durkheim, *Les formes élémentaires de la vie religieuse* (Paris, 1912).

25. I have written about medieval factions on a number of occasions, more particularly in *Vasconiana* (Madrid, 1957), pp. 15–61 ('Linajes y bandos').

26. Lamothe Langon and a number of other writers after him have referred to these trials. Cf., for example, Th. de Cauzons, *op. cit.*, II, pp. 355–8.

27. Hansen, *Quellen* . . . , p. 100, and Th. de Cauzons, *op. cit.*, II, pp. 388–9.

28. Th. de Cauzons, *op. cit.*, II, pp. 459–68.

29. Jean de Meung, *Roman de la Rose*, line 18624; Hansen, *Zauberwahn*, pp. 147–50. Cf. also Jean Français, *L'Eglise et la sorcellerie*, p. 17.

30. This is a clear allusion to the 'Waldenses' who are confused with sorcerers and witches in many other trials.

31. J. Baissac, *Le diable*, pp. 544–5.

32. There is a photographic reproduction of a fifteenth-century French miniature in Pennethorne Hughes, *op. cit.*, between pages 64 and 65.

33. Cf. more especially Jean Giraud, *L'Inquisition médiévale* (Paris, 1928), pp. 86–8.

34. The Spanish abbé, Marchena, translated and made a summary of Eymerich's work as anti-inquisitorial propaganda at the beginning of the nineteenth century: *Manual de inquisidores para uso de las inquisiciones de España y Portugal, o compendio de la obra titulada Directorio de inquisidores, de Nicolas Eymerico, Inquisidor general de Aragón. Traducida del francés en idioma castellano. Por D. J. Marchena; con adiciones del traductor acerca de la Inquisición de España* (Montpellier, 1819), pp. 104–6 especially.

35. I quote from the Lyons, 1584 edition of the *Malleus Maleficarum*, I, pp. 465–540.

36. Johannes Nider, *Formicarius*, *op. cit.*, p. 479 (Chapter III).

37. *Ibid*, pp. 484–5 (Chapter IV).

38. Johannes Nider, *Formicarius*, loc. cit.
39. *Ibid*, p. 487 (Chapter IV).
40. *Ibid*, pp. 489–91 (Chapter V).
41. *Ibid*, pp. 480–1 (Chapter III).
42. *Ibid*, p. 481 (Chapter III).
43. H. Ch. Lea, *A History of the Inquisition of Spain*, IV, p. 208.
44. Cf. Hansen, *Zauberwahn*, pp. 412–16, on the Papal Bulls of the period from 1434 to 1484.
45. This is found at the beginning of nearly all editions of the *Malleus*, after the Index.
46. 'At the same time we give instructions in our Apostolic Letters to our beloved brother the Archbishop of Strasburg, for him or others to publish this most solemnly whenever it shall seem necessary to him, or whenever one or both of the Inquisitors shall require it. Nor shall he allow the Inquisitors to be molested in their work.'
47. Hansen, *Zauberwahn*, pp. 445–70, has a good deal to say about the *Malleus*. For his comments on the Bull of Innocence VIII, see p. 467. There have been several modern editions of this.
48. *Malleus*, *op. cit.*, I, pp. 90–6.
49. *Ibid*, I, pp. 96–104 (on metamorphosis: quaestio X), and pp. 104–5 (on midwives: quaestio XI).
50. *Ibid*, I, pp. 105–42.
51. *Ibid*, I, pp. 160–9 (Part II, quaestio II, cap. II).
52. *Ibid*, II, pp. 155–160 (Part II, quaestio II, cap. II).
53. *Ibid*, I, pp. 169–247 (Part II, quaestio II, caps. III–XIII).
54. *Ibid*, I, p. 146 (Part II, quaestio I, Introduction).
55. *Ibid*, I, p. 175 (Part II, quaestio I, cap. III).
56. *Ibid*, I, pp. 333–91 (Part III, quaestiones I–XXX).

CHAPTER 7: THE RENAISSANCE CRISIS

1. A whole chapter of his classic work is devoted to superstitions in general, i.e. Chapter IV of Part VI, in the French translation of M. Schmitt—*La civilisation en Italie au temps de la Renaissance* (Paris, 1906)—pages 289–334. Cf. also pp. 315–21 of the same edition for information about the *streghe*.
2. *Ibid*, II, pp. 317–34.
3. The description is that given by Alvigia in a dialogue with Rosso in *The Courtesan*, Act II, Scene VII (*Oeuvres choisies*

275

de P. Aretin, translated into French by P. L. Jacob, Paris, 1845, pp. 117–21). The description is similar to that of the Celestina in Spanish literature and has the same overtones of classical learning. The person described, however, is essentially a Roman Renaissance figure.

4. Bernard of Como is one of the more famous witch-judges, Cf. Hansen, *Zauberwahn*, p. 419.

5. Julio Caro Baroja, 'La Magia en Castilla durante los siglos XVI y XVII' in *Algunos mitos españoles*, ed. cit., pp. 183–303.

6. Cf. the recent book of Modesto Laza Palacios—*El laboratorio de Celestina* (Málaga, 1958).

7. Cf. A. González de Amezúa's introduction to his edition of Cervantes' *El casamiento engañoso y El coloquio de los perros* (Madrid, 1912), pp. 178–83, etc. Further details are to be found in the works of Francisco Rodríguez Marín and in Sebastián Cirac Estopañón, *Aportacion a la historia de la Inquisición española. Los procesos de hechicerias en la Inquisicion de Castilla la Nueva (Tribunales de Toledo y Cuenca)*, (Madrid, 1942), I have recently published a study of a seventeenth-century Madrid witch, Doña Antonia de Acosta, whom Cirac discusses on pp. 136–51 of his book: '*Dona Antonia de Acosta Mexia, Perfil de una hechicera del siglo XVII*', 'Revista de dialectologia y tradiciones populares', XVII (1961), pp. 39–65.

8. Alfonso Martínez de Toledo, *Libro del arcipreste de Talavera llamado reprobacion del amor mundano o Corbacho*, ed. J. Rogerio Sánchez (Madrid, n.d.), pp. 275–6. See also the interesting passage on pp. 233–4.

9. J. Saroïhandy, 'El boque de Biterna en los fueros catalanes del valle de Aneu,' in the *Revista de Filologia Española*, IV (1917), pp. 33–40. The 'boque' or 'boch' is the he-goat. The documents in the municipal archives at Esterri were put in order in 1408 and some date from 1337. Two depositions were added in 1419 and 1424, the latter of which (dated 26 June) refers to witchcraft.

10. Cf. Chapter VI, The first 'Sabbath'.

11. His opinion can be found in the *Anales Salmantinos* of Fray Luis G. A. Getino, I ('Vida y obras de F. Lope de Barrientos') (Salamanca, 1927), pp. 177–9—'Tratado de la adivinanza'.

It runs as follows:

'In reply to the nineteenth Question: What answer is to be given to the belief that there are certain women called witches, who are said and believed to accompany the Pagan Goddess Diana at night, together with many other women who ride on beasts and travel through many towns and places, and are said to be able to harm animals or make use of them . . .

To this it should be answered as Raimund answers, that these things are the result of the work of evil spirits (theologically speaking) who change themselves into various shapes and forms, and deceive the souls they have in their power. Nor should anyone believe such an absurd thing as that these supposed events really take place, other than in dreams or in the imagination. Anyone who believes such things is an infidel and worse than a pagan, to judge from the way that they conceive these things. Furthermore, apart from these theological considerations, any man who has intelligence and common sense must consider what becomes of the bodies of these women, who are said to be in many places at the same time, and to be able to enter a house through the narrowest crannies. Do they leave their bodies behind, or do they take them with them? It cannot be maintained that they leave their bodies, for theologians and philosophers hold that it is impossible for the soul to leave the body when it wills. Nor can it be maintained that they take their bodies with them either. For all bodies have three dimensions: height, width and breadth, and are only able to pass through spaces which have the same dimensions as they, so that they can in no wise enter a house through crannies or small holes. And to hold that they can turn themselves into geese and enter houses to suck children is equally as absurd as to maintain that a man or a woman can leave off their natural form and take on that of some other species. So we can believe and assert that such things are the products of the imagination, and those who believe they do such things have something wrong with their minds, as we said when writing on the subject of dreams, the result of which is that their imagination loses all control and invents such things. To believe the contrary is to be lacking in common sense, failing to see the force of these arguments.

Consequently women should pay heed to their animals

and watch over them, and if they die through lack of care let them not blame it on witches who come through crannies to kill them; for to say and to maintain such a thing is to hold that these women have the bodies of those who are in Glory, and can enter as Christ entered the place where his disciples were, *januis clausis* (when the doors were shut).'

12. H. Ch. Lea, *A History of the Inquisition of Spain*, IV, pp. 209–10, quotes these views and those of other fifteenth-century writers. Hansen had earlier discussed these in his *Quellen . . .* , pp. 105–17.

13. Francisco de Vitoria, *Relecciones teológicas*, translated into Spanish by Jaime Torrubiano y Ripoll, III (Madrid, 1917), pp. 152–3 ('Relección del arte mágica').

14. Pomponazzi's *De naturalium effectuum, admirandis causis seu incantationibus liber* is prefaced with a dedicatory letter dated 14 July 1520. This would seem to suggest that the book was written before this date, although it was not printed until 1556 in Basle. There was another edition in Basle in 1567. I have also consulted the French translation by Henri Busson— *Les causes des merveilles de la nature ou les enchantements . . .* (Paris, 1930)—which has an interesting introduction on pp. 9–105. Critics and historians of philosophy have often referred to Pomponazzi and drawn attention to his rationalist approach (Victor Cousin, for example, in his *Histoire générale de la Philosophie* (Paris, 1867), p. 297). But the originality of his ideas about the powers possessed by certain people was already recognised by Bayle in his *Dictionnaire historique et critique*, XI (Paris, 1820), pp. 233–4, note D.

15. Ponzinibius was subsequently held to be a heretic by many credulous writers of later periods. But Martín del Río, in his *Disquisitionum magicarum*, p. 154 (liber II, quaest. XVI), includes him among Catholics who have held this view, like Fray Samuel, Alonso de Espina (the author of *Fortalitium fidei*) and Martín de Arles, in Spain; Porta and Alciatus in Italy; Duaren, Aerodius, Mich. Montanus (i.e. Montaigne) in France; John of Salisbury in England; and Camerarius and Molitor in Germany.

16. For information about these trials, cf. J. Baissac, *Les grands jours de la sorcellerie* (Paris, 1890), Ch. IV, pp. 34–61, and Th. de Cauzons, *op. cit.*, III, pp. 90–7.

17. Hansen, *Quellen*, pp. 263.

18. *Ibid*, p. 275.

19. I have used the Lyons, 1545 edition: *Tractatus de Hereticis: et Sortilegiis omnifarium coitu* . . . etc. There is an earlier edition, also printed in Lyons, dated 1536. The section on spells begins on f. XIV v. Bodin, del Río and Lancre, *inter alia*, constantly quoted Grillandus.

20. Grillandus, *Tractatus de hereticis et sortilegiis*, f. XLIII r.

21. *Ibid*, f. XLII r. The Italian word is 'Martinetto' or 'Martinello'.

22. *Ibid*, ff. XLI r–XLIII v. Cf. also *Magica de spectris et apparitionibus*, pp. 260–1 (Book I, No 250).

23. *Ibid*, ff. XXXIX r–XL v. Cf. also *Magica de spectris et apparitionibus*, pp. 259–60 (Book I, No 249).

24. *Ibid*, ff. XL v–XII r. Cf. also *Magica de spectris* . . . , pp. 260–1 (Book I, No 250).

25. Cf. Angelo de Gubernatis, *La mythologie des plantes ou les légendes du règne végétal*, II (Paris, 1882), pp. 248–53, the article entitled 'Noyer'.

26. Aretinus' 'The Courtesan', Act II, Scene VII (*Oeuvres choisies*, ed. cit., p. 119). For a longer exposé see 'The Philosopher', Act II, Scene XII (*op. cit.*, pp. 28–9).

27. The relevant work of Caesalpinus (1519–1603) is entitled *Daemonum investigatio peripatetica*, 2nd edition (Venice, 1593), to be found at the end of his *Quaestionum peripateticarum libri V* according to Victor Cousin (cf. *Histoire générale de la Philosophie*, p. 298). The work is also referred to by Bayle in his *Dictionnaire historique*, V (Paris, 1820), p. 19, note D, but no comment is made on its content.

28. *Hieronymi Cardani mediolanensis medici, de subtilitate libri XXI* (Basle, 1611), p. 909 (lib. XVIII, 'de mirabilibus'): 'Inde ab his natam opinionem lamiarum, quae apio, castaneis, cepis, caulibus, phaselisque victitantes, videntur per somnum ferri in diversas regiones, atque ibi diversis modis affici, prout uniuscuiusque fuerit temperies. Iuvantur ergo ad haec unguento, quo se totas perungunt. Constat ut creditur puerorum pinguedine e sepulchris, eruta, succisque apii, aconitque pentaphylli, siligineque. Incredibile dictu quanta sibi videre persuadeant: modo laeta, theatra, viridaria, piscationes,

vestes, ornatus, saltationes, formosos juvenes, concubitusque eius generis quales optant.'

29. The following paragraph is taken from the work entitled *Magica, de spectris et apparitionibus*, p. 212 (Lib. I, No 189) as quoted in Porta's book, *Magiae naturalis sive de miraculis rerum naturalium libri XX* (Naples 1589.) The earliest parts of the original date from 1558. 'Incidit mihi in manus vetula quaedam (quas a strigis avis nocturnae similitudine striges vocant, quaeque puerulorum sanguinem e cunis absorbent) sponte pollicita brevis mihi temporis spatio allaturam responsa. Jubet omnes foras egredi cum acciti erant testes, spoliisque nudata, tota se unguento quodam valde perfricuit, nobis e portae rimulis conspicua: sic soporiferum vi succorum cecidit, profundoque occubuit sommo. Fores ipsi patefacimus multum vapulat, tantaque vis soporis fuit, ut sensum eriperet. Ad locum foras redimus, jam medelae vires fatiscunt, flaccescuntque. A sommo se vocata, culta incipit fari deliria, se maria montesque transmeasse, falsa depromens responsa. Negamus, instat: livores ostendimus, pertinaciter, resistit magis.'

30. *Vita de Benvenutto Cellini scritta da lui medesimo*, ed. Adolfo Padovan (Milan, 1925), pp. 119–29 (Chapter XIII).

31. José Somoza described this episode in his booklet *El Doctor Andrés Laguna o el tiempo de las brujas* (Salamanca, 1846). The passage is taken from Laguna's *Materia medica* (Antwerp, 1555), IV, xxv, pp. 421–2, and has recently been quoted by Marcel Bataillon in his 'Contes à la première personne (Extraits des livres sérieux du Docteur Laguna)' in *Bulletin Hispanique*, LVIII (1956), pp. 204–5.

32. Ulrich Molitor, *Des sorcières et des enchanteresses per U . . . M . . . Reproduit en fac-simile d'après l'édition latine de Cologne 1489 et traduit pour la première fois en français* (Paris, 1926). The edition in question is Volume I of E. Nourry, *Bibliothèque magique des XV⁰ et XVI⁰ siècles*. There are seven illustrations altogether, but six are more especially interesting.

33. Molitor, *op. cit.*, p. 81 of the French translation. The Latin text is without pagination.

34. I have used the text given by Godelmann in his *Tractatus de magis, veneficis et lamiis* (Frankfurt, 1601), pp. 66–7 (Tractatus I, cap. VII).

35. *Magica, de spectris et apparitionibus*, pp. 223–24, 226 (Book I, Nos 206–7 and 209).

36. Cf. Del Río, *Disquisitionum magicarum libri sex*, p. 154 (Lib. II, quaestio XVI), and Godelmann, *op. cit.*, pp. 67 (I, vii), 33 (II, iv), 63 I, v), 68 (I, vii).

37. *Henrici Cornelii Agrippae ab Nettesheym. De incertitudine & vanitate omnium scientiarum & artium* (Leyden, 1614), pp. 278–9.

38. Jean de Wier, *Histoires, disputes et discours des illusions et impostures des diables, des magiciens infames, sorcières et empoissoneurs: des ensorcelez et demoniaques et de la guerison d'iceux: item de la punition que meritent les magiciens, les empoissoneurs et les sorcières*, 2 vols. (Paris, 1885): a reliable reprint of the 1579 edition.

39. *Ibid*, I, pp. 274–484.

40. *Ibid*, I, pp. 357–8 (Book III, ch. XVI).

41. Montaigne, *Essais*, IV (ed. Ch. Louandre, Paris, n.d.), pp. 192–7 (Book III, ch. XI).

CHAPTER 8: THE DEFINITIVE FORM OF THE CRIME OF WITCHCRAFT

1. H. Ch. Lea, *A History of the Inquisition of Spain*, IV, p. 210. 'El Tostado' gives the two views one after the other, while Alonso de Espina and Martín de Arles follow the *Canon Episcopi*. Cf. also Lea, *op. cit.*, II, pp. 209–10, and Hansen, *Quellen*, pp. 105–9, 113–17, 308, etc.

2. For information on Jacquier, cf. Hansen, *Zauberwahn*, pp. 446–7. On others mentioned in the passage cf. Hansen, *Quellen*, pp. 124–34, 206, 227, and Th. de Cauzons, *op. cit.*, I, pp. 390–3.

3. Jean de Wier, *op. cit.*, II, pp. 262–7 (Book VI, chapter XIII). See also pp. 268–76 (Book VI, chapter XIV) for Wier's critical views.

4. J. Baissac, *op. cit.*, pp. 339–41.

5. L. Daneau, *Les sorciers, dialogue très utile et nécessaire pour ce temps* (Geneva, 1574). There are references to a Paris edition the same year.

6. Jean Bodin, *De la Demonomanie des Sorciers* (Paris, 1580), f. 85 r (Book II, chapter IV).

7. Jean Bodin, *op. cit.*, f. 199 v. These crimes are discussed and

to some extent analysed in Michaelis, *Discours des esprits en tant qu'il est de besoin pour entendre et resoudre la matière difficile des Sorciers* (Paris, 1594), pp. 143–84, in notes on the *Extraict d'une sentence donnée en Avignon, contre dix huict Sorciers, ou Sorcières l'an de grace 1582*.

8. Bayle's article on Bodin is full of irony, as are most of the articles in his *Dictionnaire historique et critique*—cf. III (Paris, 1820), pp. 506–25. See also H. Baudrillart, *J. Bodin et son temps. Tableau des théories politiques et des idées économiques au seizième siècle* (Paris, 1853), especially pp. 183–90.

9. Jean Bodin, *De la Demonomanie des Sorciers*, ff. 218 r–252 r – 'Refutation des opinions de Jean de Wier'.

10. *Syntagma juris universi atque legum pene omnium gentium et rerum publicarum praecipuarum, in tres partes digestum* (Lyon, 1582), Part III, Book XXXIV, chapter I. There is no further information about this case other than that given by Gregory (cf. Th. de Cauzons, *op. cit.*, III, pp. 127–8. It is discussed later by Pierre de Lancre in a passage which will be examined in due course.

11. Emile Gebhardt, *Les procès pour sorcellerie à Toulouse aux XVIe et XVIIe siècles* (1583–1623) in *Les jardins de l'Histoire* (Paris, 1911), pp. 225–39.

12. Witchcraft in this region has been studied in detail by Charles Pfister and other scholars. The authority on Alsace (and other areas too for that matter) is R. Reuss.

13. *Nic. Remigii Daemonolatria lib. III, ex judiciis capitalibus noningentorum plus minus hominum, qui sortilegii crimen intra annos quindecim in Lotharingia capite luerunt* (Lyons, 1595). Another edition was published at Cologne the following year. A summary of Rémy's views was given by Jules Baissac, *op. cit.*, pp. 386–90. For further information see Jean Français, *L'Eglise et la Sorcellerie*, pp. 109–13, and for the most up-to-date bibliography Th. de Cauzons, *op. cit.*, III, pp. 156–62.

14. Suicide is often provoked by social pressures or by the desire to emulate others. Books which are in fashion can also be influential.

15. Almost all witchcraft scholars mention Boguet. For a bibliography, see J. Français, *op. cit.*, pp. 115–16, with a discussion of his views on p. 117 and ff. Cf. also Th. de Cauzons, *op. cit.*, III, pp. 162–7. The 1608 edition of his book is entitled

Discours des sorciers, avec six advis en faict de sorcellerie, et une instruction pour un juge en semblable matière (Lyons, 1608). The part containing the instruction is a later addition.

16. J. Garinet, *Histoire de la magie en France*, pp. 300–2 (note VI on page 166), gives an extract from this same passage. Boguet was rewarded by being nominated a Counsellor of the Dôle Parlement, but he had quite a struggle before he could take up the appointment, since his work did not meet with universal approval.

17. This is another instance of an old wives' tale being accepted as a fact. The case of the gentleman who shot at some cats, one of whom dropped a bunch of keys as it ran away, and turned out to be his wife, is a parallel one. Cf. Boguet, *Discours*, p. 344.

18. Bounneville and E. Teinturier made use of Boguet, Bodin and Guazzo (of whom more will be said later) when writing their booklet, *Le sabbat des sorciers*, 2nd. ed. (Paris, 1890). They include illustrations from both Molitor and Guazzo, and the same woodcuts have often been used to illustrate books on witchcraft. Their booklet was the first volume of the series entitled *Bibliothèque diabolique* which also included Jean de Wier's and Boguet's books and several trials of the sixteenth and seventeenth centuries.

19. Francis Bavoux, *La sorcellerie en Franche-Comté (Pays de Quingey)* (Monaco, 1954).

20. P. Binsfeld, *Tractatus de confessionibus maleficorum et sagarum* (Treves, 1591).

21. Cf. Menéndez y Pelayo, *Historia de los heterodoxos españoles*, III, pp. 655–9, for a lengthy discussion of Del Río. Bibliographical information can be found in *Nouvelle biographie universelle* ed. Didot-Hoefer, XIII (Paris, 1858), cols. 507–8. I have used the Venice 1616 edition of the work.

22. Martín del Río, *Disquisitionum magicarum*, pp. 159–61 (Lib. II, quaest. XVI).

23. Francesco Maria Guaccius (Guazzo), *Compendium maleficarum* (Milan, 1609).

24. Similar views are expressed by L. Maria Sinistrari d'Ameno in his *De la démonialité et des animaux incubes et succubes*, etc. (Paris, 1876), pp. 20–31 (Nos 11–23). Apparently the book was written at the end of the seventeenth century.

CHAPTER 9: THE SPIRIT BEHIND THE DECLARATIONS

1. Cf. Juan Dantín Cereceda's anthology, *Exploradores y conquistadores de Indias* (Madrid, 1922), pp. 110–11.
2. Godelmann, *op. cit.*, p. 5 (Tract. II, cap. I).
3. *Ibid*, p. 31 (Tract. II. cap. IV).
4. The Valkyrie are also closely linked to the souls of the dead. Cf. Oswald E. Erich and Richard Beitl, *Wörterbuch der Deutschen Volkskunde*, p. 852.
5. Godelmann, *op. cit.*, p. 45 (Tract. II, cap. IV). The Devil in the form of a black man, carried him.
6. *Ibid*, p. 33 (Tract. II, cap. IV).
7. *Ibid*, p. 33, loc. cit.
8. *Magia, de spectris et apparitionibus*, p. 168 (Lib. I, No 220).
9. Godelmann, *op. cit.*, pp. 34–5 (Tract. II, cap. IV).
10. The bibliography of books in German is immense. I have largely relied on the fundamental works of Soldan, Hansen and one or two others. A select bibliography is to be found in the article 'Hexe' in Erich and Beitl's *Wörterbuch der Deutschen Volkskunde*, pp. 328–9.
11. There are a large number of works in English on witchcraft in England, Ireland, Scotland and America. In the Romantic period, Sir Walter Scott wrote his *Letters on Demonology and Witchcraft* (the most accessible edition is the one printed in London, 1883) and Thomas Wright his *Narratives of Sorcery and Magic*, 2 vols. (London, 1852), *inter alia*. Prof Wallace Notestein's *History of Witchcraft in England* was published in Washington in 1911 and there have been more recent studies by L'Estrange Ewen—*Witch Hunting and Witch Trials* (London, 1929), *Witchcraft and Demonianism* (London, 1933) —as well as works by Margaret Murray and Montague Summers of a wider scope. The unfinished work of H. Ch. Lea—*Materials towards a History of Witchcraft*, 3 vols. (Philadelphia, 1939)—should also be mentioned. I have not been able to consult it.
12. Jules Baissac has already given an account of this episode in *Les grands jours de la Sorcellerie*, pp. 229–43 (Chapter X), drawing on a number of English sources. One of the best-known novels of Harrison Ainsworth, *The Lancashire Witches*,

which ran into many editions, serves as a good example of the Romantic treatment of the theme.

13. Montague Summers wrote two books on the subject which I have not been able to see: *The History of Witchcraft and Demonology* (London, 1926), and *The Geography of Witchcraft* (London, 1927). The views here are his, and they will be examined further at the end of the book.

CHAPTER 10: WITCHCRAFT AND POSSESSION BY DEVILS

1. T. K. Oesterreich, *Les possédés. La possession démoniaque chez les primitifs, dans l'antiquité, au moyen âge et dans la civilisation moderns*, translated into French by R. Sudre (Paris, 1927).

2. Some of these views have already been put forward by me in 'La Magia en Castilla durante los siglos XVI y XVII' in *Algunos mitos españoles y otros ensayos*, pp. 265–6.

3. Fray Martín de Castañega, *Tratado muy sotil y bien fundado d las supersticiones y hechizerías*, chapter XIV; Miguel Sabuco (previously Doña Oliva), *Nueva filosofía de la naturaleza del hombre* (Madrid, 1728), pp. 59–60.

4. E. E. Evans Pritchard, *Witchcraft, Oracles and Magic among the Azande* (Oxford, 1937), especially pp. 21–5.

5. Cf. Chapter 19, Personal Observation of a Typical Witchcraft Case.

6. Hieronymus Mengus, *Flagellum daemonum, exorcismos terribiles, potentissimos, et efficaces* (Lyon, 1608), pp. 164–5, 184–8, 203–7. This book, which was highly successful when it first appeared, was subsequently put on the Index.

7. Proclus's work on the mysteries of the Egyptians, Chaldees and Assyrians and his commentaries on works of Plato; Porphyry's treatise on diviners and devils; Psellus's work, and Trismegistus's *Pimander*, all had a wide circulation in Latin translations. It would be pointless to give concrete bibliographical references here. The translation in question is that of Ficino.

8. Fray. Antonio de la Peña, *El Ente dilucidado. Discurso único novísimo que muestra ay en naturaleza Animales irracionales invisibles, y quales sean* (Madrid, 1676).

9. Relevant texts on the *Celestina*, and its imitations, Rodrigo de

Reynosa's *Coplas de las comadres*, Micael de Caravajal and Luis Hurtado de Toledo's *Cortes de la muerte*, and Agustín de Rojas's *Viaje entretenido*, are quoted in 'La Magia en Castilla durante los siglos XVI y XVII' in my *Algunos mitos españoles y otros ensayos*, pp. 243–9.

10. There are large numbers of magic recipes and formulae—particularly amatory ones—in the examination of the trial of Doña Antonia de Acosta Mexía, which is amongst the documents of the Inquisition of Toledo now in the Archivo Histórico Nacional in Madrid, Leg. 91, N° 176, 9. I have published these documents in the *Revista de dialectología y tradiciones populares* (*vide* note 7 of chapter VII).

11. Fray Alonso de la Fuente, 'Memorial en que se trata de las cosas que han pasado con los alumbrados d'Estremadura, desdel año de setenta hasta el fin deste año de setenta y cinco', in *Revista de Archivos, Bibliotecas y Museos*, XII (1905), p. 268.

12. Jules Baissac, *op. cit.*, pp. 419–40 (chapter XVII). For an earlier account, see Garinet, *Histoire de la magie en France*, pp. 177–90; and for a still earlier account including details of the sentence passed, Pierre de Lancre, *L'Incrédulité et mescréance du sortilège plainement convaincue*, pp. 830–3. There are also some details of the trial in Gayot de Pitaval, *Causes célèbres*, VI (Amsterdam, 1775), pp. 152–92.

13. There is a tendencious book by a protestant author with the following suggestive title: *Histoire des diables de Loudun, ou de la Possession des religieuses ursulines, Et de la condemnation et du suplice d'Urbain Grandier, Curé de la même Ville. Cruels effets de la vengeance du cardinal de Richelieu* (Amsterdam, n.d.). Bekker analysed the more important depositions in *Le monde enchanté*, pp. 205–21 (Book IV, chapter XI). Bayle's articles on Grandier and Loudun are intelligent (cf. *Dictionnaire historique et critique*, VII, pp. 194–204, and IX, pp. 384–6, respectively). Gayot de Pitaval's account is also worth reading in his *Causes célèbres*, II (Amsterdam, 1775), pp. 273–439. Cf. also, Didot-Hoeffer's *Nouvelle biographie générale*, XX (Paris, 1857), cols. 644–53, which contains an extensive bibliography, and Jules Baissac, *op. cit.*, pp. 454–521. Michelet's *La sorcière*, pp. 225–81, is inaccurate but interesting.

14. J. Barbey d'Aurévilly, *L'ensorcelée* (Paris, 1859).
15. Cf. M. Menéndez y Pelayo, *Historia de los heterodoxos españoles*, II, pp. 556–8, for a summary account of the trial. An earlier and more detailed account is that of J. A. Llorente, *Histoire critique de l'Inquisition d'Espagne*, III, pp. 484–93; and Gregorio Marañón, in his *El conde-duque de Olivares. La pasión de mandar* (Madrid, 1936), pp. 190–3, properly distinguishes between the events of 1628 and those of 1638, when Philip IV is supposed to have been in love with a nun of the same convent, which had acquired a bad reputation and then been justifiably rehabilitated.
16. Ramón de Mesonero Romanos, *El antiguo Madrid, paseos históricos anecdóticos por las calles y casas de esta villa*, II (Madrid, 1881), pp. 263–8, gives a late account of the episode with the title 'Relación de todo lo sucedido en el caso de la Encarnación Benita, que llaman de San Plácido, de esta corte'.
17. Doña Teresa Valle de La Cerda's work was published by M. Serrano y Sanz in his *Apuntes para una biblioteca de escritoras españolas desde el año 1401 al 1833*, II (Madrid, 1905), pp. 558–66. The paragraph included here is to be found on p. 564.
18. A fairly comprehensive account of the Salem affair was given by Thomas Wright, *op. cit.*, II, pp. 284–314. Cf. also, J. Baissac, *op. cit.*, pp. 289–306.

CHAPTER 11: WITCHCRAFT AMONG THE BASQUES IN THE SIXTEENTH CENTURY

1. I have already given some information about them in my book *Los vascos*, 2nd. ed. (Madrid, 1958), pp. 431–49 (Chapter XXIII).
2. Pablo de Gorosabel, *Noticia de las cosas memorables de Guipúzcoa*, I (Tolosa, 1899), pp. 353–4 (II, 2, iii).
3. J. M. de Barandiarán, 'Mari, o el genio de las montañas', in *Homenaje a don Carmelo de Echegaray* (San Sebastián, n.d.), 245–68. Cf. also, the same author's *Mitología vasca* (Madrid, 1960), pp. 83–106.
4. Cf. Pedro Fernández de Villegas's commentary on Dante's *Inferno*, quoted by Menéndez y Pelayo in his *Historia de los heterodoxos españoles*, I, p. 620.

5. Cf. El Cartujano's 'Los doce triunfos de los doce apóstoles' in *Cancionero castellano del siglo XV*, ed. R. Foulché-Delbosc, II (Madrid, 1912), p. 306 ('Triunfo de Santiago', VII, verse II).

6. Juan de Mata Carriazo, 'Precursores españoles de la Reforma. Los herejes de Durango (1442–5)' in *Sociedad española de Antropología, Etnografía y Prehistoria. Actas y memorias*, IV (Madrid, 1925), pp. 35–69. Cf. also Justo Gárate, *Ensayos euskarianos*, I (Bilbao, 1935), pp. 114–21 (Ensayo VI).

7. Alonso de Cartagena, *Defensorium unitatis christianae (Tratado en favor de los judíos conversos)*, edited with Introduction and notes by F. Manuel Alonso (Madrid, 1943), pp. 294–5 (Part III, chapter IX, on heretics in the mountain areas and their return to pagan practices): 'sicuti etiam hiis diebus nonnulli ex montanea regione nobis propinque, qui vetustissimas opiniones et erroneos conceptus antique paganitatis noviter assumentes et pertinaci animo defendere temptantes, necnon sacratissimo corpori christi domini nostri sub devotissimo et mirabili sacramenti latenti ac sancte cruci reverentiam exhibere nolentes, et ne dicam illud adorare sed nec intueri volentes, a dyocesano suo heretici pertinaces et incorregibiles declarati per secularem potestatum iuxta severitatem legum igne legitia consumpti sunt.'

8. This view is to be found in both El Gerundense and in Fernando del Pulgar. The relevant text of El Gerundense appears in *Paralipomenon Hispaniae* f. XXIX v, in the 1545 edition (Lib. II, cap. VII), reproduced by R. Chabás in his 'Estudio sobre los sermones valencianos de San Vicente Ferrer' in the *Revista de Archivos, Bibliotecas y Museos*, VI (1902), p. 5. For Fernando del Pulgar, cf. his 'Letras' (N° XXXI) in *Biblioteca de autores españoles*, XIII, p. 59.

9. Cf. J. A. Llorente, *Histoire critique de l'Inquisition d'Espagne*, III (Paris, 1818), pp. 453–4 (Chapter XXXVII, 2, N° 41); H. Ch. Lea, *A History of the Inquisition of Spain*, IV, p. 211 (Book VIII, chapter IX); Menéndez y Pelayo, *Historia de los heterodoxos españoles*, ed. cit., II, pp. 662–3 (V, 4, ii).

10. Martín de Arles, *Tractatus de superstitionibus* (Frankfurt, 1581), pp. 362–5, 413–15. Cf. also Note 11 *infra*.

11. Cf. H. Ch. Lea, *A History of the Inquisition of Spain*, IV, p. 210, who follows Hansen, *Quellen*, p. 308.

12. Prudencio de Sandoval, *Historia del emperador Carlos V*, V (Madrid, 1847), pp. 53–7 (Book XVI, chapter V). A number of subsequent scholars have based views on this work, including J. A. Llorente, *Histoire critique de l'Inquisition en Espagne*, II, pp. 43–7 (XV, 1, Nos 6–9); Marichalar y Manrique, *Historia de la legislación y recitaciones del Derecho Civil de España*, IV (Madrid, 1862), pp. 395–6 (Section III, chapter IV), who also uses other sources; Menéndez y Pelayo, *Historia de los heterodoxos españoles*, II, p. 663 (V, 1, ii); A. González de Amezúa, *El casamiento engañoso y El coloquio de los perros* in *Novelas ejemplares de Cervantes*, critical edition with introduction and notes (Madrid, 1912), pp. 156–7 (Chapter VI).

13. There are two copies of this letter with some variants in the Biblioteca Nacional, Madrid: MSS 10122 ff. 322 r–325 v; and MSS 883 ff. 103 r–105 v. The second of these is wrongly dated 1590 and was used and translated into French by José Güell y Renté for his 'Sorciers et sorcières', in *Considérations politiques et historiques* (Paris, 1863), pp. 293–329. A third copy which is not different in many respects from this latter was published in a volume of *Relaciones históricas* in the collection of *Bibliófilos españoles*, XXXII (Madrid, 1896). I published these accounts together with others of which I shall have more to say later in my 'Cuatro relaciones sobre la hechicería vasca' in *Anuario de 'Eusko Folklore'*, XIII (Vitoria, 1933). H. Ch. Lea, in his *History of the Inquisition of Spain*, IV, pp. 214–5, speaks of a further copy in the Bodleian Library at Oxford. This information seems to be incorrect, at least in so far as the reference he gives is concerned.

14. 'Cuatro relaciones . . .' in the *Anuario de 'Eusko Folklore'*, pp. 93–4; MSS. 10122, ff. 322 r–322 v.

15. *Ibid*, pp. 94–5; *MSS. cit.*, f. 322 v.

16. *Ibid*, p. 95; *MSS. cit.*, ff. 322 v–323 r.

17. *Ibid*, p. 95; *MSS. cit.*, f. 323 r.

18. *Ibid*, pp. 95–6; *MSS. cit.*, f. 323 r.

19. *Ibid*, pp. 96–7; *MSS. cit.*, f. 323 v.

20. *Ibid*, p. 97; *MSS. cit.*, ff. 323 v–324 r.

21. *Ibid*, pp. 97–8; *MSS. cit.*, ff. 323 v–324 r.

22. *Ibid*, p. 100; *MSS. cit.*, ff. 324 v–325 r.

23. *Ibid*, pp. 98–9; *MSS. cit.*, ff. 324 r–325 v.

24. *El Crotalón* (Buenos Aires, 1945), p. 77 ('Quinto canto').
25. Gonzalo Fernández de Oviedo, *Las Quinquagenas de la nobleza de España*, I (Madrid, 1880), pp. 473–4. In Stanza IX, p. 129, he refers to the fondness for sorcery of women in general.
26. *Tratado muy | sotil y bien fundado d'las | supersticiones y hechize | rias, y varios conjuros, y | abusiones; y otras co | sas al caso tocantes y de la possibilidad ó remedio dellas* (Logroño, Miguel de Eguía, 1529). I have used the copy in the Biblioteca Nacional, Madrid, with Press-Mark R-11066.
27. Fray Martín de Castañega, *Tratado muy sotil*, Chapter III.
28. *Ibid*, Chapter IV.
29. Pedro Ciruelo, *Reprouación de las supersticiones y hechizerías* (Salamanca, 1556), f. XIX v. The first edition appeared in 1529.
30. Llorente refers to the preaching missions of Dominicans in Vizcaya in his *Histoire critique de l'Inquisition d'Espagne*, II, p. 47 (Ch. XV, 1, Nº 10). For information about the part played by Fray Juan de Zumárraga, see Fray Jerónimo de Mendieta, *Historia eclesiástica indiana* (Mexico, 1870), p. 629 (Book I, Part I, Chapter XXVII).
31. H. Ch. Lea, *A History of the Inquisition of Spain*, IV, p. 215. Note 2 refers to documents in the Archivo de Simancas, Inq. lib. 76, ff. 51, 53.
32. Cf. Pablo de Gorosabel, *Noticia de las cosas memorables de Guipúzcoa*, I, pp. 355–6 (Book II, Chapter II, § III), for information about the consultation. Lope Martínez de Isasti refers to the death of the inquisitor Ugarte: see Chapter 15 § II.
33. H. Ch. Lea, *A History of the Inquisition of Spain*, IV, pp. 219, citing Archivo de Simancas, Inq. Lib. 78, ff. 215–17, 226, 258.
34. *Ibid*, IV, pp. 221–2, citing Simancas, Inq. lib. 79, f. 226, and Inq. de Logroño, Procesos de fé, Leg. 1, Nº 8, lib. 40, f. 221.
35. Darío de Areitio, 'Las brujas de Ceberio', in *Revista internacional de estudios vascos*, XVIII (1927), pp. 654–64.
36. *Ibid*, pp. 655–7.
37. *Ibid*, pp. 657–9.
38. *Ibid*, pp. 659–60.
39. *Ibid*, pp. 660–1.
40. *Ibid*, pp. 660–2.

41. Darío de Areitio, 'Las brujas de Ceberio', in *Revista internacional de estudios vascos*, XVIII (1927), p. 662.

42. *Ibid*, pp. 663–4.

43. H. Ch. Lea, *A History of the Inquisition of Spain*, IV, pp. 222–3, citing Simancas, Patronato Real, the only existing file, ff. 86–7; Inq. lib. 83, f. 7.

44. Pablo de Gorosabel, *Noticia de las cosas memorables de Guipúzcoa*, I, p. 356 (Book II, chapter II, § III).

45. See Chapter 14, The Action taken by Inquisitor Alonso de Salazar y Frías.

CHAPTER 12: THE GREAT TRIALS OF THE SEVENTEENTH CENTURY
IN THE BASQUE COUNTRY

1. Cf. J. Bernou, *La chasse aux sorcières dans le Labourd* (1609). *Etude historique* (Agen, 1897), pp. 90–104.

2. Michelet, *La sorcière* (Paris, 1867), pp. 201, 204 and 207. Undoubtedly one of the weakest portions of the book and of scant historical interest.

3. For information on de Lancre, see Michaud's *Biographie universelle ancienne et moderne*, XXIII (Paris, 1819), pp, 328–9; Weiss's *Biographie universelle ou Dictionnaire historique*. II (Paris, 1841), p. 422; and similar reference books.

4. Pierre de Lancre, *Tableav | de l'inconstance | des mavvais anges | et demons. | Ov il est amplement trai- | cté de la Sorcelerie & Sorciers. | Livre tres curieux et tres | utile, non seulement aux juges, mais à tous ceux | qui vivent soubs les loix Chrestiennes. | Avec | Vn Discours contenant la Procedure faicte par les Inquisitions d'Espagne | & de Navarre, à 53. Magiciens, Apostats, Juifs, Sorciers, en la ville | de Logrogne en Castille le 9 Novembre 1610. En laquelle on voit, com- | bien l'exercice de la justice en France, est plus iuridiqument traicté, & | avec de plus belles formes qu'en tous autres Empires, Royaumes, Republi- | ques et Estats | . . .* (Paris, 1612).

5. Pierre de Lancre, *L'incredulité | et | mescréance | dv sortilege | plainement | convaincue. | Ov il est amplement et curievsement | traicté, de la verité ou Illusion du Sortilège, de la Fascination, de l'Attouchement, du Scopelisme, de la Divination, de la Ligature | ou liaison Magique, des Apparitions. Et d'une infinité d'autres | rares & nouveaux subjets. | . . .* (Paris, 1622).

6. *Ibid*, p. 548 (IX).

7. Other works by de Lancre are not related to the present subject.

8. Pierre de Lancre, *Tableau* . . . , p. 30 (Book I, Discourse II).

9. *Ibid*, p. 31 (I, Discourse II).

10. *Ibid*, pp. 31–7 (I, Discourse II).

11. *Ibid*, pp. 37–8 (I, Discourse II).

12. *Ibid*, p. 39 (I, Discourse II).

13. *Ibid*, p. 41 (I, Discourse II).

14. *Ibid*, pp. 41–4 (I, Discourse II).

15. *Ibid*, pp. 44–5 (I, Discourse II).

16. *Ibid*, pp. 59–60 (I, Discourse III).

17. *Ibid*, pp. 40–1 (I, Discourse II).

18. *Ibid*, pp. 66–8 (Book II, Discourse I).

19. *Ibid*, p. 69 (II, Discourse I).

20. *Ibid*, pp. 69–70 (II, Discourse I).

21. *Ibid*, pp. 71–3 (II, Discourse I).

22. *Ibid*, ff. aaij r, aaa v (in the Latin text); *L'incrédulité*, pp. 44–52.

23. *Ibid*, pp. 90–2 (II, Discourse II).

24. *Ibid*, pp. 70–1 (I, Discourse, I).

25. *Ibid*, pp. 93–4 (II, Discourse II).

26. *Ibid*, pp. 94–5 (II, Discourse II) and 132–3 (II, Discourse IV).

27. *Ibid*, pp. 95–9 (II, Discourse II).

28. *Ibid*, pp. 100–1 (II, Discourse II).

29. *Ibid*, p. 101 (II, Discourse II).

30. *Ibid*, pp. 101–2 (II, Discourse II).

31. *Ibid*, pp. 114–9 (II, Discourse III).

32. *Ibid*, pp. 128–9 (II, Discourse IV).

33. *Ibid*, pp. 138–9 (II, Discourse IV); *L'incrédulité*, p. 132 (III).

34. *Ibid*, pp. 141–3 (II, Discourse IV).

35. *Ibid*, pp. 143–4 (II, Discourse IV). Cp. *L'incrédulité*, pp. 43–4 (I).

36. *Ibid*, pp. 454–5 (VI, Discourse III).

37. *Ibid*, pp. 456 (VI, Discourse III).

38. *Ibid*, p. 456 (loc. cit.).

39. *Ibid*, p. 460 (VI, Discourse III).

40. *Ibid*, pp. 416–7 (VI, Discourse II).

41. *Ibid*, pp. 418–9 (VI, Discourse II) and 455 (VI, Discourse III).

42. *Ibid*, p. 419 (VI, Discourse II).

43. Pierre de Lancre, *Tableau* . . . , pp. 419–23 (VI, Discourse II). Cf. also pp. 433 (VI, Discourse II) and 492 (VI, Discourse IV).

44. *Ibid*, pp. 447–52 (VI, Discourse II). Cf. also p. 514 (VI, Discourse V) – La Masse, Laffon and Haritourena escaped.

45. *Ibid*, pp. 457–8 (VI, Discourse III).

46. *Ibid*, pp. 348–50 (V, Discourse I). I suspect that the person involved was a 'morisco'.

47. *Ibid*, pp. 185–7 (III, Discourse II).

48. *Ibid*, pp. 130–6 (II, Discourse IV).

49. *Ibid*, pp. 181–2 (III, Discourse II).

50. *Ibid*, pp. 184–5 (III, Discourse II).

51. *Ibid*, p. 117 (I, Discourse III), and 554 (VI, Discourse V). Cf. also Bernou, *La chasse aux sorcières*, pp. 280–7.

52. Pierre de Lancre, *L'incrédulité*, p. 50 (I).

53. *Ibid*, p. 401 (VII).

CHAPTER 13: THE WITCHES OF ZUGARRAMURDI

1. Moratín used a pseudonym when publishing the editions of this work: 'Bachiller Ginés de Posadilla, natural de Yébenes.' The first edition is undated, but is early nineteenth-century, probably the beginning of the Peninsular War period. The second dates from 1812 (Cadiz, Imprenta Tormentaria). There was another edition in Madrid (Collado) in 1820, further editions without date, and one in 1836 (Barcelona), not counting the edition in the *Biblioteca de autores españoles*, II, pp. 617–31. Page references are to this last edition; the first edition is without pagination.

2. Menéndez y Pelayo, *Historia de los heterodoxos españoles*, II, p. 667 (V, 4, ii).

3. H. Ch. Lea, *A History of the Inquisition of Spain*, IV, p. 225, citing Simancas, 'Inquisition of Logroño', Legajo 1, Procesos de fé, N° 8; Book 19, f. 85.

4. *Relación | de las personas que | salieron al Avto de la Fe qve los Se | ñores, Doctor Alonso Bezerra Holguin del Abito de Alcántara; Licenciado Iuan de Valle Aluarado: Licenciado Alonso de Salazar Frías. Inquisidores | Apostolicos, del Reyno de Navarra, y su distrito, celebraron en la Ciudad de | Logroño, en siete, y en ocho dias del mes de Nouiembre, de 1610| Años. Y de las cosas y delitos por que | fueron castigados* (Shield).

There are fourteen pages of preliminaries. (A) Title page. (B) Juan de Mongaston, the printer's preface to the reader, dated Logroño 1611. (C) Approval of the publication by Fray Gaspar de Palencia, signed at San Francisco in Logroño on January 6th, 1611. (D) Licence to print dated January 7th, 1611. (E) The text. There is a copy in the Department of Manuscripts in the Biblioteca Nacional, Madrid, lacking the last gathering (ff. 271 r–283 v), with 718 folios in all. There is a complete copy in the Department of Printed Books with the Press-Mark V/Cª 248, Nº 71. For further bibliographical information, see González de Amezúa's critical edition of Cervantes's *El casamiento engañoso y El coloquio de los perros*, pp. 155–6 (Notes 4 and 5 to chapter VI of the Introduction). Amezúa gives details of other printed and manuscript contemporary accounts of the trials. One of them, in verse, stated to be in the Biblioteca Nacional, Madrid, has disappeared (MSS. V. 1/73–12 s. A).

5. *Relación*, p. 618.
6. *Ibid*, The story is still told today.
7. *Ibid*, p. 618.
8. *Ibid*, pp. 618–9.
9. *Ibid*, pp. 620–1.
10. *Ibid*, p. 621.
11. *Ibid*, p. 619.
12. *Ibid*, pp. 623–5.
13. *Ibid*, p. 623.
14. *Ibid*, loc. cit.
15. *Ibid*, loc. cit.
16. *Ibid*, p. 626.
17. *Ibid*, loc. cit.
18. *Ibid*, loc. cit.
19. *Ibid*, pp. 626–30.
20. *Ibid*, p. 630.
21. *Ibid*, pp. 622–3.

CHAPTER 14: PRACTICAL AND THEORETICAL CONSEQUENCES
OF THE ZUGARRAMURDI TRIALS

1. The first of them is the *Discurso de Pedro de Valencia â cerca* (sic) *de los quentos de las | Brujas y cosas tocantes â Magia*

dirigido al Illm°. Sr. D. Berd°. | de Sandobal y Roxas Cardenal Arpo de Toledo Inquisidor | General de España. There is a copy with the end missing in the Department of Manuscripts of the Biblioteca Nacional, Madrid—MSS. 9087, ff. 260 v–276 r.—and another in Simancas—Lib. 939. A copy of it was published by Manuel Serrano y Sanz in the *Revista de Extremadura*, año segundo (1900), pp. 289–303, 337–47.

2. J. A. Llorente, *Histoire critique de l'Inquisition d'Espagne*, III (Paris, 1818), pp. 454–60, gives a summary of the first of the two (Chapter XXXVII, Article II, Nos. 41–51). Menéndez y Pelayo has also discussed it in his 'Apuntamientos biográficos y bibliográficos de Pedro de Valencia', in *Ensayos de crítica filosófica* (Madrid, 1918), pp. 252–4, and in his *Historia de los heterodoxos españoles*, II, pp. 668–9 (Book V, chapter IV, 2).

3. 'Segundo discurso de Pedro de Valencia acerca de los brujos y de sus maleficios', in the *Revista de Archivos, Bibliotecas y Museos* (1906), II, pp. 445–54. The manuscript itself is in the Biblioteca Nacional, Madrid—MSS 7579—and is a copy made in the nineteenth century, formerly belonging to Usoz y Río.

4. *Discurso*, I, ff. 260 v–262 r of MSS. 9087 (Biblioteca Nacional, Madrid).

5. *Ibid*, I, f. 262 v.

6. *Ibid*, I, ff. 262 v–263 v.

7. *Ibid*, I, ff. 263 v–265 r.

8. Euripides, *The Bacchi*, 668–755.

9. *Ibid*, 487.

10. J. E. Harrison, *Prolegomena to the Study of Greek Religion* (Cambridge, 1903), pp. 367–74.

11. Livy, XXXIX, 9, 13, 15 and 41.

12. *Discurso*, I, ff. 266 r–267 r.

13. *Ibid*, I, ff. 267 r.

14. *Ibid*, I, ff. 268 r–270 r.

15. *Ibid*, I, ff. 270 r–274 r.

16. *Ibid*, I, ff. 274 r–276 r. The copy is incomplete as we have already said.

17. *Discurso*, II, in *Revista de Archivos, Bibliotecas y Museos* (1906), II, p. 454.

18. H. Ch. Lea, *A History of the Inquisition of Spain*, IV, p. 229. This also has something to say about the influence of the First Discourse of Valencia.

19. H. Ch. Lea, *A History of the Inquisition of Spain*, IV, pp. 230–7, quoting Simancas, Inquisición de Logroño, Legajo 1, Procesos de fé, N° 8.

20. There is a summary account of his activities with the following title: 'Relación y epílogo de lo que a resultado de la visita q hizo el sancto offi°. en las montañas del Rey° de Navarra y otras partes con el hedito de gracia concedido a los que ouiesen yncurrido en la secta de Brujos conforme A las relaciones y papeles que de todo ello se an Remitido al Consejo.' This is to be found in MSS. 2031 of the Biblioteca Nacional, Madrid, ff. 129 r–132 v. It was published by me in *Anuario de Eusko Folklore*, XIII (1933), pp. 115–30, with one or two misprints.

The personality of this inquisitor is worth investigation. He was apparently appointed on the recommendation of Cardinal Lanfranco Margotti, to judge from two letters written by the latter to the Inquisitor General and the Papal Nuncio. Before that, he had been Procurator of the metropolitan and cathedral churches of Spain in Rome. Cf. *Lettere del Sig. Cardenale Lanfranco Margotti scritte per le più ne' tempi di papa Paolo V. A nome del Sig. Cardinal Borghese. Raccolte, e publicate da Pietro de Magistris de Calderola* (Venice, 1660), pp. 287–8.

21. Salazar, 'Relación', *op. cit.*, f. 129 r. (pp. 115–6).

22. H. Ch. Lea, *A History of the Inquisition of Spain*, IV, p. 231.

23. Salazar, 'Relación', *op. cit.*, f. 129 r. (p. 116).

24. *Ibid*, f. 129 r. (p. 116).

25. *Ibid*, f. 130 v. (p. 122).

26. *Ibid*, ff. 130 r–130 v. (pp. 119–22).

27. *Ibid*, ff. 129 v–130 r. (pp. 118–9).

28. *Ibid*, f. 131 r. (pp. 123–5).

29. *Ibid*, ff. 131 r–131 v. (pp. 125).

30. *Ibid*, ff. 130 v–131 r. (pp. 122–3).

31. *Ibid*, ff. 131 v–132 r. (pp. 127–8).

32. *Ibid*, f. 132 r. (p. 128).

33. *Ibid*, ff. 132 r–132 v. (pp. 128–30).

34. H. Ch. Lea, *A History of the Inquisition of Spain*, IV, p. 234.

35. *Ibid*, IV, p. 235.

CHAPTER 15: WITCHCRAFT IN THE BASQUE PROVINCES
AFTER THE MAJOR TRIALS

1. Pablo de Gorosabel, *Noticia de las cosas memorables de Guipúzcoa*, I, pp. 356–7 (II, 2, iii).
2. That very year, in 1617, Salazar was in Vizcaya trying to calm people down. There is some information about his visit in Martín de los Heros, *Historia de Valmaseda* (Bilbao, 1926), pp. 368–9.
3. Florencio Amador Carrandi, *Archivo de la Tenencia de Corregimiento de la Merindad de Durango. Catálogo de los manuscritos, lista de los tenientes y monografía de la Merindad* (Bilbao, 1922), pp. 66 (Nº 36) and 70 (Nº 53).
4. Juan A. de Arzadun, 'Las brujas de Fuenterrabía. Proceso del siglo XVII, el 6 de mayo de 1611 en Fuenterrabía', in *Revista internacional de estudios vascos*, III (1909), pp. 172 and ff., 357 and ff. Julio Caro Baroja, 'Las brujas de Fuenterrabía (1611)', in *Revista de dialectología y de tradiciones populares*, III (1947), pp. 189–204.
5. See Chapter 13.
6. 'Relación que hizo el Doctor don lope de ysasti presbytero y beneficiado de leço, que es en guipuzcoa acerca de las meleficas de Cantabria por mandado del Sᵒʳ Inquisidor Campofrio en Madrid,' 1618. The manuscript is in MSS. 2031 of the Biblioteca Nacional, Madrid, ff. 133 r–136 v. It was published by me in the *Anuario de Eusko Folklore*, XIII (Vitoria, 1933), pp. 131–45 ('Cuatro relaciones sobre hechicería vasca').
7. Antonio de Torquemada's book, *Jardín de flores curiosas*—first published in Lérida in 1573 with a facsimile edition in 1955—has always been reckoned to be full of fables and lies. Cervantes' view of it, when the Canon was examining Don Quixote's library, is typical. Allusions to witchcraft in the Basque country are to be found on ff. 120 r–120 v, and there are more stories about witches on ff. 137 r–144 r.
8. Lope Martínez de Isasti has the following to say about him: 'Licentiate Germán de Ugarte, Apostolic Inquisitor of Calahorra and district, Chaplain to Pope Hadrian VI, prior of Zamora, Canon of Almería, Vicar of Oyarzun and Priest-in-charge at Lezo . . . is buried in the Parish Church at Lezo

and looked upon as a Holy Martyr, for it is proved that he was poisoned by witches when investigating their crimes in 1532. He was a native of Pasaje and Lezo.' Cf. Isasti's *Compendio historical de la M.N. y M.L. provincia de Guipúzcoa* (San Sebastián, 1850), p. 326 (Book 111, Chapter III, 1).

9. Lope Martínez de Isasti, 'Relación', *op. cit.*, f. 133 r (pp. 131–2).

10. *Ibid*, ff. 133 r (pp. 132).

11. The pejorative term 'pecheligue' or 'pichilingue' (speak English?) seems to have been frequently used in the seventeenth century of foreigners, especially of English and Dutch Protestants.

12. Lope Martínez de Isasti, 'Relación', *op. cit.*, ff. 133 r–133 v (pp. 132–3).

13. *Ibid*, f. 133 v (pp. 133–4).

14. *Ibid*, f. 133 v (pp. 134–5).

15. *Ibid*, ff. 134 r–135 v (pp. 135–41).

16. *Ibid*, f. 135 r (p. 139).

17. The reference is to the sinking of four galleons of the Cantabria Squadron in 1607. Only twenty men were saved. Cf. Rafael Estrada, *El almirante Don Antonio de Oquendo* (Madrid, 1943), pp. 48–9.

18. Lope Martínez de Isasti, 'Relación', *op. cit.*, ff. 135 v (p. 141).

19. *Ibid*, f. 135 v (pp. 141–2).

20. *Ibid*, ff. 136 r–136 v (pp. 144–5).

21. *Ibid*, f. 136 v (p. 145).

CHAPTER 16: THE GREAT CRISIS

1. *Cautio criminalis, seu de processibus contra sagas liber* (Frankfort, 1632). Other Jesuits, like Father Tauner, had earlier adopted similar critical attitudes.

2. J. Tissot, *L'Imagination, ses bienfaits et ses égarements, surtout dans le domaine du merveilleux* (Paris, 1868), pp. 371–437.

3. Ecclesiastes, III, 16.

4. I have used Tissot's summary – *op. cit.*, pp. 387–96.

5. Tissot, *op. cit.*, pp. 396–437.

6. Cf. the article entitled 'Ordeal' in W. Smith and S. Cheetham's *Dictionary of Christian Antiquities*, II (London, 1880), pp. 1466–69.

7. Cf., for example, Ciruelo, *Reprouación de las supersticiones y hechicerías*, ff. XXIX r – XXX v (Chapter VII, 'De las salvas y desafíos').

8. Cf. Bekker, *Le monde enchanté, ou examen des communs sentimens touchant les Esprits, leur nature, leur pouvoir, leur administration et leurs operations* (Amsterdam, 1674), I, pp. 315–22 (Book I, chapter XXI), for information about proofs of innocence in England, Holland and Germany. See also Le Loyer's earlier book, *Discours et histoires des spectres* . . . , p. 410 (Book IV, Chapter XXI).

9. Ordeal by ducking in water is condemned by a Jesuit called Thyraeus, in his *Daemoniaci, hoc est: De obsessis a spiritibus daemoniorum hominibus, liber unus* . . . (Cologne, 1598), pp. 51–52 (Part II, chapter XIX). Pierre de Lancre also condemns certain forms of ordeal in his *L'incrédulité*, pp. 293–5 (V).

10. Pierre de Lancre himself has a great deal to say about these signs. See Chapter 12.

11. I am unable to give a concrete reference to the work in which Gassendi speaks of his experiments, but it is quoted by Tissot, etc.

12. Malebranche, *Oeuvres* ed. Jules Simon, II (Paris, 1842), pp. 210–11.

13. *Ibid*, II, pp. 212–14.

14. B. Bekker, *op. cit.*, IV, pp. 576–87 (Chapter XXIX).

CHAPTER 17: THE ENLIGHTENMENT

1. H. Ch. Lea, *A History of the Inquisition of Spain*, IV, pp. 239–42.

2. Bayle's case is well enough known for it to be unnecessary to illustrate this with specific examples. He is always slightly ironic when speaking of sorcerers and witches in his *Dictionnaire historique et critique*. Cf., for example, I, pp. 8 and 127; IV, p. 293; VI, pp. 115 and 296; XIV, p. 223, etc.

3. B. Bekker, *op. cit.*

4. Cf. articles on Bekker in Michaud's *Biographie universelle ancienne et moderne*, IV (Paris, 1811), p. 74, and Didot-Hoefer's *Nouvelle biographie universelle*, V (Paris, 1853), col. 182.

5. H. Bekker, *op. cit.*, I, the abstract of Book IV in the 'Abrégé

de tout l'ouvrage'. Book IV has thirty-five chapters and occupies the last two volumes of the work.

6. *L'histoire des imaginations extravagantes de Monsieur Oufle causées par la lecture des livres qui traitent de la Magie, du Grimoire, des Démoniaques, Sorciers, Loups-garoux, Incubes, Succubes & du Sabbat; des Fées, Ogres, Esprits, Folets, Genies, Phantômes, & autres Revenans; des Songes, de la Pierre Philosophale, de l'Astrologie Judiciaire, des Horoscopes, Talismans, Jours heureux et malheureux, Eclypses, Cometes & Almanachs; en fin de toutes les sortes d'Apparitions, de Divinations, de Sortileges, d'Enchantemens & d'autres superstitieuses practiques* ... (Amsterdam, 1710), 2 vols.

7. *Lettres de M de St André, conseiller-medecin ordinaire du Roy; à quelques-uns des ses Amis, au sujet de la Magie, des malefices, et sorciers, etc.* (Paris, 1725), p. 319, etc.

8. There is a refutation of the above with the titles: *Recueil de lettres au sujet des malefices et du sortilege; Servant de réponse aux lettres du Sieur de Saint-André, Medecin à Coutances sur le même sujet: Par le Sieur Boissier* (Paris, 1731).

9. Girolamo Tartarotti, *Del Congresso notturno delle Lammie, Libri tre* ... *S'aggiungono due Dissertazioni epistolari sopra l'Arte magica* (Rovereto, 1749).

10. Maffei's *Arte Magica dileguata* (Verona, 1749) is a pamphlet fifty-six pages long. Tartarotti's reply is entitled *Apologia del Congresso notturno delle lammie, o sia risposta di G* ... *T* ... *all' arte magica dileguata del Sig. March-Scipione Maffei* (Venice, 1751).

11. Montesquieu, *Oeuvres complètes* (Paris, 1838), p. 283.

12. Voltaire, *Dictionnaire philosophique*, IV (Paris, 1821), pp. 343–4–Volume XXXII of the Perroneau-Cérioux edition of Voltaire's *Oeuvres complètes*.

13. *Ibid*, II (Paris, 1819), pp. 71 (article 'bouc')—Vol. XXX, ed. cit.

14. B. J. Feijóo, *Cartas eruditas y curiosas*, IV (Madrid, 1774), pp. 292–3 (Carta XX).

15. *Encyclopédie méthodique*, III (Paris, 1790)—'Théologie, par M. l'abbé Bergier', article entitled 'Sorcellerie', p. 523.

16. Gaspar Melchor de Jovellanos, *Obras*, ed. *Biblioteca de Autores Españoles*, LXXXVI, pp. 18 and 19.

17. *Poetas líricos del siglo XVIII*, Vol. II, in *Biblioteca de Autores Españoles*, LXIII, p. 593. The dialogue dates from 1816.

CHAPTER 18: THE TREATMENT OF WITCHCRAFT IN ART AND LITERATURE

1. Cf. for example, the painting of Hille Bobbe with her owl and a jug of ale by Franz Hals, now in the Berlin Museum.

2. I have seen this somewhere, but am unable to find the relevant reference. In any case, Padre Sigüenza, in his *Historia de la Orden de San Jerónimo*, II (Madrid, 1909), p. 635 (Part III, Book IV, Discourse XVII), defends the painter against accusations of heresy and folly.

3. Cf. Jacques Combe, *Jerome Bosch* (Paris, 1946), p. 133 of the plates.

4. *Ibid*, pp. 45, 59, etc.

5. The work has often been reproduced.

6. F. de Quevedo, *Historia de la vida del Buscón*, ed. A. Castro (London, n.d.), pp. 29 and 32.

7. Cervantes, *El casamiento engañoso y El coloquio de los perros*, ed. González Amezúa, pp. 338-9. In Note 277 on p. 624, Amezúa suggests that Cervantes knew the account of witch-trials in Navarre published in 1590. This was, in fact, no more than a copy of that of 1527. See Chapter 11.

8. Luis Vélez de Guevara, *El diablo cojuelo*, ed. A. Bonilla y San Martín (Vigo, 1902), pp. 18-19 (Tranco segundo: ff. 12 r—12 v of the first edition).

9. Francisco Santos, *El Arca de Noé y campana de Belilla* (Saragossa, 1697).

10. Antonio Ponz, *Viaje de España en que se da noticia de las cosas mas apreciables y dignas de saberse que hay en ella*, 2nd ed. (Madrid, 1777), III, p. 261 (Letter IX, N° 10).

11. Augusto L. Mayer, *Historia de la pintura española* (Madrid, 1928), p. 472. Enrique Lafuente Ferrari, *Breve historia de la pintura española* (Madrid, 1946), pp. 291, 293.

12. Miguel Velasco y Aguirre, *Grabados y litografías de Goya. Notas histórico-artísticas* (Madrid, 1928), N° 101 (Plate 80 of the *Caprichos*).

13. A plain attack on the Inquisition is *Capricho* N° 23 ('Aquellos polbos'), which represents the accused listening to his sentence being read. The covert allusion in the title seems first to have been noted by Antonio Puigblanch, *The Inquisition Unmasked*, translated by William Walton (London, 1816) II, pp. 374-5.

14. There are references to witchcraft in *Caprichos* Nos 12 ('A caza de dientes'), 45 ('Mucho hay que chupar'), 46 ('Corrección'), 47 ('Obsequio al maestro'), 48 ('Soplones'), 59 ('¡ Y aun no se van!'), 60 ('Ensayos'), 61 ('Volaverunt'), 62 ('¡ Quién lo creyere!'), 63 ('¡ Miren qué grabes!'), 64 ('Buen viaje'), 65 ('¿Dónde va mamá?'), 66 ('Allá va eso'), 67 ('Aguarda que te unten'), 68 ('Linda maestra'), 69 ('Sopla'), 70 ('Devota profesión'), 71 ('Si amanece nos vamos').

15. Cf., for example, the etching 'Murió la verdad' (Nº 79 of the *Desastres de la guerra*) and the one which follows it, '¿Si resucitará?'. Equally horrifying is the figure writing 'Against the general good' ('Contra el bien general') in Nº 71 of the same series.

16. I refer to the one entitled 'Spanish Witches', which has frequently been published along with other works on Spanish themes by the same author.

17. Victor Hugo, *Odes et ballades* (Paris, 1862), pp. 356–61 (Nº XIV). The Ballades were written between 1823 and 1828.

18. Théophile Gautier, 'Albertus' in *Poésies complètes*, I (Paris, 1896), pp. 177–83 (stanzas CVIII–CXX).

CHAPTER 19: MODERN VIEWS OF WITCHCRAFT

1. The document is in the Municipal Archives of Fuenterrabía, Section B, Leg. 1, Series 1, Book 5, Exp. 2. I transcribed the text of it in 'La Magia en Castilla durante los siglos XVI y XVII' in *Algunos mitos españoles y otros ensayos*, pp. 277–8 303 (Note 278).

2. The Basque word 'sorguiñ' is derived from the Latin 'sors' and the Basque 'guiñ' meaning an agent: 'sorguiñ' is therefore someone who makes or tells fortunes.

3. It would be interesting to investigate the genealogical connexion between the two movements.

4. The following are the names of those interviewed by me in this connexion: Isidora Echegaray, from Oiz; Lorenza Goñi, who was born in Aranaz; Dionisia Vidaur and Benedicta Irazoqui, both from Vera; all of them now dead. Julia Aguirre, Eulalia Tellechea, María Teresa Oroz, Maximina Bereasain; all of whom were still living in 1960, when the present book was being written.

5. In a similar way J. Vinson, *Folklore du Pays Basque* (Paris, 883), pp. 223–8, affirmed that in the Basque regions of France peop... from Guéthary and Biarritz had a reputation for sorcery and witchcraft, and those from Jatsou for being cowards.

6. This event actually took place in the summer of 1916.

7. It is said that a woman from the house of Jaulei in the Berástegui region of Guipúzcoa turned into a witch because she did this. In Oñate, it is thought that those who do this are snatched into Hell, and in Zarauz, that the dead will appear to them. Cf. *Eusko Folklore*, VI, Nº LXIX (September, 1926), p. 36.

8. Hugo Schuchardt, 'Heimisches und fremdes Sprachgut', in the *Revista internacional de estudios vascos*, XIII (1922), p. 69.

9. J. M. de Barandiarán, *Mitología vasca* (Madrid, 1960), pp. 55, 67–8, and 135–6. ('Gaueko').

10. All these examples can be found in R. M. de Azkue, *Diccionario vasco-español-francés*, II (Bilbao, 1906), pp. 227–8. Many others could be given.

11. 'Cartas de algunos PP. de la Compañía de Jesús sobre los sucesos de la Monarquía entre los años de 1634 y 1648', III, *Memorial histórico español*, XV (Madrid, 1862), p. 132.

12. *Eusko Folklore, Materiales y cuestionarios*, año I, Nº X (October, 1921), pp. 38–9.

13. *Ibid*, p. 39.

14. *Ibid*, año III, Nº XXVIII (April, 1923), p. 16. For information about the spring at Narbaja, cf. año V, Nº LX (December, 1925), p. 47.

15. J. M. de Barandiarán, *Mitología vasca*, pp. 83–106, gives a good description of Mari.

16. Antonio Neira, 'El gaitero gallego', in *Los españoles pintados por sí mismos* (Madrid, 1851), p. 260.

17. J. Rodríguez López, *Supersticiones de Galicia* (Madrid, 1910), pp. 52–4.

18. Giner de Arivau, 'Contribución al folklore de Asturias: folklore de Proaza', in *Biblioteca de las tradiciones populares españolas*, VIII (Madrid, 1886), pp. 231–4. Cf. also, Aurelio de Llano, *Del folklore asturiano; mitos, supersticiones y costumbres* (Madrid, 1922), pp. 76–7, etc.

19. Menédez y Pelayo, *Historia de los heterodoxos españoles*, I,

pp. 237–8; and Rodrigo Amador de los Ríos, 'Santander', in *España, sus monumentos y artes, su naturaleza e historia* (Barcelona, 1891), pp. 263–7. Both of these writers draw on a work by the novelist Pereda.

20. Pascual Madoz, *Diccionario geográfico, estadístico, histórico de España*, II (Madrid, 1846), p. 373, describes it as 'a broad plain, a mile in circumference, called the Field of the Witches (*Campo de las Brujas*), although nobody knows how it came to be called this'.

21. *Ibid*, IV (Madrid, 1846), p. 467.

22. *Ibid*, II (Madrid, 1846), p. 95.

23. G. A. Bécquer, *Cartas desde mi celda* (Carta VII), in *Obras*, 4th ed., II (Madrid, 1885), p. 301.

24. Sometimes the places are described as 'of the sorcerers' as opposed to 'of the witches'. This is the case in Luarca, where the spot lies to the west of the Malabrigo district. Cf. Pascual Madoz, *Diccionario*, X (Madrid, 1847), p. 404.

25. Cf. Carta VI of Bécquer's *Cartas desde mi celda – Obras*, ed. cit. II, pp. 281–300. The letters date from 1864, and the murder is supposed to have taken place 'two or three years ago' (p. 281).

26. Juan Blas y Ubide, *Sarica la borda* (Madrid, 1904), pp. 361–74 (Chapter XXI), and especially pp. 365–6. The work becomes rather melodramatic from that point onwards.

27. Some writers on witchcraft have tried, at times without much success, to make contact with 'streghe'. Cf., for example, Oliver Madox Hueffer, *The Book of the Witches* (London, 1908), pp. 320–6.

28. A. Nicéforo and S. Sighele's book *La mala vita a Roma* was translated into Spanish with the title *La mala vida* ('The bad life') (Madrid, 1909).

29. Fray Gerundio, *La Brujería en Barcelona* (Barcelona, n.d.), p. 43.

30. *Le dragon rouge, ou l'art de commander les sprits celestes, aériens, terrestres, infernaux, avec le vrai secret de faire parler les morts, de gagner toutes les fois qu'on met aux Loteries, de découvrir les Trésors cachés, etc.* (Nîmes, 1825). This is one of many editions.

31. *Les véritables clavicules de Salomon, trésor des sciences occultes suivies [de] grand nombre de secrets, et notamment de la grande Cabale dite du papillon vert* (n.p., n.d.).

32. J. J. Bachofen, *Urreligion und antike Symbole*, I (Leipzig, 1926), p. 83; II, pp. 96, 347, 349, etc.

CHAPTER 20: SOME MODERN INTERPRETATIONS OF WITCHCRAFT

1. Cf. Bayle's article on him in his *Dictionnaire historique et critique*, IX (Paris, 1820), pp. 301–6.

2. Pierre le Loyer, *Discours, et histoires des spectres, visions et apparitions des esprits, anges demons, et ames, se monstrans visibles aux hommes* (Paris, 1605), p. 708 (Book VII).

3. Pennethorne Hughes, *op. cit.*, p. 91.

4. I. Bertrand, *La Sorcellerie* (Paris, 1912), p. 7.

5. André Godard, *La piété antique* (Paris, 1925), pp. 30–2.

6. See, for example, his work entitled *Witchcraft and Black Magic*, 3rd. ed. (London, 1958).

7. Stanislas de Guaita, *Essais de Sciences maudites. Au seuil du mystère*, 5th ed. (Paris, 1915), pp. 30–3.

8. Cf. for example, René Schwaeble, *Le problème du mal. La Sorcellerie practique. Astrologie-Alchimie-Magie* (Paris, 1911). p. 115.

9. Cf. Gerald B. Gardner, *Witchcraft Today* (London, 1954), for information about such groups.

10. The same example was taken by R. Benedict in his *Patterns of culture*—Spanish translation, *El hombre y la cultura* (Buenos Aires, 1944), pp. 165–213.

11. Duque de Maura, *Vida y reinado de Carlos II*, II (Madrid, 1954), pp. 294–307.

12. Juste Louis Calmeil, *De la folie considérée sous le point de vue pathologique, philosophique, historique et judiciaire*, 2 vols. (Paris, 1845).

13. Calmeil's ideas are largely taken over by A. Vigoureux and P. Juquelier in their book *Le Contage mental*, translated into Spanish by César Juarros (Madrid, 1914), pp. 269–93, ('Contagio de las formas morbosas del sentimiento religioso'). The translation is a rather free version of the original.

14. Charles Richet, *L'homme et l'intelligence. Fragments de Physiologie et de Psychologie* (Paris, 1887), pp. 261–394.

15. A. Marie, *Mysticisme et folie (Étude de Psychologie normale et pathologique comparées)*, (Paris, 1907), pp. 134–51.

16. See, for example, the cases discussed by Jean Vinchon in the

book he wrote in collaboration with Maurice Garçon, *Le Diable. Etude historique, critique et médicale* (Paris, 1926), pp. 200–17.

17. This point of view was adopted by scholars who studied so-called 'Mental Contagion'. Cf. note 13 above.

18. E. Dupré, *Pathologie de l'imagination et de l'émotion* (Paris, 1925), p. 3.

19. *Ibid*, p. 99.

20. *Ibid*, p. 54.

21. *Ibid*, p. 14.

22. *Ibid*, p. 18.

23. *Ibid*, pp. 21–2.

24. Edmond Locard, *L'enquête criminelle et les méthodes scientifiques* (Paris, 1920), pp. 28–101.

25. This is also the theory put forward by Salomon Reinach in his *Orpheus. Histoire générale des religions* (Paris, 1914), pp. 444–5.

26. H. Fühner, 'Los estupefacientes', in *Investigación y Progreso*, IV (March, 1930), N° 3, p. 37. Works on toxicology can also be consulted on this topic.

27. See Chapter 7.

28. 'Comedias escogidas de Don Francisco de Rojas Zorrilla', in *Biblioteca de autores españoles*, LIV, pp. 330–1. González Amezúa refers to this passage in a note to his edition of Cervantes's *El casamiento engañoso y El coloquio de los perros*, pp. 625–8 (Note 625), when commenting on the following sentences: 'Some say that we only go to these meetings in imagination . . . ; others disagree and claim that we really do go, both body and soul.'

29. Robert Eisler, *Man into Wolf. An anthropological interpretation of Sadism, Masochism and Lycanthropy* (London, 1951).

INDEX

307

Reginus, Abbot of Prüm, treatise
of, 61
Rémy, Nicolas, 117
Rhombus, the, 27, 30
Richet, study of witchcraft, 248–9
Río, Martin del, 119–21, 195, 211
Rojas, Fernando de, 40, 101–3,
134. *See also* Celestina

Sabbath, the: first appearance of,
84–7; origin of word, 88;
general view of, 90–1, described by del Río, 119–21;
among Basques, 147–8, 160–
5, 192–4, 197, 229–30; Church
as model for, 165–7; witches'
method of travel to, 185, 204;
in Sweden, 207–8; Hierony-
mus Bosch on, 218
Sabines, 28
Sabuco, Miguel, *Nueva filosofía*,
132
Sagae, 19
St André, letters of, 211
St Augustine, on witchcraft, 43–4,
45, 55; his authority super-
seded, 79
St Comba, 238
St Germain, Bishop of Auxerre, 64
St John Chrysostom, 46
St John's day, 5, 186
St Martin of Braga, 65
St Placidus in Madrid, convent of,
136–7
St Thomas Aquinas, 70, 79
St Walburga, 238
Salazar y Frías, Don Alonso de,
155, 172, 184–9, 236, 250, 252
Salem, witches of, 138, 252
Salic Law on witchcraft, 59–60
Salvas, 203
Sampsoun, Agnes, 127
Sandoval, Fray Prudencio de, 146,
195
Santos, Francisco, 220
Satan, Satanism, 125, 160–2, 228.
See also Devil

Schelling, 241
Schopenhauer, 9
Scot, Reginald, 129–30
Seid, 47
Selene, 26, 29–30
Simon Magus, 31
Sky, the, 4–5
Slavs, witchcraft among, 47–51
Solomon's clavicles, 240
Solstices, 5
Sorceress, The, 81
Sorguiña, the, 101, 150, 227, 228,
et passim; sorguiñ dantz, 231
Spe, Friedrich von, 201–4, 213,
252
Spain, witchcraft in, 101–2, *et
passim*
Spells, 19–20, 22, 27–8, 33, 38, 39,
43, 46, 133–4, 153, 177–8. *See
also* drugs, ointments
Spina, Bartolommeo de, 104
Spiritual leaders, 134–5
Stedingerland, 75–7
Strabo, *Geography*, 7
Streghe, in Italy, 99–100
Striga, Stria, Strix, 33, 36–8, 45, 56
'Succubi,' 94, 95, 133, 249
Summers, Montague, 245–6
Summis desiderantes affectibus Bull,
94
Sun, the, 5, 8
Super illius specula Bull, 84
Sweden, witch trials in, 207–8

Tacitus, on witchcraft, 40; *Ger-
mania*, 47–8
Talavera, Archpriest of, 102
Talmud, on witchcraft, 80
Tartarotti, G., 211
Tertullian, *Apology*, 42
Theodosian Code, 43
Theocritus, 26, 29–30, 32, 33
Theophilus, story of, 73–4
Thessaly, 26, 28, 31
Thiers, J. B., 55
Throgmorton family, 128–9
Tissot, J., 202